International Aid and South Korea

This book explores South Korea's experience as an aid recipient, as an aid donor, and as an inter-Korea aid provider.

Analysing case studies of international aid both received and dispensed by South Korea, from the end of the Korean War until the present day, this collection provides a novel lens through which to explore South Korea's development pathway. While it examines the cases of Italian and German aid to South Korea during its early economic development period, this volume also delineates South Korea's international aid in the health and gender sectors. It also discusses the South Korean experience of providing aid to the Mekong region and North Korea. The latter specifically analyses whether this policy represents international altruism or reveals a novel method of international validation for South Korea over its neighbour.

Featuring an exploration of South Korea's development on the international stage through the lens of aid, this book will appeal to both students and scholars in the fields of Korean studies, East Asian studies, and Asia Pacific studies, as well as in the disciplines of Development Studies and International Relations and Political Economy, particularly that of aid policies and practices.

Sojin Lim is a Professor (Reader) at the University of Central Lancashire, UK. She is the author of articles and book chapters on *Sustainable Development and Political Economy*. Her recent publication includes her monograph *International Aid and Sustainable Development in North Korea: A Country Left Behind with Cloaked Society* (2023). She frequently discusses changes in the Korean Peninsula in media interviews.

Routledge Research on Korea
Series Editors: Niki Alsford and Sojin Lim,
University of Central Lancashire, UK.

The Research on Korea series surveys key topics in the study of North and South Korea (both on the peninsula, and in the diaspora). It is a prestigious series that is multidisciplinary, covering the social sciences and arts and humanities. The series seeks to publish best new research from both senior and junior scholars.

3 **Korea and the Global Society**
Yonson Ahn

4 **Politics, International Relations and Diplomacy on the Korean Peninsula**
Edited by Sojin Lim

5 **International Aid and Sustainable Development in North Korea**
A Country Left Behind with Cloaked Society
Sojin Lim

6 **South Koreans and the Politics of Immigration in Contemporary Australia**
David Hundt

7 **Soviet-North Korean Relations During the Cold War**
Unruly Offspring
Fyodor Tertitskiy

8 **Korean Film and History**
Hyunseon Lee

9 **The Forgotten Political Elites of North Korea**
Woe to the Vanquished
Fyodor Tertitskiy

International Aid and South Korea

Experience from Recipient to Donor

Edited by
Sojin Lim

Routledge
Taylor & Francis Group
LONDON AND NEW YORK

First published 2025
by Routledge
4 Park Square, Milton Park, Abingdon, Oxon OX14 4RN

and by Routledge
605 Third Avenue, New York, NY 10158

Routledge is an imprint of the Taylor & Francis Group, an informa business

This work was supported by the Core University Programme for Korean Studies through the Ministry of Education of the Republic of Korea and the Korean Studies Promotion Service of the Academy of Korean Studies (AKS-2020-OLU-20200045).

British Library Cataloguing-in-Publication Data
A catalogue record for this book is available from the British Library

ISBN: 978-1-032-80287-9 (hbk)
ISBN: 978-1-032-80479-8 (pbk)
ISBN: 978-1-003-49703-5 (ebk)

DOI: 10.4324/9781003497035

Typeset in Times New Roman
by codeMantra

Contents

Figures

Tables

Contributors

Max Altenhofen teaches history at Sungkyunkwan University, South Korea. He received his PhD in Korean Studies from the University of Tübingen, Germany, and is especially interested in global history, history of development, and environmental history. Based on his thesis, he is currently writing a monograph in German on the *Technical Development Cooperation of West Germany and South Korea during the Cold War*.

Queralt Boadella-Prunell is a PhD candidate at the University of Central Lancashire, UK. She earned her MA degree in International Relations and Political Economy of Development at the Institut Barcelona d'Estudis Internacionals (IBEI). Her primary research focuses on the impact of transnational activities on international migration and political economy in North Korea. Her publications include *The Spaces in Between: The Impact of Remittances on North Korean Mobility and Border Economy* (2024).

Patricia Chica-Morales is an Assistant Professor in the Area of East Asian Studies-Korean Studies at the University of Malaga, Spain. She published her research on South Korean ODA, gender policies in South Korea, and women's issues in Mongolia. She is currently a member of the research project AKS-2021-INC-22500025 *Path to Equality: Korean Studies Network on Inclusiveness*.

Antonio J. Doménech is a Full Professor in the Area of East Asian Studies-Korean Studies at the University of Malaga, Spain. He is an author and translator of works on Korean thought, society, and intercultural exchanges. He was awarded the *Order of Cultural Merit Hwangwan* by the President of South Korea and currently serves as a principal investigator of the research project *Path to Equality: Korean Studies Network on Inclusiveness*.

Juhee Jeong is a PhD candidate at Heidelberg University, Germany. Her research interests include role theory, foreign policy analysis, the domestic politics of South Korea and Japan, and their Indo-Pacific strategy. Her doctoral research focuses on the *'Self-Assertive' Roles of South Korea and Japan in Relation to ASEAN Amidst the Strategic Rivalry between the US and China*.

Sojin Lim is a Professor (Reader) at the University of Central Lancashire, UK. She is the author of articles and book chapters on Sustainable Development and Political Economy. Her recent publication includes her monograph *International Aid and Sustainable Development in North Korea: A Country Left Behind with Cloaked Society* (2023). She frequently discusses changes in the Korean Peninsula in media interviews.

Jae-Eun Noh is a Research Fellow at the Australian Catholic University, Australia. Her research explores development policies and practices from human rights perspectives. Her publications include *Themes on NGO Advocacy for Health Justice* (2024), *Development Ethics* (2023), and *Emotions in Korean Aid* (2023). She is currently working on a global research project to enrich understandings and practices of solidarity for health equity and justice.

Lauren Eloise Robertson is a PhD candidate at the University of Central Lancashire, UK. Her research focuses on the role of development assistance in building climate adaptation and resilience in North Korea. She recently co-authored *Compliance with Global Norms: A Case of North Korea and the United Nations Sustainable Development Goals* (2023).

Marco Zappa is an Assistant Professor at Ca' Foscari University of Venice, Italy. His research focuses on *International Cooperation in East and Southeast Asia*, particularly on *Human Resource Development, Knowledge Transfer, and Policy Circulation in the Development Industry in Asia*. He published several articles and volume chapters on *the History of International Relations and Development in Northeast and Southeast Asia*.

Commentary

Since I joined the Ministry of Foreign Affairs of the Republic of Korea in 1985, I have been closely involved in and observed the development process of South Korea becoming an Organisation for Economic Co-operation and Development (OECD) Development Assistance Committee (DAC) donor country. Right after the government of Korea became a member of the OECD DAC, I was fully involved in the process of shaping Korea's official development assistance (ODA) policy in my capacity as a Director-General for Development Cooperation in the Ministry between 2011 and 2013. I was responsible for organising the Fourth High-Level Forum of the OECD DAC on Aid Effectiveness, which took place in Busan in November 2011. I also undertook the OECD DAC's special review and peer review processes that the DAC members are required to participate in.

Prior to that, from 2006 to 2009, I served as Minister-Counsellor in the Korean Permanent Mission to the United Nations, where I contributed to the work of the international development cooperation community, focusing on human rights, women's status and empowerment, and refugee issues. Before I retired as a diplomat in 2022, I also served as an ambassador of South Korea to the UK with a great interest in climate change, including COP26. As such, it is my honour and great pleasure to contribute to the commentary of this scholarly discussion on the issue to which I devoted most of my career path.

As it is widely known, South Korea has achieved unprecedented economic growth as a war-torn, fragile country. The country's development cannot be decoupled from the history of international aid that helped the country transition from a recipient to a donor. Accordingly, 'we owe the international community; thus, we return the favour to those who need our help' is a widely shared sentiment among Koreans when it comes to the reason why the government of South Korea is willing to provide ODA.

Based on this background, the government of South Korea escalated its efforts to become an official ODA-providing member. Accordingly, South Korea joined the OECD in 1996 and became an official ODA donor as a DAC member in 2010. In 2021, the OECD introduced Korea as a country 'from emerging donor to global development partner'. It was about ten years after when Korea was considered an emerging donor country. Before and after Korea entered into its OECD DAC membership, we were rather at the stage to learn the experience of other DAC members in their ODA policies and practices; however, the country has now become a partner that shares its own donor experience with other members of the DAC, including lessons learnt in its development discourse.

As such, I believe that this particular edited volume that explores South Korea's experience of past, present, and future in the context of international aid recipients and donors will contribute not only to the scholarly debates but also to those of the international aid policymakers and practitioners.

Enna Park
Former South Korean Ambassador to the United Kingdom

Preface

The Republic of Korea (ROK, or South Korea) is known as a country that achieved its economic development from a war-torn, fragile country to a high-income country in about half a century. Accordingly, an extensive amount of research work has been conducted about its economic development and industrialisation experience. It includes a recent body of literature on South Korea as an official development assistance (ODA) donor, in line with the success story of the national economic achievement. However, its experience as an aid recipient has not been equally explored, and thus, a limited number of book publications deal with how the ODA during its early stage of economic development played its role, especially those written in English (Lim, 2021). And it is more limited to finding a publication that navigates South Korea's experience as a donor as well as a recipient at the same time.

With this in mind, this edited volume aims to examine the case of South Korea as an aid recipient, as an aid donor, and as an inter-Korea aid provider. In doing so, the first two chapters explore the experience of South Korea as an aid recipient after the Korean War, from the perspectives of donors. In more detail, Marco Zappa covers the period of the 1950s, focusing on Italian aid to South Korea in Chapter 1, while Max Altenhofen deals with the period of the 1960s with the case of German aid to South Korea in Chapter 2. As a war-torn, fragile state, South Korea received humanitarian aid first before it received development aid. Zappa's chapter mostly discusses the former case—humanitarian aid, focusing on the interactions between Italy and South Korea. Then, Altenhofen explores German technical assistance to South Korea, which can be understood as grant development aid. ODA can be provided in different forms, including humanitarian aid and development aid. While humanitarian aid consists of grant aid, development aid is composed of grant aid and loan aid. Technical assistance is one of the grant aid modalities (see Lim, 2021).

In comparison, the next three chapters examine the experience of South Korea as an aid donor. In Chapter 3, Jae-Eun Noh explores the limitations of global cooperation, focusing on health-related issues, and argues that South Korea as an ODA donor should play a stronger role in global development cooperation in addressing global inequalities and justice. Both Patricia Chica-Morales and Antonio J. Doménech then analyse the case of the Korea International Cooperation Agency (KOICA)'s gender approach to its aid project in Mongolia in Chapter 4. South

Korea's ODA architecture is divided between grant and loan aid. While the grant aid is executed mostly by the KOICA, under the Ministry of Foreign Affairs, along with other ministries and their sub-bodies, the loan aid is solely operated by the Economic Development Cooperation Fund (EDCF) of the Export-Import Bank of Korea (KEXIM), commissioned by the Ministry of Economy and Finance (Lim, 2021: 126–128; OECD, 2024: 16). In the following Chapter 5, Juhee Jeong discusses South Korea's development cooperation approach in the Mekong region. She argues that the development policy direction of South Korea towards the Mekong region, largely through the ODA, needs to be balanced between its domestic cope conceptions and the expectations of the Mekong countries.

Lastly, Chapter 6 discusses South Korea's aid to its sister country, North Korea. The aid from South Korea to North Korea is not considered an ODA due to the constitutional interpretation: North Korea is a part of South Korea; thus, South Korea's aid to North Korea is not an aid from one country to the other. Thus, South Korea's ODA statistics reported to the Organisation for Economic Co-operation and Development (OECD) do not include its assistance to North Korea, except for multi-bi aid, which is not channelled directly from South to North Korea but through international organisations (see Lim, 2023: 98–100). Rather, the government of South Korea established the Inter-Korean Cooperation Fund (IKCF) and has operated the fund by the KEXIM. For this reason, not much research on South Korea's ODA deals with the case of its aid to North Korea. In light of this, Queralt Boadella-Prunell and Lauren Eloise Robertson analyse this case in terms of inter-Korea cooperation. In doing so, Boadella-Prunell and Robertson give particular attention to the motivations of both South Korea and North Korea in their inter-Korean exchange and cooperation.

All in all, this particular edited volume intends to provide different aspects of South Korea's ODA experience that have not been fully investigated from the existing research at once. South Korea has been one of the best cases that managed to develop its initial humanitarian aid to the stage of development aid and made it successfully work for democratic and economic development (Lim, 2021). Therefore, we intend that the South Korean experience shared in this volume can benefit international aid policymakers and practitioners, especially those working on the humanitarian-development-peace nexus, thus achieving sustainable and peaceful development targets in countries.

References

Lim, Sojin (2021). The Evolution Story of South Korea from a Fragile State to an International Actor. In: Sojin Lim and Niki Alsford (eds). *Routledge Handbook of Contemporary South Korea*. London, Routledge. 118–135.

Lim, Sojin (2023). *International Aid and Sustainable Development in North Korea: A Country Left Behind with Cloaked Society*. London, Routledge.

OECD (2024). *OECD Development Co-operation Peer Reviews: Korea 2024*. Paris, OECD.

1 From 'Donor' to 'Friend'

Italy's Humanitarian Aid and South Korea's Middle Power Diplomacy in the Wake of the Korean War[1]

Marco Zappa

Introduction

In October 2018, the President of the Republic of Korea (ROK, or South Korea) Moon Jae-in visited Italy as the first Asian head of state to meet with the newly elected Conte government. On that occasion, the leaders of the two countries signed a joint declaration, paving the way for a strategic partnership to respond to the challenges of a new era. Ahead of Moon's visit, the ROK Ambassador to Italy, Choi Jong-hyun, contributed an op-ed to Italy's major newspaper, *Il Corriere della Sera*. The title read, 'Korea and Italy "Together we are stronger"'. In the article, Choi illustrated the main aims of his government's strategy towards the European partner, describing the evolution of the bilateral relation: 'Thanks to Italy's contribution during the Korean War, our countries have strengthened their unique relation guaranteeing permanent peace' (Choi, 2018: 30).

Although largely symbolic in nature, Italy's humanitarian aid to the ROK during the Korean War and in the immediate aftermath of the conflict can be considered a cornerstone in the rebuilding of friendly relations between the two countries after the Second World War (WWII). The Italian efforts in support of the ROK have been greatly appreciated by Seoul. A blog managed by ROK's Ministry of Patriots and Veterans Affairs, for instance, celebrates the Italian Red Cross 'hospital No 68' (*itallia je 68 jeoksipja byoungwon*), exhibiting pictures of the Red Cross volunteers, of the field hospital that was installed in Ushin Elementary School, in Yeongdong-po district, and of a 1951 stamp commemorating the Italian participation in the Korean War (Ministry of Patriots and Veterans Affairs, 2019). South Korean scholars, observers, and officials, in fact, point at the Italian support and humanitarian relief initiative during the conflict as the beginning of 'substantive' relations between Rome and Seoul, putting particular emphasis on the fact that at the time, Italy was not a member of the United Nations (UN) and that it was struggling with its economic reconstruction (Oh, 2016: 74). Recently, in the wake of the COVID-19 pandemic, South Korean medical historians have highlighted the importance of the Italian initiative in building positive ties, resulting in the government in Seoul sending medical equipment to Italy in 2020 and 2021 through its Embassy in Rome (Lee and Yoon, 2020; Gu, 2022).

DOI: 10.4324/9781003497035-1

Italian humanitarian efforts in South Korea in the early 1950s might be considered a turning point in Italy's diplomacy and a step further in the country's postwar path towards middle power status. Through its Red Cross (Croce Rossa Italiana, CRI), at the time under the jurisdiction of its Ministry of Defence, in 1951, the country joined the United States (US)-led Korean campaign and UN-coordinated international humanitarian effort along with other European allies (namely, Sweden, Denmark, and Norway) (Kim and Yang, 2022; Midtgaard, 2011; Park, 2010). As illustrated below, with this effort, the Italian government expected to enhance its international status and economic role in the ROK and the Asia Pacific. Although unsuccessful, Rome came to be recognised by the ROK leadership led by President Syngman Rhee as a 'friend' and ally against the 'Red Devil' of communism, notwithstanding Rome's cautious Atlanticism. After the 1953 armistice, a series of visits to Europe by ROK high-level state officials and diplomats were conceived to broaden the scope of the country's alliances at a time of strained relations between Rhee and the US administration, which wanted primarily Seoul to normalise its relations with Japan, the region's rising economic powerhouse.

With this in mind, this chapter has addressed the following research questions: given both Italy and ROK's asymmetrical relations with great power (the US) in the early phases of the Cold War, how the two nations pursued their foreign policy goals independently; and considering its interactions with European nations and specifically with Italy, whether the label of 'client state' is still pertinent to the ROK in the 1950s. Based on these, this chapter contributes to a better understanding of interactions between two lesser powers in the context of the early phase of the Cold War. Particularly, on the one hand, it aims to reassess Italy's role as an international donor in this historical phase, which has been neglected in the scholarly debate. Although several outdated studies delineating the main principles of Rome's international economic cooperation in the context of an emerging international effort to ameliorate the conditions of developing countries are available (Magliano, 1962; Papi, 1962; Parrillo, 1966), more recent ones focus mainly on economic aspects such as performance and efficiency of Italian aid in comparison with the Organisation for Economic Co-operation and Development (OECD) standards (Bertoli, Cornia and Manaresi, 2007). Few other studies, instead, have offered useful insights into the history of Italian international cooperation and its institutional arrangements with regard to economic and military cooperation (Calandri, 2003; Giacomello and Magnani, 1993). On the other hand, this chapter aims to identify the emergence of the ROK as a middle power well before it was in the international spotlight in the late 2000s (Choi, 2009; Lee and Park, 2017; Mo, 2016; Shim and Flamm, 2012).

This chapter thus presents how the ROK has strategically negotiated its subordinate role vis-à-vis the US at a time when the superpower seemed to be restricting the ROK's policy options, particularly in regard to ROK-Japan normalisation (Cha, 2016, 2011), or even plotting against it (Lee, 2011). Specifically in this phase, by strengthening its ties with Western European partners such as Italy, the ROK arguably attempted to pursue a sort of middle power diplomacy, whose traits have been discussed below, well ahead of the emergence of the ROK as a global middle power in the late 2000s.

The Middle Powers That Be: Italy and the ROK in the Context of the Early Cold War

South Korea and Italy are today considered by many observers as two regional powers or middle powers (Andreatta, 2001; Colombo and Palm, 2019; Snyder et al., 2015; Verbeek and Giacomello, 2011). While Italy has been trying to play a role as a regional middle power in the Mediterranean and North Africa since the early postwar era (Andreatta, 2001; Varsori, 2022), the ROK has been characterised as a middle power in the scholarly debate much more recently (Choi, 2009; Lee and Park, 2017; Mo, 2016; Shim and Flamm, 2012). These studies pointed out ROK's enhanced activism in various fields such as human security, regional economic development, and US-centred multilateralism as key factors in the nation's rise in the international arena since the late 1990s and early 2000s. At the same time, the ROK's middle power diplomacy cannot be disentangled from its military strength and its soft power potential built upon the global success of South Korean popular culture (Lee, 2011).

However, defining a middle power can be a hard task, and the very concept of middle power needs to be problematised (see Beeson and Higgott, 2014: 220). According to Beeson and Higgott (2014: 223), a classical definition of middle power emphasises the 'in-betweenness' of one country in terms of location (between Great Power systems), size (not too big nor too small), and ideology (adopting a middle ground position between two conflicting ideologies or socio-political systems). The middle power status has to do with the limitations of one country's natural and military resources leading said country to pursue its interests and foreign policy goals using 'non-material assets' (Beeson and Higgott, 2014: 223–224; Siddi, 2019: 124). Persuasion, for instance, is a key element in middle power diplomacy, being the cornerstone of its capacities to identify common issues or challenges and, consequently, create coalitions to tackle them, using bilateral or multilateral channels and specific, even technical skills. In this regard, Beeson and Higgot (2014: 224) stress that:

> a successful middle power player might facilitate associational, collaborative and coalitional activity. It is here that superior diplomatic ability (a skill not to be under-rated or assumed to be possessed by every foreign office) to plan and convene meetings and provide technical support (declaration drafting and the like) ought to become important.

Ultimately, successful middle powers contribute to the creation of new institutions, such as new norms, conventions, and organisations, which become diffused and accepted internationally. Adopting a structuralist perspective, however, it is clear that the ability of one nation to establish itself as a middle power does not depend exclusively on the persuasion skills of its diplomats and their capacity to catalyse and mobilise consensus internationally. In fact, a series of structural conditions have to be met for a middle power to act and be recognised as such.

First, 'hegemonic decompression' may favour the middle power's initiatives. In such historical phases, visible after the collapse of the Cold War world system, the established superpower(s) may decline, leaving the international system with no apparent hegemon, thus allowing middle powers to be more effective. Second, the prospective middle power has to exhibit a 'purposeful willingness' to act independently of the constraints posed by its relationship with one or multiple great powers. Third, the country's leadership must pursue its diplomatic goals based on a middlepowermanship self-awareness, that is, on the construction and crystallisation of a specific identity as a middle power within the state's bureaucratic apparatus and outside of it (Beeson and Higgot, 2014: 225–226). In fact, as highlighted by constructivist theorists, identity construction is an open-ended and socially determined process that does not forcibly reflect the position of one country within the structures of the contingent international system (Beeson and Higgott, 2014: 232), and in this process, the use of language and discourse becomes a key.

Although middle power diplomacy seems less feasible in times of extreme hegemonic compression with at least two great powers hindering the capacities of other states (being both middle powers or small) to exercise independent and meaningful agency vis-à-vis great powers or overt patron states (Beeson and Higgott, 2014), the possibility of it is not entirely precluded.

However, as the Italian case clearly shows, thanks particularly to its first republican cabinets, and particularly its Prime Minister Alcide De Gasperi and Foreign Minister Carlo Sforza's diplomatic activism, Rome was relatively successful in regaining a status of middle power in the context of the US-Union of Soviet Socialist Republics (USSR) confrontation over Europe, emerging regional economic, trade, and political coordination, and in the region's defence system through its joining of the North Atlantic Treaty Organization (NATO) in 1949 (Andreatta, 2001; Varsori, 2022). As poignantly pointed out by Andreatta (2001: 48), Italy's foreign policy during the Cold War was 'heterodox' involving 'a sophisticated mixture of orthodox and eccentric measures' aimed at maintaining strong relations with the US-led Western coalition without alienating the Communist bloc (and a large part of the Italian public opinion supporting the Italian Communist Party).

Undeniably, from 1945 until the mid-1950s, Rome was dependent on foreign and specifically US economic and military aid. Moreover, the US political influence was conspicuous. However, while keeping a low profile diplomatically and exercising remarkable military restraint until the late 1980s (Andreatta, 2001), the Italian government could effectively pursue a series of diplomatic goals to achieve equal status compared with other Western European partners (Varsori, 2022: 130). Topping the agenda was the restoration of Italian sovereignty over disputed territories at the borders with Jugoslavia and, partially, over its former African colonies. Nevertheless, in the geopolitical context of the time, Rome attempted to expand by means of humanitarian assistance its strategic and commercial interests in the Asia-Pacific region in the context of Washington's engagement in the Korean War. For these reasons, even in a context of hegemonic compression, Italy's international standing seems to escape the definition of a client state and confirm the country's characterisation as a middle power.

By contrast, the ROK at the outset of the Cold War has often been characterised as an overt US client state, for instance, a smaller actor seeking additional resources to increase its own security to its patron, a major power with considerable military and economic resources, through formal agreements (Carney, 1989; Kim and Woods, 2022). Nevertheless, Seoul's attempt to establish a middle power diplomacy can be identified in the early phase of the Cold War, particularly when friction emerged between the US and ROK administrations in the aftermath of the 1953 armistice. In this regard, it is possible to agree with Shin (1994: 122), who argues that the relationship between the two nations was only partially characterised by clientelism while admitting the power asymmetry between the ROK and the US. Upon the end of WWII, South Korea was included in the regional order reshaped by the US to contain both the USSR and China, the region's major communist powers. This order, which Chijiwa (2022: 48) labels the US-led '1905 East Asian system' with the US occupying the role of the regional hegemon instead of imperial Japan after its 1905 victory over Russia, was centred around Japan's economic recovery and the US's provision of economic and military aid to both the ROK and Taiwan.

However, a 'regional security complex' that could effectively support the US' regional strategy and military operations in Asia was attained only in the mid-1960s after the South Korean-Japanese normalisation, which, in turn, was made possible by a regime change in the ROK (Shin, 1994: 123). In fact, under Syngman Rhee, despite its dependency on US aid, the ROK administration, at least until the 1960 military coup, was able to resist Washington's political pressures to establish peaceful relations with the country's former coloniser. In addition, as it will be shown in detail below, the Rhee administration seemed keen to establish friendly relations with other partners in 'the West', particularly European middle powers such as Italy, agitating the threat of the communist 'Red devil' to win support and thus potentially creating at least a discursive coalition against it. Against this backdrop, ROK-Italy interactions during the first years of the Cold War are revealing of the attempts of both nations to affirm their middle power status vis-à-vis the US. Concomitantly, the case analysed hereafter demonstrates how middle power diplomacy was still possible, although in a very limited scope, despite structural limitations to smaller powers' agency in the context of the US-USSR confrontation (Beeson and Higgott, 2014; Duara, 2011).

In the following paragraphs, this chapter illustrates the strategisation of humanitarian needs by Syngman Rhee's administration and the role played by Italy in enhancing the ROK's legitimacy and reaching out to new audiences in the face of an emerging competition for international recognition with the Democratic People's Republic of Korea (DPRK, or North Korea). It also dealt with the constraints to which both Seoul and Rome were subject against the backdrop of their institutionalised alliances with the US and how this limited the effectiveness of Italy's diplomatic efforts in postwar ROK. The following discussion is largely based on a preliminary analysis of declassified documents produced by the Italian Ministry of Foreign Affairs and International Cooperation,[2] General Direction Political Affairs Bureau (Direzione Generale Affari Politici, DGAP), fifth and sixth sections (V and VI Ufficio [brief: Uff.]). In addition to the state perspective, by keeping track of the correspondence with other ministries and organisations such as the CRI, reports from ambassadors and representatives, as well as documents related to South Korean officials visiting Italy, DGAP documents offer an original and multi-layered perspective, offering a complex representation of Italy-ROK relations since the early 1950s. Considering the above, the following paragraphs clarify the historical background of the Italian engagement with South Korea during the Korean War.

Common Constraints: The Alliance with the US, Domestic Diplomatic Agendas, and the Role of Humanitarian Aid

In the aftermath of WWII, both Italy and the ROK emerged as two client states of the US. On the one hand, following the collapse of the fascist regime led by Benito Mussolini in September 1943, the emerging Italian leadership opted to side with the Anglo-Americans, aspiring to be recognised as 'a member in the community of Western democracies' (Brogi, 2002a: 19). General Pietro Badoglio went as far as to declare in 1944 that the US should 'use' Italy as a 'secure base' to project their power in the Mediterranean region and, concomitantly, in the country's domestic affairs (Brogi, 2002a: 20). Therefore, after May 1945, international cooperation and loyalty to the US leadership became key to Italy's 're-conversion to democracy' (Brogi, 2002a: 21–22). This does not mean that Italian post-war leaders, and particularly conservative Prime Minister Alcide De Gasperi and his Foreign Minister Carlo Sforza, had submitted *in toto* to the patron-state's directives, but rather that they strived to pursue an independent international agenda. Despite being often influenced by domestic political and economic considerations, this agenda needed to be aligned with the European neighbours and within US hegemony (Brogi, 2002b; Mammarella and Cacace, 2006).

In exchange, Rome obtained generous US aid through the European Recovery Programme (ERP), which kickstarted the country's economic recovery, post-war growth, and military protection through its affiliation with NATO. In this context, at the end of the 1940s, the De Gasperi cabinet, which could benefit from direct US financial support against the socialist and communist parties at the 1948 elections, reoriented its diplomacy towards favouring Italy's accession to the UN. Despite their 'informal' role as observers (Mower, 1966: 267–268), Italian representatives were granted access to the organisation in New York in the context of multilateral discussions over Italian colonies in Africa, eventually leading to, among other things, the concession of a ten-year trusteeship over Somaliland in 1950 (Mammarella and Cacace, 2006: 183). Nonetheless, the international community, and particularly the US and Great Britain, remained wary of Italy.

On the other hand, after the 1948 contested establishments of the ROK and the DPRK, both Seoul and Pyongyang claimed to be the only legitimate representatives of the Korean nation with neither of the two controlling or exerting jurisdiction over the entire territory of the peninsula and competed the one with the other to win over allies and, thus, international recognition (Gills, 2005: xix). Tensions exploded when, in May 1949, border fights erupted in the Ongjin Peninsula, northwest of Seoul, leading to the beefing up of both ROK and DPRK troops. A year and a few weeks later, skirmishes escalated to a full-scale war. After the fall of Seoul at the end of June 1950, the US rapidly intervened in the conflict in defence of the ROK, first by offering military aid and then by mobilising its army and navy and allies with a UN Security Council mandate (Cumings, 2011).

Against this backdrop, international support with military, economic, and humanitarian means to both the ROK and the DPRK inevitably reflected Cold War arrangements. In other words, international aid became key to both regimes' survival. Specifically, Syngman Rhee saw US intervention as an opportunity to unify the peninsula, leveraging on US military power to achieve his unification plan (*bukjin tongil*) (Cha, 2011: 6). According to Rhee, unification was a goal to be achieved regardless of the hardships and sacrifices the Korean people might encounter (Lee, 2011: 38). Regardless of the ROK President's ambitions, US direct involvement in the conflict offered Washington the opportunity to prevent possible unilateral aggression on the DPRK by the ROK enacting the powerplay strategy that has characterised the US approach to its 'rogue allies' in the Asia Pacific during the Cold War (Cha, 2016, 2011). Reporting on late 1950s White House deliberations, Cha (2011: 9) clearly illustrates how the US administration of the time was prepared to remove Rhee and even give up its alliance with the ROK in case of a deliberate action against the North. Fearing US abandonment in the ROK's long-standing competition for legitimacy against the DPRK, it is likely that after the armistice Seoul began looking beyond the patron–client relation, resorting to a sort of multilateralism with other Western democracies against the global threat of Communism (see Kim and Woods, 2022; Lee, 2011).

These considerations led us to reassess the role of humanitarian aid in international relations along with the theoretical lines that were illustrated above. Upon this, the following paragraphs clarified how this form of aid has played out in building mutual trust between two client states within US hegemony. Despite their negligible material results, particularly with respect to the economic ties that the Italian government was particularly keen to establish in the context of an expanding economy, Italian humanitarian aid was nevertheless symbolically consequential as the cornerstone of contemporary Italy-ROK relations. In its final years in power, Rhee was in fact able to co-opt, at least rhetorically, another European ally in his enduring fight against Communism (see Kim and Woods, 2022; Lee, 2011).

Upon the outbreak of the Korean conflict, the Italian public was divided. If the Christian-Democrat-led government sought an opportunity to enhance its international status vis-à-vis its patron-state and disillusioned European allies, the Italian Communist Party, which had a strong influence on the political opposition, rallied for the DPRK, wishing that its forces might teach a lesson to the American imperialists so that they could also be chased out of Asia and ultimately of Italy (The New York Times, 1950). Nonetheless, the Italian government officially started planning the dispatch of a unit of volunteers and military doctors of the CRI to Korea in September 1950. Between August and September 1950, through the Italian Embassy in Washington, the Italian and US governments reached an agreement in principle over Italian humanitarian aid to Korea and established the CRI unit under the direct control of the UN command in Korea, presided by General

Douglas MacArthur. The unit would be able to exhibit the Italian flag as per the Geneva Convention and would also assist prisoners of war (POW).

The agreement between Rome and Washington involved that the United Nations Command (UNC) provided for the transport of the Italian unit to Korea and supplied equipment and necessary services. Part of these expenses would be reimbursed by the Italian government to the UNC (MAE DGAP Uff. VI, 1950a). The Ministry of Foreign Affairs (Ministero degli Affari Esteri, MAE) in Rome rapidly signalled that the Italian government expressed support for the decision of the CRI to send a relief unit to Korea, comprising 100 beds, doctors, volunteers, and military nurses, to the Italian representative at the UN in New York. In addition, it demanded that the news be reported to the UN Secretary-General. The CRI had reportedly responded to a call by the International Red Cross Society expressing its willingness to participate in the 'international relief action' in Korea and to 'bring tangible aid' to the ailing civilian population and military personnel dispatched to Korea (MAE DGAP Uff. VI, 1950b). By confirming its support for the CRI's decision, the Italian government appealed to the UN Secretary-General, showing its commitment to the multilateral military endeavour (MAE DGAP Uff. VI, 1950b). It might be worth stressing that in this phase, Italy was not a full UN member but only, although not formally, an observer country (Mower, 1966).

Italy's decision was communicated to the UN Secretary-General Trygve Lie in December by the Italian observer's office at the UN. Urged by the UNC, Lie asked the Italian part to grant permission to the CRI unit to aid North Korean and Chinese POW captured by the UN troops in Korea. The MAE quickly replied, stating the government's decision to grant permission to the CRI unit to follow the UNC's instructions (MAE DGAP Uff. VI, 1950a). A note by the US Embassy in Rome from January 1951 reports that the Italian offer has been accepted by the UNC, describing it as 'anxious to arrange immediate transportation' of the unit to Korea (Embassy of the United States of America to Italy, 1951a: 1).

Besides allocating an ITL 155 million fund (USD 250,000)[3] to the Ministry of Defence to support the mission, Rome would refund the costs of the unit transport from Italy to Korea to the US government (Ministero del Tesoro, 1951). At the same time, it demanded that the CRI prepare a financial plan based on which needs could be assessed and further financial support by the UN and US authorities could be provided. In responding to the MAE's requests, the CRI President at that time, Mario Longhena,[4] detailed a monthly estimated cost of slightly more than ITL 16 million for the field hospital operation and management. Therefore, the Italian government decided to allocate monthly ITL 204 million for the financial year 1951/1952 and ITL 190 million for the following year (Ministero del Tesoro, 1953: 2). He also demanded that a specific fund of no less than USD 100,000 be created to support the activities of the hospital and continuous financial support for the volunteers after they return to their civilian lives by the Italian state. In fact, the mission was sent to respond to international war contingencies, and thus, subject to specific directives from the Italian Minister of Defence (CRI Comitato Centrale Direzione affari internazionali, 1951). Most relevantly, the CRI President reminded his counterpart at the MAE that the field hospital could not be dispatched in support of the combatants due to the nature of the structures and supplies in any way (CRI Comitato Centrale Direzione affari internazionali, 1951).

Later, in April, the Italian government reported that the 69-people-strong CRI unit was ready to be dispatched despite technical discussions still underway between competent ministries, and that the Ministry of Defence had to issue the mobilisation order being the CRI an auxiliary organisation in compliance with the Italian law (MAE DGAP Uff. VI, 1951a). Furthermore, in his correspondence with the Italian Representative at the UN, Pasquale Simone Jannelli, then Director General of the Political Affairs Bureau at the MAE, stresses the fact that 'Italy is not in a state of war and is not a member state of the United Nations', adding that, 'according to the national legislation, CRI's duties are exclusively territorial and that only the Military Health Service can operate as embedded with armed forces' (MAE DGAP Uff. VI, 1951b), reiterating once more the impossibility for the unit to join combat divisions on the frontline, as expressed by Longhena in his first communication with the MAE. In early September, after a few months' hiatus, the Ministry of Defence finally gave the mobilisation order, and later that month. The Italian unit received the UNC permission to fly the UN flag together with the Italian and the Red Cross flags (MAE DGAP Uff. V, 1951a). The concession of the UN flag to an agency of a UN non-member state was an exceptional achievement for the Italian government, which was engaged in negotiations for its own access to the international multilateral organisation, which materialised only four years later, in December 1955.

In the meantime, through an exchange of notes between the US Embassy in Rome and MAE, arrangements had been made for the CRI unit to be transported to South Korea from Naples on the US Navy Military Sea Transportation Service (MSTS) General W. C. Langfitt on 16 October 1951 (Embassy of the United States of America to Italy, 1951b; MAE DGAP Uff. V, 1951b). The field hospital arrived in South Korea a month later. The Italian Embassy in Tokyo came to supervise the establishment of the hospital. As agreed by Italian and US authorities, the hospital was installed outside the combat area in Yeongdong-po which was in the outskirts of Seoul, and tasked with the assistance of solely civilian victims of the conflict. However, in an attempt to show Italy's willingness to partake in the multilateral effort facing pressures from the UN Command, though 'in perfect harmony with the American authorities' in South Korea, Italy's Ambassador to Japan, Blasco Lanza D'Ajeta's, upgraded the mandate of the CRI hospital to respond to both 'civilian and second-line military needs', an interpretation espoused by DGAP Director Jannelli (Ambasciata d'Italia Tokyo, 1951: 2; MAE DGAP Uff. V, 1951c).

After a year in service, the original budget allocated to the CRI hospital was increased by ITL 138 million, and the financing was kept stable until 1955 when the unit was disbanded and repatriated to Italy. The US Department of State attempted to institutionalise the cooperation with the Italian counterpart, proposing an administrative agreement that would have regularised the relation between US military authorities and the CRI hospital based on similar operational agreements signed with Denmark, Sweden, and Norway. In fact, despite the CRI hospital being a second-line hospital, during the first year of operation, it received from the

US military several goods, such as food, drugs (not supplied by United Nations Civil Assistance Corps Korea (UNCACK) and Italy), fuel, equipment, and services (such as works for the installation of the hospital and trips for the Italian medical personnel, authorities, and journalists) on the promise of a reimbursement paid by the Italian authorities to the US government (MAE DGAP, 1952: 1). At the same time, the hospital No 68 had operated primarily with the UNCACK, supporting the distribution of relief goods (and thus gratuitous) to the civilian population and having access at the same time to their use (mainly medicines as disinfectants, antibiotics, goods as sheets and blankets, and hospital food) (68th Italian Red Cross Field Hospital, 1953). In this regard, signing of a formal agreement would have required parliamentary approval and posed political obstacles to the allocation of funds on the part of the Italian Treasury. Therefore, after an interministerial meeting and various consultations with diplomats and envoys, the hypothesis of a formal agreement between Italy and the US was dropped in favour of an exchange of notes, a more flexible tool that could allow the Italian government to speed up procedures for the reimbursements of hospital-related expenses sustained by the US military (Ambasciata d'Italia Tokyo, 1952a; Ambasciata d'Italia Washington, 1952; MAE DGAP Uff. V, 1952).

Despite several delays in the transfer of funds for the field hospital operation (CRI Comitato Centrale, 1953a; Presidenza del Consiglio dei Ministri, 1953a, b), CRI efforts in South Korea received public praise[5] and contributed to enhancing Italy's international standing in the arena of the Korean conflict. In early 1953, weeks after having suffered a dramatic fire[6] that destroyed its main building, the hospital had treated 74.5 thousand people, particularly around 350 surgical operations and 6.6 thousand radiological exams. The hospital was visited, among others, by UNC commander General Mark W. Clark, who bestowed the UN commemorative medal on the hospital personnel, by the UN Vice Secretary General Andrew Cordier, by the Minister of Health of the ROK, by the Apostolic Vicar of Seoul Paul Roh Ki-nam, and, most importantly, by the ROK President Syngman Rhee (CRI Comitato Centrale, 1953b). According to an Italian medical official's report, Rhee complimented the field hospital No 68 for assisting the civilian population of Korea and awarded the 'Presidential Unit Citation', the highest decoration established by the Korean government (MAE DGAP, n.d.). Nonetheless, the author of the document, Gianluigi Ragazzoni, lamented that 'while our relief action is for its own sake, other similar units, for instance the hospitals of the Scandinavian countries, the German hospital and the English one, and so on., have also an economic and political dimension, beside the humanitarian one' (MAE DGAP, n.d.: 1).

Gianluigi Ragazzoni went on reporting on training courses and internship opportunities for South Korean graduates of medicine and nursing organised by other international hospitals. Ragazzoni maintains that these opportunities help to create a sense of friendship and sympathy towards the international unit where they have been trained or have interned with their attendees and participants. In this regard, he denounces Italian backwardness due to 'bureaucratic inefficiency'. In fact, during its service in South Korea, the Italian unit could employ just one Korean surgeon and two nurses (MAE DGAP, n.d.: 1). Moreover, in contrast with other international hospitals, he regretted the lack of a store of Italian products annexed to the field hospital. Italian products, such as cameras, radiographic film, typewriters, food, and wine, might be 'sold out (*vendutissimi*)' and would serve to publicise 'our products' to the allied troops and civilian population and, eventually, win public procurement contracts (MAE DGAP, n.d.: 1). On top of this, Ragazzoni lamented that the Italian diplomatic action had been largely inconsequential despite several President Rhee's public calls for enhanced relations between Italy and the ROK (MAE DGAP, n.d.). Requests aimed at taking similar steps as other international missions are evident in D'Ajeta exchanges with the Ministry in regard to the purchase and distribution of Christmas gifts to the CRI hospital personnel and Korean assistants between 1952 and 1953, which required an MAE contribution of USD 1,000 (Ambasciata d'Italia Tokyo, 1953: 1, 1952b: 2).

Seoul's New Ally and Italy's Northeast Asian Bounty

In February 1953, the CRI Hospital was rebuilt and expanded to a maximum capacity of 200 beds. Despite the progressive scaling down of the activities at the hospital in the light of the military stalemate leading to the armistice in July 1953, it continued its activities until 1955, when the unit was demobilised and repatriated.[7] According to the Korean Minister of Patriot and Veteran Affairs, a further 35,000 patients were treated in the CRI Hospital. With the end of hostilities, the 68th field hospital became a civilian-only hospital focused on the treatment of parasite-caused diseases (Ministry of Patriots and Veterans Affairs, 2023). Nonetheless, the image of Italy as a reliable ally against the 'illegal aggression of the communists' was gaining momentum among the South Korean leadership. In early July 1953, after attending the crowning ceremony of Queen Elizabeth II in London, Shin Ik-hee (presented as Patrick Henry Shinicky), Speaker of the National Assembly of the ROK, soon to become a presidential candidate against Rhee, became the highest South Korean official to visit Italy. Shin was welcomed by Consul Mario Filo Della Torre, who escorted him to meet the Speakers of the Senate and House of Deputies. During the meeting, Shin, accompanied by Deputy Kim Dong-sung, thanked his hosts and commanded the 'active part taken by Italy in alleviating the sufferings that the Korean people had to endure for several years'. He further added that the entire Korean people wanted the unification of the nation and that he would fight with all his energies towards that goal and introduced to his counterparts the current situation in the institution he presided over: 100 seats have been left vacant for North Korean deputies until the country will be reunited (MAE DGAP Uff. V, 1953: 3). He also mentioned that his government was struggling to take 40 deputies that were deported to North Korea during the brief occupation of Seoul by Pyongyang's military back to South Korea, but at that moment had no information on their fate. During a private meeting with Filo della Torre, however, Shin shied away from further commenting on the political situation of his country but stressed that Rhee 'may have made some mistakes' in his rule (MAE DGAP Uff. V, 1953: 4). In a letter that Shin sent to Filo della Torre in September after returning to Korea at the end of his Thank You tour to Europe, he defined Italy as 'a great nation' and cheered his addressee by hoping that the ROK would receive Italy's 'continuous generosity and sympathies in helping us for freedom [sic] of the world' (Shinicky and Kim, 1953: 1).

Similar tones regarding the enduring friendship between Italy and South Korea can be observed in MAE records regarding the 1957 visits of several ROK political personalities. Against the backdrop of re-emerging tensions on the 38th parallel due to North Korea's military development programme supported by the USSR and the People's Republic of China (RPC) in December 1956, Italy and the ROK re-established official diplomatic relations (Ambasciata d'Italia Washington, 1957a). Rome had appointed a provisional charge d'affaires, Giuseppe Brigidi, former Italian consul in Tianjin and Northern China, to head the Italian ligation in Seoul, amidst several difficulties. A few months later, in March 1957, Cho Kyung Kyoo, Vice-Speaker of the ROK National Assembly, arrived in Rome as part of a 'goodwill tour' in Western Europe after visiting Western Germany, Switzerland, and France. While in Italy, Cho met with the Speakers of the House and Senate, whom he thanked again for Italy's humanitarian efforts in assisting the civil population affected by the war.

If the 68th field hospital still remained Italy's most important contribution in support of Seoul's cause during the Korean War in the eyes of the ROK leadership, another key decision by Rome in this regard was the allocation of ITL 200 million (USD 320,000) to the United Nations Korean Reconstruction Agency (UNKRA) in July 1955, a month ahead of Italy's official accession to the UN in December of the same year. Furthermore, at a January 1957 session of the UN General Assembly, Rome expressed its support to a US-led resolution asking the Security Council to re-examine the ROK's accession to the organisation vetoed by the Soviet Union. Along with other sponsor countries, such as Japan and the Philippines, in fact, Italy produced a supporting statement in favour of the ROK, which, in the words of the then US delegate Edward Greenbaum, had become a 'symbol of the first great effort of the free world to take collective action against aggression' (Teltsch, 1957: 6). In light of these facts, an MAE internal memo underlines that:

> The destruction caused by the recent conflict has been partially made up for and now the efforts of Seoul's government are to improve the country's industrial equipment. There are numerous opportunities for export into Korea of our machinery. Regarding Italian textiles (already dominating the local market) and fertilisers, we could further enhance their export. It could also be possible to sell conspicuous quantities of rice to Korea, given that local demand is higher than the production. Furthermore, there is no lack of opportunities for our specialised industry, technicians, particularly in the fishing industry which is extremely important for the Korean economy.
>
> (MAE DGAP, 1957a: 3).

Probably more consequential was, in May of that year, a visit to Italy by the ROK ambassador to the US and representative at the UN, Yang You-chan. Yang engaged in a goodwill tour of Western Europe as a Special Representative of the President of the ROK to rally moral support for the ROK's cause amongst major US allies. Through the Italian Embassy in Washington, he demanded to meet 'your Chief of State, your Premier and your Foreign Minister' to convey President Rhee's regards (Yang, 1957: 1). According to MAE internal exchanges, Yang is a man of trust for the ROK President that had been sent to Europe to strengthen 'economic and cultural ties between Korea and European nations' and thus his requests should be agreed upon (Ambasciata d'Italia Washington, 1957b: 2). As illustrated above, Italian authorities hoped that the humanitarian aid provided during the Korean War through the mobilisation of a CRI unit could lead to economic gains for Italian enterprises and, in general, favour Rome's national interests, particularly with regard to Italy's accession to the UN. The results of this effort were only limited. In several documents that have been analysed for this research, however, MAE officials appear aware of the political, rather than economic, scope of Yang's diplomatic mission to Italy. Another ministerial memo stresses that:

> The government in Seoul did not miss any opportunity to signal to the external world the repeated violation of the armistice clauses by the Pyongyang government and its allies and the continuous threat of aggression lingering on the country (trying to communicate the idea of a Soviet aggression in Korea would be in effect an aggression against the whole free world).
>
> (MAE DGAP Uff. V, 1957a: 4)".

In addition, the author of the note suggests adopting a discreet approach during the diplomatic exchange over the international situation in East Asia (for example, by avoiding any reference to Seoul's strained relations with Japan) and encourages a discussion on trade possibilities in the machinery, textile fibres, and fertilisers (MAE DGAP Uff. V, 1957a: 6). Speaking to Italy's Prime Minister Antonio Segni, who voiced his 'expectations' for enhanced economic ties with the ROK, Yang stressed that Italian firms were granted contracts for the development of chemical and ammunition plants but swiftly moved to political considerations over communism and the need to 'proactively defend democracy' (MAE Cerimoniale, 1957). At a press conference, Yang once more stressed that communism represented a 'persistent danger' for his country and called for renewed attention on political evolutions in the Far East, where the advance of communism was more worrying (MAE DGAP, 1957b: 2). To show his country's resolve to contrast it, Yang stressed that the ROK was 'one of the first peoples to send relief goods to Hungary's freedom fighters' in the face of the Soviet repression of political protests in Budapest (MAE DGAP, 1957c: 1). In conclusion, he added:

> It is up to us of the free world to forget our minor individual differences in the face of this global annihilation and unite in order to preserve our various individualities and remain free men. If we do not work together as a unit, we shall all be lost, and become slave of brutal communist tyrant.
>
> (MAE DGAP, 1957c: 2).

Pledges for political unity and friendship between Rome and Seoul were again reinforced by the ROK Ambassador Kim Young-kee, who, meeting Italian Prime Minister Adone Zoli ahead of his official installation, thanked Italy for its humanitarian aid during the 1950–1953 conflict and confirmed that his country looked with sympathy at Italy's political role to achieve the Korean people's goal to see their country finally reunited (Corriere della Sera, 1957: 7). Despite this political alignment in principle, domestic conditions on both sides prevented further enhancing bilateral cooperation in the time interval here taken into consideration. In particular, from a close reading of MAE archival materials, a sense of disappointment towards ROK's customs in regard to the chargé d'affaire Brigidi's accreditation as Ambassador and US-dominated trade policies emerges (Legazione d'Italia Seoul, 1957b, 1957c; MAE DGAE Uff V, 1957a). On the one hand, Brigidi, the *de facto* Italian representative in the ROK since December 1956, devoted much energy to gathering information on the economic and political situation of the ROK and wooing the Korean authorities in order to boost economic ties with Rome. On the other hand, he complained of being 'severely limited in his diplomatic action' given his lack of official status (a problem which he claimed was partially overcome by the intercession of US Ambassador Walter Dowling) and residence (he established his 'office' in the Bando Hotel in the ROK capital) that made it impossible for him to directly exchange express official notes with Rome (having to do that through Tokyo) and meet his diplomatic and business counterparts in restaurants or kisaeng as required by the Korean custom of the time (Legazione d'Italia Seoul, 1957d: 2).

However, Brigidi's service was key to the establishment of friendly relations with the ROK in the late 1950s. In one interview given to the Korean press before his departure from Hong Kong, he compared President Rhee to the Italian patriot Giuseppe Mazzini, one of the heroes of Risorgimento, credited with the invention of the liberation and unification movement of Italy in the late 19th century (Legazione d'Italia Seoul, 1957c). Then, once in Seoul, he acknowledged the possibility of meeting cabinet ministers, establishing relations with the ROK Foreign Minister Cho Chung-hwan, and taking part in formal diplomatic events. His apparent appreciation of Rhee won him the possibility to meet the President in private form during the celebrations for Rhee's 82nd birthday in March 1957. Brigidi describes Rhee as a man of 'benevolent and fatherly kindness', expressing his love for Italy, a country that he visited in his youth. Meeting Brigidi, Rhee thanked the Italian authorities for the warm welcome reserved to his envoys and discussed the threat of the 'Red Devil', for example, communism, stressing again the need for further cooperation and mutual knowledge among free countries (MAE DGAE Uff V, 1957b). Nonetheless, in 1957, despite Brigidi's presence serving as a means for enhanced communication between Rome and Seoul, trade relations between Italy and the ROK remained negligible in size, directly managed by private actors through the Italian Trading Office in Seoul, the sole Italian company operating in the ROK at the time, and not sanctioned by any provision of international law. In addition, the delay in the appointment of an official representative rather than a *de facto* one, such as consul Brigidi until late 1957, was deemed to further prevent Italian exporters from successfully participating in tenders for the supply of goods and services managed by the US International Cooperation Administration (ICA), which administered reconstruction funds for the ROK on behalf of the ROK Reconstruction Ministry and the US Office Economic Coordinator (OEC) (Legazione d'Italia Seoul, 1957b). Particularly, this diplomatic and administrative hindrance seems to have affected Italian business operators in the sectors of textiles, chemicals, and car parts (tyres) (Esportatori italiani, 1957).

However, in addition to the aforementioned development projects, the Italian representative had engaged in discussions over possible Italian participation in tenders for the supply of Fiat automobiles to the Seoul Police (deemed more suitable for the city's conformation) in the development of the Chinhae naval base since 1957 (MAE DGAE Uff V, 1957c, 1957d) and in the establishment of a technical cooperation for the development of ROK's fishing industry (MAE DGAE Uff V, 1957e, 1957f). In regard to the Chinhae base, Brigidi refers to his exchanges with a 'Colonel J. S. An' of the ROK Naval Engineering Corps, a graduate of the University of Genoa, who 'speaks and writes in Italian with me and showed me the most sincere and devoted friendship for Italy' (MAE DGAP Uff. V, 1957b). On that occasion, Brigidi inquired about the possibility of sending Italian technicians to support the development of the basis and showed his counterpart a catalogue of precision machinery manufactured by Italian companies that could be installed in the facility. From these documents emerges a certain sense of urgency among the Italian authorities in South Korea and Japan to foster economic ties with the ROK. In a July 1957 message, in the light of a soon-to-be-signed trade agreement between Japan and South Korea, the Italian Embassy in Tokyo suggested that:

> The organisation of trade exchanges with South Korea be enhanced [...] in order to benefit from the current contingencies to boost our exports in that market, that is, before an ROK-Japan agreement enters into force and creates a very dangerous competitor for our major export goods.
>
> (Ambasciata d'Italia Tokyo, 1957: 1).

In addition to international competition, Italian trade ties with ROK were further hindered by specific policies enacted by the government of the ROK to exclude cargo ships that had previously made port calls in 'communist countries' from its ports (Legazione d'Italia Seoul, 1957e: 2). According to Brigidi's final report, during his one-year tenure as chargé d'affaires in Seoul, Italian textile companies kept their dominant position on the Korean market, though they were increasingly exposed to competition from German and Japanese operators and could grab a nearly 6-million-dollar-worth procurement deal through the ICA funds. Furthermore, chemical and pharmaceutical companies had made profits of USD 500,000 and nearly USD 400,000, respectively. By contrast, carmaker Fiat could take part in a public tender for the supply of 1,500 jeeps to the Seoul Police but entered the Korean car market only two decades after when it sold licenses for its 124 model to Asia Motors, later included in the Kia group (Lee, 2009). Similarly, an agreement on the fishing industry development was reached only in 1962, when the Italian government agreed to lend USD 100,000 to purchase 950 Italian fishing boats (The New York Times, 1962).

Conclusion

Based on the aforementioned, it is possible to draw a few conclusions. Broadly, on the basis of a close reading of archival materials of the Ministry of Foreign Affairs and International Cooperation in Rome, this chapter has shown how ties between the ROK and Italy have been constructed since the early 1950s, strategising their respective positions vis-à-vis each other, the international community, and their patron state. On the one hand, by sending humanitarian aid to the ROK, Rome consistently pursued its long-term goal to regain prestige as a regional middle power on an equal standing with other European partners. On the other hand, the ROK's leadership in the 1950s attempted to establish a sort of middle power diplomacy centred on multilateralism and anti-communism at a time when the US support for the nation seemed flickering due to strategic divergences. Particularly, it has been pointed out how the two countries have partially worked around their unbalanced relations with the US to pursue their respective national interests and diplomatic agendas. In this regard, this chapter has reassessed the role of the ROK in the early phases of the Cold War as an overt US client state while shedding light on its emerging middlepowermanship. The attempt to create an anti-communist coalition in support of the ROK constitutes a piece of evidence of the ROK's leadership's attempt to deploy affective, immaterial means to catalyse sympathy and support towards the anti-communist cause.

In fact, in the 1950s, Rome and Seoul were mutually instrumental in achieving the two governments' respective foreign policy aims. On the one hand, by contributing to the UN multilateral efforts in the Korean peninsula through the Italian Red Cross (at that time under the state's jurisdiction), Italy has kept its promise to work together with the international community to enhance its international standing in the early phases of the Cold War. On the other hand, facing the risk of being abandoned by the US in the late 1950s, the Rhee administration included Italy in its diplomatic strategy to gather all possible support from the 'free world', to use ambassador Yang's words (MAE DGAP, 1957c: 2). At the same time, wooing Italy's support was an important part of the ROK's international strategy to foster its legitimacy in the face of competing claims in this regard by the DPRK, along with that of other Western European US allies. Although the original aims were only partially achieved on both ends, the case of the construction of the ROK-Italy alliance during the 1950s clearly illustrated the enduring symbolic value of humanitarian aid and its eminent political character. Finally, by focusing on post-war diplomatic interactions between the ROK and Italy, this chapter has attempted to clarify the behaviour of lesser and middle powers in the context of the Cold War. States with fewer capabilities and resources, and even client states such as the ROK in the historical contingency analysed above, can have room for political and diplomatic manoeuvring notwithstanding their patron states' preferences. Particularly, the case of ROK-Italy relations in the 1950s shows how Seoul could achieve its diplomatic goals (for example, contributing to the creation of a sense of an international Communist threat) by leveraging the memory of the Korean War and the legacy of Italian aid.

Notes

1 This chapter would not have been written without the immensely valuable help of Filippo Manara and the 'Farnesina' Historical Diplomatic Archive staff, particularly Riccardo Andreozzi, Paola Busonero, and Federica Onelli, who kindly accommodated my needs and requests, allowing me to access the archival materials in a very limited amount of time. This chapter has also benefitted from a series of invaluable insights from Kevin Gray, Sojin Lim, and Marco Milani.

2 The Italian Ministry of Foreign Affairs (Ministero degli Affari Esteri, MAE) has changed its name to Ministry of Foreign Affairs and International Cooperation (Ministero degli Affari Esteri e della Cooperazione Internazionale, MAECI) in 2014.

3 Currency conversion is based on data collected by Werner Antweiler, University of British Columbia. Available at https://fx.sauder.ubc.ca/etc/USDpages.pdf (Last accessed on 26 February 2023).

4 As a former socialist local administrator in Bologna since the late 1930s, Longhena was forced into clandestinity and joined the anti-fascist resistance. After the war, in 1948, he was appointed by Prime Minister Alcide De Gasperi as President of the CRI. As CRI president, besides the activities of Hospital 68 in South Korea, he coordinated the relief activities during the Polesine flood in northeastern Italy in 1951. He kept the post until 1957.

5 Particular recognition was given to the 68th field hospital medical personnel's prompt response to a train accident in Yeongdong-po that killed 17 people and left 200 injured in September 1952 (Corriere della Sera, 1952).

6 In the morning of 30 November 1952, a violent fire erupted in the CRI hospital No 68, probably caused by a fuel leak from a fuel-powered water boiler. Thanks to the prompt response by the hospital personnel, no victims were reported except for the brick-and-wood building in which the hospital's first surgery division was hosted (CRI 68th Italian Red Cross Field Hospital, 1952).

7 The MAE archival documents indicate that one of the members of the CRI mission, Dr Enrico Bosetti, stayed in Seoul after the decommissioning of the 68th Field Hospital, opening an Italian hospital. The hospital was transferred into the central Jongno district, in a three-story building. In May 1957, it had 26 beds and employed several Korean nurses who were instructed and coordinated by Bosetti (Legazione d'Italia Seoul, 1957a).

References

68th Italian Red Cross Field Hospital (1953). Protocollo 1096/C Schema Convenzione forniture Ospedale (schiarimenti). Archivio Storico Diplomatico, Ministero degli Affari Esteri e della Cooperazione Internazionale. Roma.

Ambasciata d'Italia Tokyo (1951). Telegramma 13837/2- Unità ospedaliera CRI in Corea. Archivio Storico Diplomatico, Ministero degli Affari Esteri e della Cooperazione Internazionale. Roma.

Ambasciata d'Italia Tokyo (1952a). 1E-Ospedale CRI in Corea. Archivio Storico Diplomatico, Ministero degli Affari Esteri e della Cooperazione Internazionale. Roma.

Ambasciata d'Italia Tokyo (1952b). Telespresso N. 2370. Archivio Storico Diplomatico, Ministero degli Affari Esteri e della Cooperazione Internazionale. Roma.

Ambasciata d'Italia Tokyo (1953). Telespresso N. 3192/2370. Archivio Storico Diplomatico, Ministero degli Affari Esteri e della Cooperazione Internazionale. Roma.
Ambasciata d'Italia Tokyo (1957). Telespresso N. 1203/837. Archivio Storico Diplomatico, Ministero degli Affari Esteri e della Cooperazione Internazionale. Roma.
Ambasciata d'Italia Washington (1952). Telespresso N. 14805/6555. Archivio Storico Diplomatico, Ministero degli Affari Esteri e della Cooperazione Internazionale. Roma.
Ambasciata d'Italia Washington (1957a). Telespresso N. 478. Archivio Storico Diplomatico, Ministero degli Affari Esteri e della Cooperazione Internazionale. Roma.
Ambasciata d'Italia Washington (1957b). Telespresso urgente N. 4933/040. Archivio Storico Diplomatico, Ministero degli Affari Esteri e della Cooperazione Internazionale. Roma.
Andreatta, F. (2001). Italy at a crossroads: The foreign policy of a medium power after the end of bipolarity. *Daedalus*, 130(2), 45–65.
Beeson, M., and R. Higgott (2014). The changing architecture of politics in the Asia-Pacific: Australia's middle power moment? *Int. Relat. Asia-Pac.*, 14(2), 215–37.
Bertoli, S., G. A. Cornia, and F. Manaresi (2007). Aid performance and its determinants. A comparison of Italy with the OECD norm. *Banca Naz. Lav. Q. Rev.*, 60, 271–321.
Brogi, A. (2002a). *A Question of Self-esteem: The United States and the Cold War Choices in France and Italy, 1944–1958*. Westport: Greenwood Publishing Group.
Brogi, A. (2002b). Ike and Italy: The Eisenhower Administration and Italy's "Neo-Atlanticist" agenda. *J. Cold War Stud.* 4, 5–35. https://doi.org/10.1162/152039702320201058
Calandri, E. (2003). Italys foreign assistance policy, 1959–1969. *Contemp. Eur. Hist.* 12, 509–525. https://www.cambridge.org/core/journals/contemporary-european-history/article/italys-foreign-assistance-policy-19591969/00D9C0DDE4F6A1F412E1BC6619959324#.
Carney, C. P. (1989). International patron-client relationships: A conceptual framework. *Stud. Comp. Int. Dev.*, 24(2), 42–55.
Cha, V. D. (2011). Rhee-straint: The origins of the U.S.-ROK alliance. *Int. J. Korean Stud.*, XV, 1–15.
Cha, V. D. (2016). *Powerplay: The Origins of the American Alliance System in Asia*. Princeton: Princeton University Press.
Chijiwa, Y. (2002). Japan's Postwar Security: From the US-Japan Alliance and the Constitution's Article 9 to the NSC. Tokyo: Chūō kōron sha [Chijiwa, Y. (2002). Sengo Nihon No Anzen Hoshō: Nichibeidōmei, Kenpō Dai 9 Jō Kara NSC].
Choi, J. H. (2018). Tra Corea e Italia "l'unione fa la forza" (Between Korea and Italy, "union is strength). Corriere della Sera 15 October, p. 30. Retrieved from https://archivio.corriere.it/ (accessed: March 20, 2024).
Choi, Y. J. (2009). South Korea's regional strategy and middle power activism. *J. East Asian Aff.*, 23(1): 47–67.
Colombo, S., and A. Palm (2019). *Italy in the Mediterranean*. Brussels and Rome: FEPS, Fondazione EYU.
Corriere della Sera (1952). Salta in aria in Corea un treno carico di scolari. 17 September, p. 5. Retrieved from https://archivio.corriere.it/ (accessed: March 20, 2024).
Corriere della Sera (1957). Zoli riceve l'ambasciatore della Corea de Sud. 15 September, p. 7. Retrieved from https://archivio.corriere.it/ (accessed: March 20, 2024).
CRI 68th Italian Red Cross Field Hospital (1952). Relazione dell'incendio del Reparto ospedaliero dell'Ospedale C.R.I. n. 68. Archivio Storico Diplomatico, Ministero degli Affari Esteri e della Cooperazione Internazionale. Roma.
CRI Comitato Centrale (1953a). Protocollo N. 02616 Forniture all'Ospedale n. 68 Corea da parte del Governo Americano. Archivio Storico Diplomatico, Ministero degli Affari Esteri e della Cooperazione Internazionale. Roma.

CRI Comitato Centrale (1953b). Protocollo N. 4602 Ospedale della C.R.I. In Corea. Archivio Storico Diplomatico, Ministero degli Affari Esteri e della Cooperazione Internazionale. Roma.

CRI Comitato Centrale Direzione affari internazionali (1951). Protocollo N. 7923 Risposta al Piano finanziario dell'ospedale CRI per la Corea. Archivio Storico Diplomatico, Ministero degli Affari Esteri e della Cooperazione Internazionale. Roma.

Cumings, B. (2011). *The Korean War: A History*. New York: Random House Publishing Group.

Duara, P. (2011). The cold war as a historical period: An interpretive essay. *J. Glob. Hist.,* 6(3), 457–480.

Embassy of the United States of America to Italy (1951a). F.O. No. 6483. Archivio Storico Diplomatico, Ministero degli Affari Esteri e della Cooperazione Internazionale. Roma.

Embassy of the United States of America to Italy (1951b). F.O. No. 8173. Archivio Storico Diplomatico, Ministero degli Affari Esteri e della Cooperazione Internazionale. Roma.

Esportatori italiani (1957). Telegramma 888. Archivio Storico Diplomatico, Ministero degli Affari Esteri e della Cooperazione Internazionale. Roma.

Giacomello, G., and E. Magnani (1993). Italian peace-keeping operations: A brief history. *Peace Res.,* 25, 85–94.

Gills, B. (2005). *Korea versus Korea: A Case of Contested Legitimacy*. New York: Routledge. https://doi.org/10.4324/9780203975282

Gu, J. (2002). Italian Red Cross and the Korean War - In the case of Italian 68 Medical Units support activities. Korean J. Eur. Integr., 13, 107–145. [구지훈 (2002). 이탈리아 적십자와 한국전쟁. 통합유럽연구, 제13권 2집. 107–145.].

Kim, D. W., and H.-S. Yang (2022). Seojeon Byungwon, Jutlandia, and NORMASH: UN's Scandinavian Allies at the Korean war and beyond (1950s–1960s). *East Asia Piscataway NJ,* 39, 127–147. https://doi.org/10.1007/s12140-021-09369-8

Kim, I., and J. Woods (2022). Survival politics: Regime security and alliance design on the Korean Peninsula. *J. Glob. Secur. Stud.*, 7, ogac001. https://doi.org/10.1093/jogss/ogac001

Lee, H. (2009). The old, reliable Fiat 124-except made in Korea [WWW Document]. Korea JoongAng Dly. https://koreajoongangdaily.joins.com/news/article/article.aspx?aid=2910295 (accessed: March 20, 2024).

Lee, H., and S. Yoon (2020). Republic of Korea: Korean War veteran's son in Italy thanks Korea for protective masks. *Korea.net*. https://www.korea.net/NewsFocus/policies/view?articleId=185940 (accessed: October 1, 2024).

Lee, S. H. (2011). Syngman Rhee's vision and reality: The establishment of the nation and thereafter. *Rev. Korean Stud.*, 14, 33–60. https://doi.org/10.25024/REVIEW.2011.14.3.002

Lee, S. H., and Y. C. Park (2017). Korea's middle power diplomacy for human security: A global and regional approach. *J. Int. Area Stud.*, 24(1), 21–44.

Legazione d'Italia Seoul (1957a). Telespresso N. 308/1. Archivio Storico Diplomatico, Ministero degli Affari Esteri e della Cooperazione Internazionale. Roma.

Legazione d'Italia Seoul (1957b). Telespresso N. 74/42. Archivio Storico Diplomatico, Ministero degli Affari Esteri e della Cooperazione Internazionale. Roma.

Legazione d'Italia Seoul (1957c). Telespresso N. 40/28. Archivio Storico Diplomatico, Ministero degli Affari Esteri e della Cooperazione Internazionale. Roma.

Legazione d'Italia Seoul (1957d). Telespresso 693/324. Archivio Storico Diplomatico, Ministero degli Affari Esteri e della Cooperazione Internazionale. Roma.

Legazione d'Italia Seoul (1957e). Telespresso N. 560/245. Archivio Storico Diplomatico, Ministero degli Affari Esteri e della Cooperazione Internazionale. Roma.

MAE Cerimoniale (1957). Appunto. Archivio Storico Diplomatico, Ministero degli Affari Esteri e della Cooperazione Internazionale. Roma.
MAE DGAE Uff V (1957a). Telespresso N. 0310. Archivio Storico Diplomatico, Ministero degli Affari Esteri e della Cooperazione Internazionale. Roma.
MAE DGAE Uff V (1957b). Telespresso N. 15/4118/C. Archivio Storico Diplomatico, Ministero degli Affari Esteri e della Cooperazione Internazionale. Roma.
MAE DGAE Uff V (1957c). Telespresso N. 45/05700. Archivio Storico Diplomatico, Ministero degli Affari Esteri e della Cooperazione Internazionale. Roma.
MAE DGAE Uff V (1957d). Telespresso N. 16478. Archivio Storico Diplomatico, Ministero degli Affari Esteri e della Cooperazione Internazionale. Roma.
MAE DGAE Uff V (1957e). Fonogramma in partenza N. 5442. Archivio Storico Diplomatico, Ministero degli Affari Esteri e della Cooperazione Internazionale. Roma.
MAE DGAE Uff V (1957f). Telespresso N. 15285. Archivio Storico Diplomatico, Ministero degli Affari Esteri e della Cooperazione Internazionale. Roma.
MAE DGAP (1952). Appunto circa le forniture americane all'ospedale della C.R.I. In Corea. Archivio Storico Diplomatico, Ministero degli Affari Esteri e della Cooperazione Internazionale. Roma.
MAE DGAP (1957a). Appunto. Oggetto: Corea. Archivio Storico Diplomatico, Ministero degli Affari Esteri e della Cooperazione Internazionale. Roma.
MAE DGAP (1957b). Conferenza stampa dell'ambasciatore Yang. Archivio Storico Diplomatico, Ministero degli Affari Esteri e della Cooperazione Internazionale. Roma.
MAE DGAP (1957c). Statement by Ambassador You Chan Yang. Archivio Storico Diplomatico, Ministero degli Affari Esteri e della Cooperazione Internazionale. Roma.
MAE DGAP (n.d.). Pro Memoria. Archivio Storico Diplomatico, Ministero degli Affari Esteri e della Cooperazione Internazionale. Roma.
MAE DGAP Uff. V (1951a). Telespresso N. 16/15036. Archivio Storico Diplomatico, Ministero degli Affari Esteri e della Cooperazione Internazionale. Roma.
MAE DGAP Uff. V (1951b). Telespresso N. 1659/2. Archivio Storico Diplomatico, Ministero degli Affari Esteri e della Cooperazione Internazionale. Roma.
MAE DGAP Uff. V (1951c). Telegramma N. 10180. Archivio Storico Diplomatico, Ministero degli Affari Esteri e della Cooperazione Internazionale. Roma.
MAE DGAP Uff. V (1952). Telespresso N. 15/18705. Archivio Storico Diplomatico, Ministero degli Affari Esteri e della Cooperazione Internazionale. Roma.
MAE DGAP Uff. V (1953). Appunto. Archivio Storico Diplomatico, Ministero degli Affari Esteri e della Cooperazione Internazionale. Roma.
MAE DGAP Uff. V (1957a). Telespresso urgente 4480/15 (allegato). Archivio Storico Diplomatico, Ministero degli Affari Esteri e della Cooperazione Internazionale. Roma.
MAE DGAP Uff. V (1957b). Telespresso N. 15/5585. Archivio Storico Diplomatico, Ministero degli Affari Esteri e della Cooperazione Internazionale. Roma.
MAE DGAP Uff. VI (1950a). Telespresso urgente 21/24144. Archivio Storico Diplomatico, Ministero degli Affari Esteri e della Cooperazione Internazionale. Roma.
MAE DGAP Uff. VI (1950b). Telegramma 7999. Archivio Storico Diplomatico, Ministero degli Affari Esteri e della Cooperazione Internazionale. Roma.
MAE DGAP Uff. VI (1951a). Nota verbale No. 04962/41. Archivio Storico Diplomatico, Ministero degli Affari Esteri e della Cooperazione Internazionale. Roma.
MAE DGAP Uff. VI (1951b). Telespresso N. 21/05386. Archivio Storico Diplomatico, Ministero degli Affari Esteri e della Cooperazione Internazionale. Roma.
Magliano, M. (1962). L'assistenza ai paesi in via di sviluppo. *Riv. Studi Polit. Internazionali* 29, 28–46.

Mammarella, G., and P. Cacace (2006). *La politica estera dell'Italia: dallo stato unitario ai giorni nostri*. Roma: Laterza.

Midtgaard, K. (2011). National security and the choice of international humanitarian aid: Denmark and the Korean War, 1950–1953. *J. Cold War Stud.*, 13, 148–174.

Ministero del Tesoro (1951). Telegramma N. 11193. Archivio Storico Diplomatico, Ministero degli Affari Esteri e della Cooperazione Internazionale. Roma.

Ministero del Tesoro (1953). Telespresso N. 11/C 105726 Unità ospedaliera della Croce Rossa Italiana in Corea. Archivio Storico Diplomatico, Ministero degli Affari Esteri e della Cooperazione Internazionale. Roma.

Ministry of Patriots and Veterans Affairs (2019). The story of the UN participants in the Korean War - Italy: The last country to dispatch a medical support unit, Italy's 68th Red Cross Hospital. Official Blog. https://blog.naver.com/mpvalove/221592395043 (accessed: September 27, 2024). [국가보훈처 (2019). 6.25 전쟁 유엔참전국 이야기 - 이탈리아편. 마지막으로 의료지원부대를 파견한 나라, 이탈리아 제68적십자병원. 국가보훈부 공식 블로그, 보훈정책 소식].

Ministry of Patriots and Veterans Affairs (2023). Background of participation and activity of each forces [WWW Document]. https://www.mpva.go.kr/english/contents.do?key=1311 (accessed: February 25, 2023).

Mo, J. (2016). South Korea's middle power diplomacy: A case of growing compatibility between regional and global roles. *Int. J.,* 71(4), 587–607.

Mower, A. G. (1966). Observer countries: Quasi members of the United Nations. *Int. Organ.*, 20, 266–283.

Oh, T. H. (2016). 130 years between Korea and Italy: Evaluation and prospect. In: Korea's Economy. Washington, DC: Korea Economic Institute of America, PP 73–81.

Papi, G.U. (1962). Paesi in via di sviluppo. *Riv. Studi Polit. Internazionali*, 29, 189–210.

Park, J. (2010). The medical assistance of Swedish Red Cross field hospital in Busan during and after the Korean War. *Korean J. Med. Hist.*, 19, 189–208.

Parrillo, F. (1966). La cooperazione economica internazionale e i paesi in via di sviluppo. *G. Degli Econ. E Ann. Econ.*, 25, 56–88.

Presidenza del Consiglio dei Ministri (1953a). Telespresso N. 45663/260. Archivio Storico Diplomatico, Ministero degli Affari Esteri e della Cooperazione Internazionale. Roma.

Presidenza del Consiglio dei Ministri (1953b). Telespresso N. 260/104. Archivio Storico Diplomatico, Ministero degli Affari Esteri e della Cooperazione Internazionale. Roma.

Shim, D., and P. Flamm (2012). *Rising South Korea: A Minor Player or a Regional Power?* German Institute of Global and Area Studies (GIGA). https://www.jstor.org/stable/resrep07649 (accessed: July 18, 2023).

Shin, W. (1994). Geopolitical determinants of political economy: The cold war and South Korean political economy. *Asian Perspect.*, 18(2), 119–40.

Shinicky, P. H., and D. S. Kim (1953). Letter of P. H. Shinicky and Kim Dong Sung to Mario Filo della Torre. Archivio Storico Diplomatico, Ministero degli Affari Esteri e della Cooperazione Internazionale. Roma.

Siddi, M. (2019). Italy's 'Middle Power' approach to Russia. *Int. Spect.*, 54(2), 123–38.

Snyder, S., C. Bradford, T. Dalton, B. Howe, K. J. O'Donnel, and A. O'Neil (2015). Middle-Power Korea. Council on Foreign Relations. https://www.cfr.org/report/middle-power-korea (accessed July 18, 2023).

Teltsch, K. (1957). U.S. Bids U.N. Seat Seoul and Saigon. New York Times, 24 January, p. 6. Retrieved from https://archive.nytimes.com/ (accessed: March 20, 2024).

The New York Times (1950). Togliatti Rallies Italy against U.S., 31 July, p. 12. Retrieved from https://archive.nytimes.com/ (accessed: March 20, 2024).

The New York Times (1962). Seoul to Get Ship Loan. 13 February, p. 56. Retrieved from https://archive.nytimes.com/ (accessed: March 20, 2024).

Varsori, A. (2022). *Dalla rinascita al declino. Storia internazionale dell'Italia repubblicana.* Bologna: Il Mulino.

Verbeek, B., and G. Giacomello eds. (2011). *Italy's Foreign Policy in the Twenty-First Century: The New Assertiveness of an Aspiring Middle Power.* 1st edition. Lanham, MD: Lexington Books.

Yang, Y. (1957). Letter to Manlio Brosio, Ambassador Extraordinary and Plenipotentiary of Italy, Washington D.C. Archivio Storico Diplomatico, Ministero degli Affari Esteri e della Cooperazione Internazionale. Roma.

2 German Economic Advisory Group (DVB) to Korea, 1962–1968[1]

Max Altenhofen

Introduction

This chapter focuses on the early period of development cooperation between the West German and South Korean governments. While the government of the United States (US) provided significant material and technical support to South Korea (hereinafter, Korea) in the 1950s, it started to transfer more responsibility to its partners, including West Germany (hereinafter, Germany), in the early 1960s (Hein, 2006: 31–34). The new Korean government under Park Chung-hee attempted to expand the list of donor countries to overcome dependency on the US. In 1961, Germany and Korea signed the first protocol on technical and financial cooperation. This bilateral cooperation lasted until 1993, and Germany provided a total of DM 590 million in financial loans and DM 209 million in technical support, making it the third largest bilateral partner after the US and Japan (Köllner, 1998: 30 & 32).

For the early period of this bilateral cooperation, the activities of the German Economic Advisory Group (Deutsche Volkswirtschaftliche Beratergruppe, DVB) in Korea played a significant role. The DVB was working within the newly established Economic Planning Board (EPB) of the Korean government from 1962 to 1968 and consisted of three young German economists and one engineer on site, as well as the senior project manager Walter Rau, who was commuting between Seoul and Bonn. Originally, the advisory group was dispatched for two years, but the contract was subsequently extended by four more years. The advisors were involved in shaping Korean economic policy through their work on the five-year plans, the preparation of sectoral studies, as well as consulting on infrastructure projects and business cooperation. However, the DVB also reported information on the Korean economy and specific projects to the German ministries, banks, and companies to enable decisions on funding within the framework of bilateral cooperation. Although the DVB usually worked closely with Korean and American economists, they also criticised them and set their own accents in economic policy.

As the development of the Korean economy that started in the 1960s has been regarded as an ideal case for developing countries, the analysis of bilateral cooperation during the development period plays an even more important role (Kim, Kim and Kim, 2013). While the US and United Nations (UN) support for Korea

DOI: 10.4324/9781003497035-2

is well known (Han, 2017; KOICA, 2004), research on smaller donors like West Germany has so far not been sufficiently conducted. Especially during the 1960s, the role of Germany as a donor country became more important, and with the state visit of Korean President Park Chung-hee in 1964, Korean policymakers regarded Germany as a model for economic development with the 'Miracle of the Rhine River' (Noh, 2011).

In this chapter, West German technical assistance in Korea is historically critically examined as a global phenomenon at the local level. This 'glocal' approach focuses on 'concepts, constellations, institutions and practices where they were developed, in their application on site and above all in their mutual interdependence' (Büschel and Speich, 2009: 9). This chapter deals with the transfer of economic know-how from Germany to Korea, specifically from the perspective of the actors. Therefore, this chapter employs no theoretical approach and rather lets the sources and actors speak, to trace the creation of economic knowledge during the Cold War. This also provides a new perspective on bilateral development cooperation in the field of economic advisory today.

This chapter first provides a background to the role of economics during the Cold War, specifically the West German and South Korean economists. Then, the activities of the advisory group are analysed more in detail. This chapter focuses on how economic policy influence was exerted through this advice. Finally, international cooperation with American economic consultants on site and within the framework of the multilateral economic advisory group, the International Economic Consultative Group for Korea (IECOK), will be considered.

Economist's Influence in West Germany and South Korea during the Cold War

The economy, and thus, economics, played an important role because the two superpowers and their respective blocks were in economic competition. While the communist bloc stuck to the centrally planned economy, several paradigm shifts took place in the West from the neoclassical school of Keynesianism and ordoliberalism to neoliberalism (Loth, 2010). Because neither West German nor South Korean economic policy was clearly and permanently oriented towards one of these theories, tracing their influence in actual politics proves difficult, making it inevitable to look at the actors involved.

Due to the high complexity of economic policy issues, the Federal Ministry of Economic Affairs (Bundesministerium für Wirtschaft, BMWi) and the Korean EPB had a high proportion of economists as employees. Even if the largest number of officials in the BMWi were lawyers, economists, and scientists from business administration followed in second place. Also, most of the early West German ministers for economic affairs had received a comparable education in either business administration or economics, including Ludwig Erhard, Karl Schiller, and Helmut Schmidt (Nützenadel, 2005; Löffler 2016). In South Korea, most EPB employees were economists too, generally trained at Seoul National University (Kim, 1992). At the same time, external consultants such as professors played an important role.

In Germany, for example, the Advisory Council for the Assessment of Overall Economic Development, which was created in 1963 and whose members, also known as the 'five wise men (fünf Wirtschaftsweise)', still advise the federal government today (Nützenadel, 2005: 152–174; Hesse, 2016: 427–435). For the Korean EPB, next to the DVB, not only American advisors but also individual Korean professors and the International Advisory Group should be mentioned, and, from 1968, the IECOK played an important role in economic advice (Park, 2007).

On the one hand, the influence of the so-called Freiburg school of ordo-liberalism in the Federal Republic of Germany (FRG) is classically emphasised in research, which was different from Anglo-American economics. Above all, the catchphrase 'social market economy' is normally used in this context. Keynesianism or neoclassical economic theory, on the other hand, were more likely to be seen as 'American imports' and were therefore less successful in the beginning (Nützenadel, 2005: 18). At the same time, historians have emphasised the rising influence of American theories on German economics because, especially in the 1960s, many West and East German economists were invited for training at American universities (Bianchini, 2020). In addition, recent research also highlights the early influence of the neoliberal school on German economics, primarily through consulting activities and the influential Mont Pèlerin Society (Bank, 2013; Plehwe and Schmelzer, 2015: 488–499).

There is little research literature on the development of economics in Korea, though. Historian Eric Helleiner (2021) outlined the transnational transfers of (neo-)mercantilism starting with German economist Friedrich List, for example, employed by thinkers of the Gaewha Group under the late Choson dynasty, which shows some early influences of German economic thinking in Korea. However, he also emphasised the historical traditions of mercantilism in East Asia (Helleiner, 2021: 261–281). As in other fields of science, many Korean economists were educated in Japan during the colonial period. After 1945, most professors in economics at Korean universities were left-wing and trained their students accordingly. However, after the division and with the influence of the US, a large number of economists were sent to the US for further training and conformed to the South Korean government's anti-communist ideology. Also, modernisation theory became popular in the 1960s in Korea (Lee, 2012). Regarding the Park Chung-hee government's first five-year plan, Park Hui-beom is described as the most influential Korean economist and advisor to the Korean government. Park Hui-beom's proximity to institutional economics met with disapproval, especially among American advisors, who considered it to be socialist planning.

Irrespective of the various economic theories, there was a tendency of economists to differentiate themselves more strongly from the humanities and to make their research more scientific by increasingly applying econometric, for example, quantitative approaches and appropriating models of natural sciences or engineering. This aimed for greater political neutrality. Similar tendencies can be found in other sciences, such as demography, nutritional science, or agricultural science (Nützenadel, 2005: 99; also see : Latour, 1999). In the FRG, non-university research institutes for applied economics with a focus on topics such as consumer research, econometrics, or statistics developed, which produced various sectoral and economic studies for politics and the free economy. These included, for instance, the German Institute for Economic Research or the Kiel Institute for the World Economy (Nützenadel, 2005: 90–122). Similarly oriented consulting activities were also carried out by DVB, as below.

DVB: Politics and Economy

Although economic advice played an important role in so-called developed countries after the end of the Second World War for reconstruction within the framework of the Marshall Plan, the economic advisory groups deployed in developing countries exhibited a form of geopolitical hegemony and influence—mostly by the US—that did not exist in the industrialised countries (Burton, 2021; Calvo-Gonzales, 2006; Schiffman, Young, and Zelkha, 2017; Simpson, 2008). The political importance of the DVB in Korea against the background of the Cold War was also emphasised at various points. As early as 1962, the head of DVB, Walter Rau,[2] made a detailed statement on the political and economic situation in Korea in a first overview report. On the one hand, Korea was 'by no means completely safe from communism or immune to it' (Rau, 1962a: 1). The 'peasant proletariat' and the intellectuals could easily be influenced by 'communist demagogues' (Rau, 1962a: 1–2). The military government under Park Chung-hee, on the other hand, was trying to create a 'corruption-free administration' and to promote economic development (Rau, 1962a: 1–2). This represented a general view of the situation in Korea at the time, as similar statements by German Ambassador Karl Bünger show (German Embassy Seoul, 1963: 2). In this context, Rau emphasised the political importance of the DVB:

> The Park government has a few years to prove itself. If it does not pass this test, the political stability of this country is in question. The danger of self-mutilation and communism is then within reach. Passing this test depends mostly on the economic success of the government. Economic success would be Western success.
>
> (Rau, 1962b: 3)

The deployment of the DVB was therefore characterised by the competition with communism and pursued political goals. The rhetoric showed clear parallels to Konrad Adenauer's and Ludwig Erhard's policy of economic stability, which was later taken up by the Korean government under the Park administration (Noh, 2011). Furthermore, Rau saw the possibility of German 'influence on South Korean economic policy' (Rau, 1962b: 3). Interestingly, however, he emphasised that direct influence by the German advisory group should be avoided and that it should only go unnoticed:

> An economic advisory group faces a particularly difficult psychological task. Any developing country would be willing to admit that it had no geological

> or engineering experience. No developing country will readily admit that it is making economic policy mistakes. It is therefore important to skilfully 'sneak' into the mentality of the country in question and imperceptibly influence the process design. This requires a special kind of intellectual independence (…)
>
> (Rau, 1962b: 4)

The behaviour of the German consultants in Korea differed from that of other developing countries. Burton (2021: 420) describes the West German economic and financial advisors in Tanzania as 'more self-confident, sometimes even brash and aggressively demanding' compared to the East German experts in the same field. Above all, the choice of words such as 'sneak into' and 'imperceptibly' portrays the activities of the DVB as a secret mission, as shown above. Direct actions or even attempts to interfere in Korean politics would have been regarded negatively, and thus, the German consultants adapted to the circumstances in Korea. This might be a reason why it proves difficult to come across the direct influence of the advisors on actual policy.

Externally, it was emphasised that the consultants were not concerned with imposing Western values, institutions, or technology. Rau, for example, wrote that although such acceptance is necessary to a certain extent, many values and institutions in Korea do not impede economic development. At the same time, he emphasised the reciprocity of technical assistance, an idea that is only reflected later by the term 'development cooperation'. In an article for the *Korea Journal*, Rau (1963a: 37) wrote: 'Learning and teaching is a matter of reciprocity and mutuality. In a 'reversed technical assistance programme' Korea might teach something to the Western countries of her arts and her skills'. However, the actual practice of this rhetoric was not visible in the DVB's activities.

Typically for economists at the time, the influence of modernisation theory on the DVB was strong. Rau attributed Korea's 'backwardness' to an economic theory called the 'vicious circle of poverty', which was a popular model at the time, as follows:

> The most important domestic obstacle can be subsumed in this connection under the general heading: vicious circle, thus showing that (…) many obstacles to development are both cause and consequence. The basic vicious circle in the sense of a circular relationship is: backwardness – low productivity – low income – low level of saving – low level of capital formation – backwardness.
>
> (Rau, 1963a: 36)

According to this model, foreign capital in the form of development assistance was needed to break out of this circle. Rau (1966a: 11) cited Israel, Taiwan, and Hong Kong as successful examples of development in the 1960s, where state intervention was minimal. Even if the recourse to the modernisation theory, which was widespread in Korea at the time, initially seems appropriate, mentioning the model countries can be seen as a criticism of the direct interventions and planning methods of the EPB and the government under Park Chung-hee. At the same time, DVB was actively involved in the government's planning efforts by revising and drafting the five-year plans, as analysed in the following section of this chapter.

Elsewhere, German economists criticised the econometric orientation of economics in the Korean EPB (Kraus, 1966: 2–4; Rau, 1962a: 3). They attributed this imprint to the fact that many Korean officials had studied in the US.[3] However, as mentioned above, a tendency towards a more scientific approach to economics through econometric approaches could also be observed in Germany. Rau (1966a) also noted that German advice and influence on qualitative issues would only be possible if the DVB gained recognition in the quantitative approach. For this reason, quantitative calculations were transferred to the Institute for Applied Economic Research (Institut für Angewandte Wirtschaftsforschung, IAW) in Tübingen. For example, the institute carried out special calculation assignments for the five-year plans (Rau, 1962c: 1–2, 1963b: 19–20). Like the research institutes mentioned above, the institute in Tübingen had a focus on econometrics.

Germanifying Korea's Economic Policy and Practice

The main tasks of the group consisted of advising the Korean government on economic and technical questions, examining projects of German and foreign development assistance, and advising German companies. The DVB covered a wide variety of areas in business and industry (Boucherie, 1967: 2–3). The first and probably most important task of the DVB was the close cooperation with the EPB in the revision of the first and the development of the second five-year economic plan. The DVB also prepared a long-term forecast for Korean economic development. The EPB reports highlight this advisory activity rather positively (EPB, 1964: 4–5). At first glance, economic planning under President Park Chung-hee's administration is very closely linked to the five-year plans. However, almost all five-year plans were revised by adjusting the figures, discarding projects, or adding new ones. In historical research, the preparation of the plans is therefore also understood as part of symbolic politics since the original planning and political reality did not correspond one to one (Kim, 2019).

As mentioned above, the head of the German advisory group, Rau, criticised the strong focus on planning by the Korean officials in the EPB right from the start, calling them 'plan-obsessed' (Rau, 1962a: 4). Most of the officials at the EPB were trained in the US and therefore adhered to a 'mathematical direction in economics', which means their economic planning was only focused on quantitative aspects. In his opinion, however, the balance of the planning left a lot to be desired (Rau, 1962a: 3–4). Similar criticism was also voiced internally by Korean economists and in talks with American experts (Kimiya, 1991; Park, 2007). Rau (1963b: 28) comments on the first five-year plan as follows: 'In the end, despite all the apparent economic brilliance, the plan is neither homogeneous nor realistic'. The planning was 'too demanding' and 'supersised' from a macroeconomic point of view, since according to DVB advisors, a degree of capital assistance, own capital formation, and productivity growth was assumed that could not be realised (Rau, 1963b: 29). DVB, therefore, attempted to draft the plans more realistically.

In the first year, the effects of the failed currency reform and rice import crisis showed that the plan had various shortcomings, which is why a revision was initiated, also under pressure from the US (Park, 2007). The revision process began in November 1962 and was based on the actual experiences of the first year of the plan. In July 1963, the plan up to the third year was first published, and then in February 1964, the plan for the remaining two years was released under the title 'Supplement to the first five-year economic plan' (Park, 2007: 321).[4]

For the drafting of the second five-year plan, the German advisory group and the American economic advisors participated in weekly meetings of the economic cabinet, which were also known as the '10.30 AM meeting' (Boucherie, 1965: 7–8). In addition to the EPB, the DVB also worked closely with the finance and trade ministries and the Korean central bank (Glaeser, 2021). In contrast to the first five-year plan, foreign consultants were involved right from the start, and greater cooperation between the individual departments was achieved (Cole and Lyman, 1971). For example, the DVB developed a capital coefficient and a model for estimating the growth rate for the second five-year plan in close cooperation with IAW in Tübingen. The DVB also criticised the lack of quantitative guidelines for investment distribution. While export goals, import substitution, and exchange rates had been realistically planned, there was no coordination of the detailed planning. Therefore, the German and American consultants worked out a more specific investment plan together (Boucherie, 1965: 6).

During the five years of activity, the consultations shifted from fundamental macro-economic issues to more differentiated issues related to individual projects and economic sectors. The DVB compiled several project reports and sector studies.[5] The following classification can be found in an expert opinion on the activities of DVB:

> The working area of the group is extremely broad. It extends to all economic policy issues and planning tasks. This means that the group may be involved with matters ranging from dewatering to the tax system, from a project appraisal to the completed law. Nevertheless, the planning of the production structure is at the centre of the consulting work.
>
> (Kraus, 1966: 2)

Due to the complexity and variety of issues, close cooperation between the DVB employees was essential. Because the topics were not narrowed down, the group showed great flexibility and initiative, according to the expert's report (Kraus, 1966: 5). In particular, the latter helped to increase their influence on Korean economic planning and legislation. The advisers were able to contact ministries directly from the EPB and attended important meetings on economic planning, including the cabinet meetings. Nevertheless, the DVB was not free from minor internal conflicts either.[6]

The preparation of reports and studies on individual sectors was similar to the consulting work of the above-mentioned private institutes for applied economics. However, contemporaries also criticised the large number of reports and their low impact on actual politics. The West German economist Gerhard Weisser, for example, spoke of a 'survey cemetery' already in the 1950s (Nützenadel, 2005: 130). It remains unclear which DVB studies and reports had an impact on the political decisions of the Korean actors. It has also not yet been clarified whether the macroeconomic or the sectoral reports played a more important role. Regardless of its effect, expert opinions still represent a crucial component of consultancy work in development policy in general.

Furthermore, several institutions of the German government relied on the DVB's reports and studies. Although the embassy's economic attaché oversaw assessment and decision-making on German development assistance projects, the Bundesministerium für wirtschaftliche Zusammenarbeit und Entwicklung (BMZ), the BMWi, or the Kreditbank für Wiederaufbau (KfW) bank often turned to the DVB because its members seemed to have a better knowledge of the Korean economic situation (Rau, 1963c: 16). The position of the DVB is therefore divided from the beginning. On the one hand, it was emphasised that the experts should advise the Korean government independently of the FRG or German private companies, and they were supposed to pass on knowledge and neutral opinions on German development assistance projects (GAWI, 1965). Statements were made on the Yeongnam II thermal power plant and the German-Korean dairy farm projects, which played an important role as political leverage during the so-called East Berlin spy-ring incident (Bösch, 2024: 211–212; Lee, 2017; Spiegel, 1967; Wichelmann, 1966).[7] The DVB had an advisory function and a corresponding influence on the posting of Korean interns to Germany, for which the embassy made the final decisions (German Embassy Seoul, 1967). This important role of the DVB led to conflicts with the embassy and the foreign office. For instance, in one meeting, Rau criticised that his role as head of the DVB was repeatedly questioned by the German embassy in Seoul. He also stated that Ambassador Karl Bünger hated him 'like the plague' but had to recognise his work in Korea (German Foreign Ministry, 1966: 3). The embassy ultimately accepted the DVB's role, probably also due to the professional knowledge of the DVB employees.

In an oral history interview, the Korean economist Yeong-hun Baek (2009), who completed his doctorate in Germany and thereafter worked in the EPB, mainly remembered DVB's statements and reports on financial assistance projects rather than their advice on the five-year or sectoral plans. Baek, who misdated DVB's starting date of the advisory activities in the interview, named four main areas of capital assistance that were relevant to economic development at the time: coal mining, fertiliser production, cement production, and telephone lines. The German government supported the Korean government's first and second five-year plans with financial loans or Hermes guarantees in all these sectors (Köllner 1998: 30–32). However, DVB also examined projects in other sectors, such as the textile and steel industries. The oral history interview outlines another view of the DVB, namely it being connected to the German government's economic investments and technical assistance in Korea (see Baek, 2009).

In addition, the advisory group was often contacted by German businesspeople throughout Asia. They assumed that the group primarily represented German export interests in Korea, which the advisory group rejected. Still, they consulted with the companies informally in case they deemed it necessary (Kraus, 1966: 1). However, according to the DVB reports, the Korean authorities were aware that the advisory group had no direct links with the German export industry, which increased their importance to the Korean government. Japanese or American consultants, in comparison, were more likely regarded to have a business interest (Kraus, 1966: 6). This also shows how the DVB saw itself as politically neutral and more scientifically oriented, especially compared to Korea's other partners.

However, notwithstanding such claims, the DVB represented German business interests as well. For example, the DVB established contacts between German and Korean companies, selected Korean companies for German trade fairs and prepared them for the visit, and they conducted market assessments and studies for individual large companies (Boucherie, 1965: 17–18). According to a DVB consultant, the cooperation with German companies was above all a 'mutual exchange of opinions and ideas' (Glaeser, 2021). The reports do not show how companies were selected and whether, for example, separate consultancy fees were paid. Presumably, however, contacts were also made through private relationships, as in the case of other German projects (Altenhofen, 2024: 73).

The example of the ceramics industry underlines the close connection between the private interests of German companies, official development assistance (ODA) and DVB's consulting work. The German ceramics company 'Villeroy & Boch' entered private cooperation with a Korean ceramics company as early as 1962 and sent a technical consultant at its own expense. However, due to the Korean company's financial difficulties, further cooperation failed (Villeroy & Boch, 1965: 1). From 1965 onwards, the president of Villeroy & Boch finally got in touch again with various Korean companies by the BMZ and DVB, travelled to Korea personally, and inquired specifically about direct investments (Villeroy & Boch, 1965: 1). As a result, the Korean government requested the dispatch of an expert for the ceramics industry, and an employee of the Villeroy & Boch Company was selected for this task and sent to Korea for three years from 1967 to 1970 at the expense of the FRG (Glaeser, 1965). Although the DVB claimed otherwise, there is no distinct boundary between private interests and German development assistance in this field. As Burton (2021: 376 & 402) has shown for the case of Tanzania, the close cooperation between German businesses, development assistance, and economic advisory in the 1960s was common. According to Bösch (2024: 12; 202–203), the German government at the time cooperated with developmental dictatorships like South Korea to secure export markets.

The field of bilateral business cooperation (betriebliche Kooperation in German) as part of advisory groups in development cooperation was expanded starting in the 1980s. Two German and Korean advisors, respectively, supported the closure of contracts on technology transfer or joint ventures between German and Korean companies, mostly in the industry sector. While these were traditionally fields of the German Chamber of Foreign Trade or the Korea Trade-Investment Promotion Agency (KOTRA), ODA projects played an increasingly important part. As the number of cases in the 1960s was rather small and the above-mentioned chamber was not yet active in Korea, the DVB advisors had to deal with the cases on their own, even though they were not experts on business joint ventures (Koch, 1986; Uhlig, 1985: 278–279).

Another important task of the DVB consisted of symbolic activities such as lectures and presentations to the officials of the EPB. Above all, these revolved around the economic development of the FRG and dealt with general economic topics. The German consultants hoped this would allow them to indirectly influence Korean economic policy (Rau, 1963b: 22). Two advisors of the DVB gave a joint English-language lecture at Sungkyunkwan University to around 30 economics students, which dealt with general 'economic problems of underdeveloped countries' (Rau, 1963d: 22). One advisor also published an article on German economic development in the university magazine of the *Hankuk University of Foreign Studies* (Glaeser, 1966). Hence, the officials of the EPB as well as economics students at Korean universities were not only brought closer to German economic development but also to their economic approaches in general. This might have enforced the prevailing discourses on the German economic 'Miracle of the Rhine River' and highlighted once again Germany as an economic role model for Korea (Noh, 2011). The positive view of Germany and German values at the time was strongly connected to the craft system and ordo-liberalism, as Noh (2007) and Yu and Chung (2016: 11–12) have analysed. Further analysis of the economic models in 1960s Korea would highlight not only their symbolic but also practical importance amongst Korean intellectuals and economists.

Furthermore, the BMZ and the head of the DVB, Rau, made it possible for a Korean counterpart at the EPB, Kang Shin-joe, to conduct research at a German university. Kang mentioned his study abroad in an oral history interview (Kang, 2012) but did not go into specifics. During his two-year studies in Hamburg and Kiel, which did not lead to a degree, he wrote the monograph *Economic Integration in* Asia (Kang, 1969). In the interview (Kang, 2012), Kang emphasised that studying economics in Germany was rather an exception and that the Korean government subsequently sent him to Europe again for further missions as he had developed a certain expertise there. Compared to projects in the fields of vocational training or rural development with similar advisory groups, however, little attention was given to counterpart training in the DVB project, probably also because there were already many trained economists in Korea. For example, as part of the advisory group for the vocational training sector, several counterparts from the Office of Labour Affairs (OLA), the current Ministry of Labour, were sent to Germany every year (KOICA, 2004: 146). Due to this lack of counterpart training, there is also less information on the Korean economists in the EPB and their working relationship with the German advisors.

Cooperation with American Economic Advisors Comparing to the German Case

The United States Operations Mission to Korea (USOM) and the United States Agency for International Development (USAID) have been strongly represented in Korea since the end of the Korean War. The American consultants worked closely with the Korean authorities, such as the finance and economic ministries. Their advice was primarily aimed at economic issues, which should help promote Korea's economic development and strengthen the interests of American companies in Korea (Rau, 1962a: 5).[8] The American consultants were involved in the development of a fundamental economic programme in 1954 and the forerunner of the first five-year plan. During the transition period from Rhee Syngman to Park Chung-hee government, 1959–1961, the Oregon Advisory Group served at the Korean Economic Development Council (Nathan, 1954; Park, 2007: 35–42; The Oregon Advisory Group to Korea, 1961). With Park Chung-hee coming to power, personal economic advisors exerted more direct influence. As early as 1961, Park requested an American consultant for his private services. Albert Boucher was initially selected for this post, and USAID director for Korea, Joel Bernstein, took over the position later. Park asked the consultants directly about development projects, their chances of success, and possible problems. The American economists at the time, therefore, emphasised the extraordinary role of the USOM and USAID in Korea since it normally did not have a direct advisory function (Brazinsky, 2005; Cole and Lyman, 1971; USAID, 2011).

In addition, in the 1960s, several American short-term experts were dispatched to provide economic advice on various subjects, including Edward S. Shaw, John G. Gurley on the development of financial institutions, Irma Adelman on planning models and concepts, Richard A. Musgrave on tax and fiscal policy, Peggy B. Musgrave on foreign trade policy, Edward Hollander and Edgar McVoy on manpower planning, and Alan Strout on general planning models (Cole and Lyman, 1971: 205). DVB refers to these experts in its reports and particularly emphasises that they were well-known and esteemed scholars. The German experts also acted as external advisors on the Adelman study to calculate the distribution of investment areas (Boucherie, 1965: 9–10). Comparatively, few individual experts were sent by the German side. Only two experts were dispatched for coal mining and one for the ceramics industry, while the DVB consultants covered other topics such as the textile industry or export marketing by themselves. This shows the different scope of advisory activities by the two countries with less known and fewer economists from Germany.

In addition to the official advisors, private advisors, including R. Nathan, were also active in Korea on behalf of the American government. The advisory group around him was known as the Nathan Advisory Group. Nathan states he also had close ties to officials at the EPB and President Park himself. In an oral history interview, he summarised his activities (Nathan, 1989: 83): 'We worked with them on all these policies. We worked with every five-year plan; we were in Korea until '75, from '52 to '54–55, and then again from '60 to '75, resident teams'. Historian

Brazinsky (2005: 102) also mentioned that Nathan played an important role in the revision of the second five-year plan in June 1966.[9] At the same time, he states that the five-year plans were not necessarily reflected in the policies of the Korean government as they were modified while conducted (Brazinsky, 2005: 102, see also, Park, 2007). This presents a similar problem as in the case of DVB because it is difficult to prove the actual influence of the experts on economic policies.

The activities and possible influence of non-American consultants in Korea and especially the DVB are not mentioned in either the Korean or the English-language research. However, German and American documents show that the advisory groups from both countries cooperated closely, reviewed each other's advice, or supplemented it.[10] Rau was already in contact with USOM during the government negotiations while preparing for the project and described the overall relationship as good (BMZ, 1964: 1; Boucherie, 1968: 3–4). Apparently, USOM also considered DVB's role to be important. USOM's head advisor J. Killen reportedly told W. Boucherie that DVB should 'not underestimate its influence on Korean economic policy' (Boucherie, 1964: 12). According to Killen, they had better chances of influencing the Korean government than USOM itself (Boucherie, 1964: 12).

Later on, both sides carried out joint consultations in the EPB and exchanged their studies or project reports (Rau, 1963b: 18). There were also some overlaps, such as a German and an American mining expert, respectively (Rau, 1963c: 1), although a German report initially described that 'neither the Koreans nor the Americans nor we have the slightest concern that the areas of activity of the American and our group could overlap, which could result in personal or material difficulties' (Boucherie, 1964: 1). In later years, the advisory groups of the two countries tried to decide on a clear distinction of their activities. The Nathan Advisory Group took over the financial policy sector, while the DVB advised the EPB on export promotion and industrial development (Nittscher, 1965a: 5).

From an economic point of view, many aspects could probably be analysed. However, it is noticeable that, for example, the advice on the role of small and medium-sized companies is similar. Both the American and the German advisors recommended that the Korean government should not focus too much on large companies (Rau, 1966a: 13). They also jointly advised development based on the 'balanced growth model', for instance, with an expansion of agriculture (Nittscher, 1965b). Although Korean economic planners included this in the five-year plan under pressure from the US, they ultimately did not implement it (Park, 2007). A German consultant also remembers that the promotion of small and medium-sized companies was mentioned in his job advertisement as a focus of the activities, but in reality, it did not play a role (Glaeser, 2021). This shows once again the gap between economic advice and actual policies.

Regarding consultations on technical and financial development assistance, the two groups cooperated. But, at the same time, they also competed to a certain extent, especially in the realm of private investments. Therefore, it was important to exchange information about the project applications, their examination, and rejection to prevent the Korean government from submitting double applications (Nittscher, 1965c: 7). This also simplified work for the BMWi and KfW. In comparison, the American side was not pleased when a German consortium of investors granted private loans to Korea in 1962 and announced that they would subsequently make larger investments (Brazinsky, 2005).

However, despite close cooperation, there were also differences of opinion between the German and American consultants. Above all, Rau repeatedly criticised the recommendations of the American consultants in his reports. The American authorities were not critical enough regarding the Korean government's economic planning:

> Contrary to the opinion of American economists and independent experts, who have recognized these dangers and warned of them, the American officials (especially USOM) play down these dangerous 'plan excesses'. They mostly overlook the Korean government's problematic inclination for overly capital-intensive measures (…). There is therefore a danger that, under the impression of American sales interests, American development aid for Korea will be largely converted from consumer aid to capital aid but will still be determined too strongly by American ideas about export aid.
>
> (Rau, 1962a: 5)

This assessment from 1962 addresses the change in American development aid, which has been extensively described in previous research (Lee, 2020; Park, 1999). Rau also criticised American sales interests, while researchers emphasised the criticism of the American consultants of Korean planning (Park, 2007). In addition, the American consultants see the Korean economic development as too positive, which Rau attributes to 'exaggerated optimism' because effective Korean economic development would lead to a gradual reduction in American development aid (Rau, 1966b: 2–3).

In addition to the American consultants, advisors by the Japanese government and international organisations as well as banks later became important partners for DVB in Korea (Boucherie, 1965: 11–12).[11] However, until the founding of the joint international advisory group IECOK, cooperation with the American authorities seems to play the most important role. Although there was also repeated exchange with other projects of bilateral and multilateral partners in Korea in other sectors of technical assistance, the cooperation in economic policy advice seemed to have been closer because the American authorities dominated this sector in the early 1960s.

Globalising Korean Economic Assistance with the International Economic Consultative Organization for Korea

The idea of setting up an international advisory group for economic planning came up early on and was finally realised with the foundation of the IECOK in 1966. From the side of the donor countries, economic advice and development assistance for Korea were supposed to be coordinated better and made more efficient (Kraus, 1966: 7). The proposal to found IECOK seemed to be based on an idea from the

American side and discussed diplomatically at various levels, for example, between the US, Germany, Japan, and Korea (Boucherie, 1965: 11–12; German Foreign Ministry, 1965a, 1965b; Rau, 1966b; Ulshöfer, 1965). After various meetings with representatives of the EPB, the American Nathan Advisory Group, and USOM, Rau summarised the political intentions of the parties involved in a memo for the BMZ. In this, he explained that the American authorities primarily tried to strengthen their development assistance policy through the involvement of other advisors and wanted to 'objectify' and moderate Japan's influence (Rau, 1965: 1). The US had too often been accused of 'meddling in internal affairs' (Rau, 1965: 1). In comparison, Japan tried to distract attention from the fact that it was acting 'again in the style of a colonial power' in Korea (Rau, 1965: 2). At the same time, they intended to negotiate multilaterally with the US. The foundation of IECOK was also in the interests of the Korean government since an international advisory group meant greater neutrality (Rau, 1965: 2).

In the case of Japan, they were initially sceptical about the proposal, following a statement from the German Embassy in Tokyo (1965: 1). Even in the German government, the founding of the group did not meet with approval from the start. For example, there were fears in the Foreign Office that the founding of the group would result in institutionalisation of development assistance and that the donor countries would have to take on more responsibility for Korea's finances. Besides, they argued, there were not enough qualified experts available. Therefore, trilateral agreements should be made with the other two major donors, the US and Japan (German Foreign Ministry, 1965b: 1–2).

However, from the talks with the other foreign consultants, Rau concluded that the FRG would play a key role in the decision for or against the establishment of an international consulting group and thus started advocating for such a group. The group could 'correctively influence Korea's unhealthy, problematic investment policy', which would also bring advantages for German business (Rau, 1965: 3). But Rau also mentioned (Rau, 1966a: 14): 'The Federal Republic of Germany will not hesitate to leave such a group if the Korean government merely intends to squeeze its foreign economic partners for more capital assistance and more support'. The assumption that Korea was mainly interested in increasing capital loans and development assistance was later confirmed. According to the report by the Comptroller General to the US Congress, the Korean delegation brought 'a shopping list of projects for which foreign assistance is desired' to the meetings (US Comptroller General, 1973: 10; 64). From the point of view of the Korea International Cooperation Agency, the group intended to attract foreign capital, which is why the Korean government lobbied for its establishment (KOICA, 2004: 60–61).

In December 1966, the constitutive meeting of IECOK took place in Paris, chaired by the World Bank. In addition to the three countries mentioned, France, Canada, Australia, Belgium, Italy, the United Kingdom, and Taiwan also participated. The Asian Development Bank, International Monetary Fund, and United Nations Development Programme had an observer role (BMZ, 1967: 1). After the Korean government presented its economic plan on the first day and the participating nations discussed it, the tasks of the advisory group were discussed on the second day. In addition, the American representative, among others, presented the financial assistance provided by his government. The German delegation consisted of officials from the BMZ, BMWi, and BMF, headed by Rau. According to the joint report by the BMZ, there was initially no clear plan for the group's tasks, and thus, the German delegation expressed its ideas, which the other countries eventually agreed to, and they, therefore, rated their role at the first meeting as decisive (BMZ, 1967: 4–5).

The participants decided to meet (bi-)annually to discuss Korean economic planning, in particular the five-year plans and investment laws, and to coordinate development assistance (BMZ, 1967: 4–5). The procedure at the meetings was similar to the constitutive meeting. After an introduction by the World Bank, the Korean delegation presented a report on the economic situation and the economic planning and reforms that were carried out, which were then discussed by all participants. Concrete proposals were made to solve economic problems, such as those caused by the first oil crisis (Obermüller, 1974: 2). The group then determined the required foreign funds and exchanged views and project plans of their respective technical and financial assistance. In the early 1970s, for example, the agricultural sector was at the forefront of the third five-year plan, which is why the donor countries' projects also covered this sector (Obermüller, 1974: 1–2). This orientation was also reflected in actual German financial and technical assistance, which supported a reforestation project, research on grassland, and the construction of grain storage facilities (German Embassy Seoul, 1976: 1–4).

The Korean government cooperated with various countries and organisations in various sectors from the late 1960s, which required the coordination of individual bilateral and multilateral projects. The founding of the IECOK as an international advisory group of donor countries and organisations seemed, therefore, necessary to make this expanded development assistance more effective. This made DVB's advisory work superfluous, as it would not have been able to provide such coordinated advice. Thus, the DVB was gradually replaced by the IECOK. In the same way, IECOK adapted to external circumstances. With the arguably steady Korean economic growth, the delegates finally decided at their meeting in 1984 to transfer IECOK's tasks to the Korean government and dissolve the group (World Bank, 1984).

Conclusion

Viewing DVB as just one of many advisory groups in Korea falls short. DVB worked at the EPB during a critical phase of early economic development under the new and still unstable government of Park Chung-hee, fulfilling important tasks. The consultants were involved in shaping Korean economic policy by working on the five-year plans, the preparation of reports and studies, and giving advice to the EPB. They usually cooperated closely with the Korean and American authorities but also criticised them and set their accents. Although the Korean side particularly emphasised the mid-term forecasts and cooperation on the five-year plans, sectoral and project studies represented a large part of the activity. The DVB fulfilled a double function. On the one hand, they served the Korean government by analysing the situation of specific industry branches, assessing projects, and coordinating economic policies. On the other hand, BMZ, BMWi, and KfW were able to make decisions on the funding of projects within the framework of technical and financial assistance. In addition to the German Embassy in Seoul, the West German government had a tool to assess the situation on site. At the same time, DVB advised German and Korean companies and was also active in the private sector, which benefitted German foreign trade interests.

The early projects of German technical assistance not only had an outstanding symbolic effect but also had a lasting influence on the general direction of German development assistance in Korea. While the German-Korean Skilled Workers School in Incheon was the first in a series of projects in the vocational training sector and can be seen as a starting point for German development assistance in this area, DVB has played an important role in selecting projects for German technical and financial assistance in the different sectors, such as the ceramics industry, electricity and telephone infrastructure, and stock breeding. Its efforts were later continued in the form of bilateral business cooperation with consultants from both countries, strengthening the technology transfer and joint ventures between the German and Korean private industries.

At the same time, DVB was not only active on a purely bilateral basis but also relied on close cooperation with its 'First World' partners, primarily the US and later Japan. For the Korean government, the German advisory group represented (in their own view) a neutral authority since the US primarily exercised economic hegemony in Korea, while Japan, as a former colonial power and direct neighbour, also seemed to be pursuing political power claims. However, the DVB experts were still deeply embedded in the ideological system of the Cold War and aimed for South Korean economic development as a landmark against Communism. Only the founding of IECOK enabled the internationalisation of economic policy advice and the better coordination of development assistance for Korea.

Until now, the case of Korean economic development has been unprecedented, which made Korea a model for many developing countries. Especially, the Korea Development Institute (KDI) researches and promotes the Korean 'Miracle of the Han River' and provides services like K-Developedia or the Korean Knowledge Sharing Programme (KSP) to provide lessons from the Korean development experience. However, the KDI does not or only rarely refer to the experience of Korea as a recipient of ODA. A notable publication on lessons from ODA to Korea is compiled in a report by KOICA (2004), and a limited number of academic research has discussed Korea's experience as a recipient of international aid (for example, see Lim, 2022). For the case of Germany, this report highlights merely the assistance in the sector of vocational education, while other projects like the DVB are not mentioned. This shows the high potential of further analysis of West German projects in other sectors to complete the view of the so-called Korean experience and employ it for developing countries and ODA policies today. This chapter on the DVB as a key project of West German assistance in Korea during the 1960s can therefore contribute to further research on bilateral economic cooperation, especially since in the 1970s many more bilateral projects were launched.

Notes

1 This chapter is a translated and revised version of a subchapter from the author's PhD Thesis, 'Altenhofen, Max (2024). Technische Entwicklungszusammenarbeit zwischen Westdeutschland und Südkorea, PhD. Thesis. University of Tübingen, chapter 2: 234–259', which deals with most German-Korean technical projects during the 1960s and 1980s.

2 For a short biographical note on Walter Rau, see the website of the Bundesarchiv, Kabinettsprotokolle der Bundesregierung: URL: https://kabinettsprotokolle.bundesarchiv.de/register/person/cae5ba10-a24d-43d6-b6fb-cc55514a6208 [last accessed on 15 March 2024].

3 This can also be seen in various United States Agency for International Development (USAID) documents, which are available in digitised form on the website of the *National Library of Korea*, such as NARA RG 286 Records of the Agency for International Development, Korea Subject Files, FY 71, Official Files of USAID/Korea-Participant Training Files (PIO/Ps) Covering Period FY 1970.

4 See also the *National Archives of Korea* topic page on the Five-Year Plans: https://theme.archives.go.kr/next/economicDevelopment/primary.do [last accessed 15 March 2024].

5 The consultants divided the responsibilities as follows: iron and steel industry and pharmaceutical industry for one expert; shipbuilding and electricity for another expert; textile industry for the other expert; and petrochemical, American, and Japanese development aid for the vice director.

6 Especially at the beginning of the project, the DVB employees complained about the poor performance of the Deutsche Fördergesellschaft für Entwicklungsländer (GAWI) and the lack of overseas commissary and exchange privileges. In addition, there were various conflicts about the (re-)classification of employees in appropriate salary levels and their taxes. The unclear status of the deputy project manager, W. Boucherie, also led to a conflict with the other employees (Rau, 1963e).

7 The DVB vice chair, Wilhelm Boucherie, commented on this affair in an interview with the German weekly magazine *Spiegel* (1967).

8 Rau wrote: 'The previous American aid was a failure, primarily because it was granted to a large extent as "consumer aid" in the interest of selling American surplus goods'.

9 Although the plan's text and its direction in general were examined to establish the influence of the American advisors, Brazinsky relied primarily on R. Nathan's own assessments, particularly his diary, which is part of the *Nathan Papers* in the Archives of Cornell University: *Nathan Papers at Cornell University*. https://rmc.library.cornell.edu/EAD/htmldocs/RMM04410.html#subjects [last accessed on 15 March 2024].

10 The American government instructed USOM in Seoul, among other things, to work more closely with the German advisers of DVB (Department of State, 1965).

11 Boucherie made two visits to Japan and held talks at the Japanese Ministry of Economy and Foreign Affairs on Japanese loans and reparations. The talks were organised through the German Embassy in Tokyo.

References

Altenhofen, Max (2024). Technische Entwicklungszusammenarbeit zwischen Westdeutschland und Südkorea, Ph.D. Thesis, University of Tübingen.

Bank, Max (2013). Stunde der Neoliberalen? Politikberatung und Wirtschaftspolitik in der Ära Adenauer, Ph.D. Thesis, University of Cologne.

Bianchini, Mario (2020). 'Theoretical Soldiers: German Economists in the Cold War', *German Studies Review* 43(1), pp. 41–58.

Bösch, Frank (2024). *Deals mit Diktaturen: Eine andere Geschichte der Bundesrepublik*, München: C.H. Beck.

Brazinsky, Gregg A. (2005). 'From Pupil to Model: South Korea and American Development Policy during the Early Park Chung Hee Era', *Diplomatic History* 29(1), pp. 83–115.

Burton, Eric (2021). *In Diensten des Afrikanischen Sozialismus: Tansania und die globale Entwicklungsarbeit der beiden deutschen Staaten, 1961–1990*, München: De Gruyter Oldenbourg.

Büschel, Hubertus and Daniel Speich (ed.) (2009). 'Einleitung: Konjunkturen, Probleme und Perspektiven der Globalgeschichte von Entwicklungszusammenarbeit', in: *Entwicklungswelten: Globalgeschichte der Entwicklungszusammenarbeit*, Frankfurt am Main/ New York: Campus, pp. 7–32.

Calvo-Gonzales: Oscar (2006). 'Neither a Carrot Nor a Stick: American Foreign Aid and Economic Policymaking in Spain during the 1950s', *Diplomatic History* 30(3), pp. 409–438.

Cole, David C. and Princeton N. Lyman (1971). *Korean Development: The Interplay of Politics and Economics*, Cambridge: Harvard University Press.

Glaeser, Rolf (1966). 'Die Wirtschaftliche Entwicklung in der Bundesrepublik Deutschland', *The Argus*, 15 November.

Han, Bongseok (2017). 1950nyeondae migugui daehan gisul wonjo yeongu (A Study on the Technical Assistance of the U.S. for Korea during the 1950s), Ph.D. Thesis, Sungkyunkwan University.

Helleiner, Eric (2021). *The Neomercantilists: A Global Intellectual History*. Ithaca: Cornell University Press.

Hein, Bastian (2006). *Die Westdeutschen und die Dritte Welt: Entwicklungspolitik und Entwicklungsdienste zwischen Reform und Revolte 1959–1974*. München: R. Oldenbourg.

Hesse, Jan-Otmar (2016). 'Wissenschaftliche Beratung der Wirtschaftspolitik: Das Bundeswirtschaftsministerium und die Volkswirtschaftslehre', in: Werner Abelshauser, Stefan Fisch, Dierk Hoffmann, Carl-Ludwig Holtfrerich and Albrecht Ritschl (eds.): *Wirtschaftspolitik in Deutschland 1917–1990*, vol. 4, München: De Gruyter Oldenbourg, pp. 390–481.

Kang, Shin Joe (1969). *Economic Integration in Asia*, Hamburg: Verlag Weltarchiv.

Kim, Bo Hyeon (2019). 'Bak Jeong-hui jeongbusigi gyeongjegaebal 5gaenyeongyehoegui sujeonge gwanhan yeongu: Gyehoeg hamniseonginga, seongjang sungbaeinga?' (The Revised Five-Year Economic Development Plans in the Park Chung-Hee Government Era: Plan Rationality or Growth Fetishism?), *Gyeongjewa sahoe* 124, pp. 228–256.

Kim, Byung-Kook (1992). 'Economic Policy and the Economic Planning Board (EPB) in Korea', *Asian Affairs* 18, pp. 197–213.

Kim, Eun Mee, Pil Ho Kim, and Jinkyung Kim (2013). 'From Development to Development Cooperation: Foreign Aid, Country Ownership, and the Developmental State in South Korea', *The Pacific Review* 26(3), pp. 313–336.

Kimiya, Tadashi (1991). Hangugui naepojeog gongeopwajeollyagui jwajeol: 5.16gunsajeongbuui gukkajayulhwaui gujojeog hangye (Frustration of Korea's Intrinsic Industrialization Strategy – 5.16 Structural Limitations of Military Government's National Autonomy), Ph.D. Thesis, Korea University.

Koch, Harald (1986). 'Auswahl des richtigen Partners ist für die mittelständische Industrie wichtig', Handelsblatt, 08 April.

Köllner, Patrick (1998). 'Die deutsch-koreanischen Beziehungen von 1945 bis zur Gegenwart', in: Köllner, Patrick (ed.): *Korea 1998: Politik, Wirtschaft, Gesellschaft*, Hamburg: Institut für Asienkunde, pp. 19–56.

Korea International Cooperation Agency (2004). *Hanguge daehan gaebal wonjowa hyeomnyeog: Urinaraui suwon gyumowa bunya hyogwa sarye deunge gwanhan josayeongu*

(Study on Development Aid and Cooperation for South Korea: Size, Scope, and Exemplary Effects), Seoul: KOICA.

Latour, Bruno (1999). *Pandora's Hope: Essays on the Reality of Science Studies*, Cambridge: Harvard University Press.

Lee, Hwihyeon (2020). '1960nyeondae choban migugui daeoewonjojeongchaeg jojeonggwa daehanwonjoui jeongsanghwa' (Adjustment of U.S. Foreign Aid Policy and 'Normalization' of U.S. Aid to Korea in the early 1960s), *Hangungmunhwa* 92, pp. 295–331.

Lee, Jeongmin (2017). 'Handok gyeongjehyeomnyeokgwa dongbaengnim sageon' (South Korean-West German Economic Cooperation and the East Berlin Incident), *Yeoksabipyeong* 119, pp. 160–184.

Lee, Sangcheol (2012). 'Hangug gyeongjegwallyoui ilje singminji giwonseol geomto: 1950nyeondae~1960nyeondae jeonban' (The Colonial Origin of Economic Bureaucrats in Korea: During 1950s-Early 1960s), *Minjusahoewa Jeongchaegyeongu* 21, pp. 202–247.

Lim, Sojin (2022). 'The evolution story of South Korea from a fragile state to an international actor', in: Sojin Lim and Niki J. P. Alsford (eds.): *Routledge Handbook of Contemporary South Korea*, London: Routledge, pp. 118–135.

Löffler, Bernhard (2016). 'Personelle und institutionelle Strukturen des Bundeswirtschaftsministeriums 1945/49 bis 1990', in: Werner Abelshauser, Stefan Fisch, Dierk Hoffmann, Carl-Ludwig Holtfrerich and Albrecht Ritschl (eds.): *Wirtschaftspolitik in Deutschland 1917–1990*, vol. 4, München: De Gruyter Oldenbourg, pp. 95–192.

Loth, Wilfried (2010). 'The cold war and the social and economic history of the twentieth century', in: Leffler, Melvin P. and Odd A. Westad (eds.): *The Cambridge History of the Cold War*, Cambridge: Cambridge University Press, pp. 503–524.

Nathan, Robert R. (1954) *An Economic Program for Korean Reconstruction – Prepared for the UNKRA*, Seoul: UNKRA.

Noh, Meung-Hoan (2007). '1980nyeondae ihuui segyehwa sidae seodogui munhwakodeuwa dogilmodello jeongchakdoen gyeongjemunhwa teukjingui byeonhwa: Dogil modelui wigiwa jeonmangeul jungsimeuro' (Globalization and Cultural Changes in Germany since 1980s: Focused on the discussions of 'German Model'), *Yeoksamunhwayeongu* 27, pp. 341–386.

Noh, Meung-Hoan (2011). 'Naengjeon sidae hanguksaneopwa jeongchaekkwa seodogui uimiwa yeokal, Naengjeon sidae hanguksaneopwa cjeongchaekgwa seodogui uimiwa yeokal, 1961–1967' (The Meaning and Role of the Federal Republic of Germany for the Industrialization of the Republic of Korea at the Beginning of the Park Chung Hee Era under the International Cold War System 1961–1967), *Sarim* 38, pp. 289–323.

Nützenadel, Alexander (2005). *Stunde der Ökonomen: Wissenschaft, Politik und Expertenkultur in der Bundesrepublik 1949–1974*, Göttingen: Vandenhoeck & Ruprecht.

Oregon Advisory Group to Korea (ed.) (1961). *A Report on the University of Oregon Advisory Mission to the Korean Economic Development Council, 1959–61*, University of Oregon: Eugene.

Park, Tae-Gyun (1999). 'Change in U.S. Policy Toward South Korea in the Early 1960s', *Korean Studies* 23, pp. 94–120.

Park, Tae-Gyun (2007). *Wonhyeonggwa byeonyong: Hangug gyeongjegaebalgyehoegui giwon (Archetype and Metamorphosis: The Origins of Korea's Economic Development Plans)*, Seoul: Seoul National University Press.

Plehwe, Dieter and Matthias Schmelzer (2015). 'Marketing Marketization: The Power of Neoliberal Expert, Consulting, and Lobby Networks', *Zeithistorische Forschungen* 12, pp. 488–499.

Rau, Walter (1963a). 'Obstacles of Economic Growth', *Korea Journal* 3(9), pp. 34–37.

Rau, Walter (1966a). 'Economic Development in Korea', *Korea Journal* 6(8), pp. 10–15.

Schiffman, Daniel, Warren Young, and Yaron Zelkha (2017). *The Role of Economic Advisers in Israel's Economic Policy: Crises, Reform and Stabilization*, Cham: Springer.

Simpson, Bradley R. (2008). *Economists with Guns: Authoritarian Development and U.S.-Indonesian Relations,* 1960–1968, Stanford: Stanford University Press.

Spiegel (1967). 'Affären – Lage des K.', 27 August.

Uhlig, Christian (1985). 'Aspekte der unternehmerischen Kooperation zwischen Industrie- und Entwicklungsländern in Südost- und Ostasien', *Internationales Asienforum* 16, pp. 267–287.

USAID (2011) 'Case Study South Korea – From Aid Recipient to Donor: USAID's role in South Korea's extraordinary transformation', Report Number: PDACY151.

World Bank (1984). 'News Release: Consultative Group for Korea', 16 July, Report Number: 151500, https://documents.worldbank.org/curated/en/683251596708868077/Announcement-of-Consultative-Group-for-Korea-on-July-16-1984 [last accessed 15 March 2024].

Yu, Jinyoung and Kiseob Chung (2016). 'Dogil gisulgyoyuk jiwonui gyoyuksajeok uiui: Incheon handoksireopakgyo seollipgwa uimireul jungsimeuro (1960–1970)' (The Significance of the German Technical Education Support: Focusing on the Meaning and the Establishment of Incheon-German Vocational School (1960–1970)), *Han'gukkyoyuksahak* 38(2), pp. 1–26.

Interviews

Baek, Y. (2009). 'Oral History Interview – Part 4-3'. Interview by Noh Meung-Hoan, 12 November, Seongnam: Academy of Korean Studies – Oral Archives of Modern History.

Glaeser, R. (2021). 'Oral History Interview'. Interview by Max Altenhofen [telephone], 13 July.

Kang, S. (2012). 'Oral History Interview – Part 1-1'. Interview by Hong Hyeonung, 25 April, Seongnam: Academy of Korean Studies – Oral Archives of Modern History.

Nathan, R. (1989). 'Oral History Interview'. Interview by Niel M. Johnson, 22 June, Independence: Harry S. Truman Library.

Archival Sources

BMZ (1964). Note on the Outcome of the Meeting of 06 April 1964 concerning Korea (German Advisory Group). 10 April, File Number: B 102/102239, Koblenz: Bundesarchiv [*Vermerk über das Ergebnis der Besprechung vom 06.04.1964 betreffend Korea (deutsche Beratergruppe)*].

BMZ (1967). Joint Report on the Constituent Meeting of the International Consultative Group for Korea on 12–13 December 1966 in Paris. 04 January, File Number: PA AA, B 37, Bd. 56, Berlin: Politisches Archiv des Auswärtigen Amtes [*Gemeinsamer Bericht über die konstituierende Sitzung der Internationalen Beratungsgruppe für Korea am 12.-13.12.1966 in Paris*].

Boucherie, Wilhelm (1964). Memorandum on the Composition of the Staff and the Differentiation to the Area of Activity of the American Group. 13 April, File Number: B 213/11968, Koblenz: Bundesarchiv [*Aktennotiz über die personelle Zusammensetzung und die Abgrenzung des Tätigkeitsbereiches der amerikanischen Gruppe*].

Boucherie, Wilhelm (1965). Report on the Period from 01 June to 01 October 1965. 30 October, File Number: B 213/11968, Koblenz: Bundesarchiv [*Bericht für die Zeit vom 01.06. bis zum 01.10.1965*].

Boucherie, Wilhelm (1967). Overview of the Activities of the German Economic Advisory Group in Korea. 11 January, File Number: B 213/11968, Koblenz: Bundesarchiv [Überblick über die Tätigkeiten der Deutschen Volkswirtschaftlichen Beratergruppe in Korea].

Boucherie, Wilhelm (1968). Report on the Activities of the German Advisory Group in Seoul. 01 April, File Number: B 213/11960, Koblenz: Bundesarchiv [*Bericht über die Tätigkeit der DVB in Seoul*].

Department of State (1965). Aid Coordination Korea. 19 February, File Number: RG 59 8, KOR S, 1/1/64, Seoul: National Library of Korea.

EPB (1964). Status of Economic and Technical Cooperation between the Federal Republic of Germany and the Republic of Korea and Proposal for Further Cooperation. 26 June, File Number: BA0084353, Seongnam: National Archives of Korea.

GAWI (1965). Letter to the BMZ: DVB Korea – Report from 01 June to 01 October 1965. 07 December, File Number: B 213/11968, Koblenz: Bundesarchiv [*Schreiben an das BMZ: DVB Korea, Bericht vom 01.06–01.10.1965*].

German Embassy Seoul (1963). Letter to the German Foreign Ministry: Meeting with Park Chung Hee. 28 May, File Number: B 58–407/Abt 8/III B1–3, 886, Berlin: Politisches Archiv des Auswärtigen Amtes [*Schreiben an das AA: Unterredung mit Park Chung Hee*].

German Embassy Seoul (1967). Letter to the German Foreign Ministry: Further Training for Members of the Developing Countries in the 1967 Fiscal Year. 23 March, File Number: B 58–407/Abt 8/III B1–3, 1162, Berlin: Politisches Archiv des Auswärtigen Amtes [*Schreiben an das AA: Fortbildung von Angehörigen der Entwicklungsländer im Haushaltsjahr 1967*].

German Embassy Seoul (1976). Note on Project Manager Meeting on 25 February 1976 in Seoul. 03 March, File Number: B 213/8760, Koblenz: Bundesarchiv [*Vermerk zur Projektleitertagung am 25.02.1976 in Seoul*].

German Embassy Tokyo (1965). Letter to the German Foreign Ministry: Korean Request to form an Advisory Group for Development Assistance. 12 August, File Number: B 58–407/Abt 8/III B1–3, 886, Berlin: Politisches Archiv des Auswärtigen Amtes [*Schreiben an das AA: Koreanischer Wunsch auf Bildung einer Beratergruppe für Entwicklungshilfe*].

German Foreign Ministry (1965a). Letter to the BMWi, BMF and BMZ: Korea – American Proposal to form a 'Consultative Group'. 05 May, File Number: B 58–407/Abt 8/III B1–3, 886, Berlin: Politisches Archiv des Auswärtigen Amtes [*Schreiben an das BMWi, BMF und BMZ: Korea – Amerikanischer Vorschlag zur Bildung einer ‚Consultative Group'*].

German Foreign Ministry (1965b). Note from the Foreign Ministry: Korea – American Proposal to Form a Consultative Group, Departmental Meeting on 12 May 1965. 14 May, File Number: B 58–407/Abt 8/III B1–3, 886, Berlin: Politisches Archiv des Auswärtigen Amtes [*Aufzeichnung des AA: Korea – Amerikanischer Vorschlag zur Bildung einer, Consultative Group', Ressortbesprechung am 12.05.1965*].

German Foreign Ministry (1966). Internal Note: Departmental Meeting at the BMZ on 26 August 1966 on the Extension of the Agreement on the Dispatch of the German Economic Advisory Group to Korea. 29 August, File Number: B 58–407/Abt 8/III B1–3, 1114, Berlin: Politisches Archiv des Auswärtigen Amtes [*Interner Ergebnisvermerk: Ressortbesprechung im BMZ am 26.08.1966 über Verlängerung der Vereinbarung über die Entsendung einer deutschen volkswirtschaftlichen Beratergruppe nach Korea*].

Glaeser, Rolf (1965). Ceramics Industry in Korea; Dispatch of a German Ceramics Expert as Part of Technical Assistance. 30 November, File Number: B 213/11969, Koblenz: Bundesarchiv [*Keramische Industrie in Korea; Entsendung eines deutschen Keramikfachmanns im Rahmen der technischen Hilfe*].

Kraus, Willy (1966). Statement on the Activities of the German Advisory Group in South Korea, 17 July, File Number: B 213/11968, Koblenz: Bundesarchiv [*Stellungnahme zur Tätigkeit der deutschen Beratergruppe in Südkorea*].

Nittscher, Werner (1965a). Report on the Period from 01 November 1964 to 31 January 1965. 17 February, File Number: B 213/11968, Koblenz: Bundesarchiv [*Bericht für die Zeit vom 01.11.1964 bis zum 31.01.1965*].

Nittscher, Werner (1965b). Letter to the German Foreign Ministry: Technical Assistance for Korea – Agriculture. 30 March, File Number: B 58–407/Abt 8/III B1–3, 886, Berlin: Politisches Archiv des Auswärtigen Amtes [*Schreiben an das AA: Technische Hilfe für Korea – Landwirtschaft*].

Nittscher, Werner (1965c). Report on the Period from 01 February to 31 May 1965. 03 June, File Number: B 213/11968, Koblenz: Bundesarchiv [*Bericht für die Zeit vom 01.02. bis zum 31.05.1965*].

Obermüller, Heinz (1974). Note on the 7th Meeting of the World Bank Consultative Group for Korea, 25–27 March 1974 in Paris. 02 April, File Number: B 213/8744, Koblenz: Bundesarchiv [*Vermerk zur 7. Tagung der Weltbankberatungsgruppe Korea vom 25. bis 27.03.1974 in Paris*].

Rau, Walter (1962a). On the Political and Economic Situation in South Korea. 06 April, Number: B 213/11968, Koblenz: Bundesarchiv [*Zur politischen und wirtschaftlichen Lage Südkoreas*].

Rau, Walter (1962b). Note for Dr. Stedtfeld and Dr. Daniel on the Issue of Partnership Services in Connection with the Dispatch of an Economic Advisory Group. 30 April, File Number: B 102/102239, Koblenz: Bundesarchiv [*Vermerk für Dr. Stedtfeld und Dr. Daniel zur Frage der partnerschaftlichen Leistung im Zusammenhang mit Entsendung einer wirtschaftlichen Beratergruppe*].

Rau, Walter (1962c). Letter to the Federal Minister for Economic Cooperation and Development: Funds for Research in the Field of Development Aid; Here: Financing of a Research Project. 24 August, File Number: B 102/102239, Koblenz: Bundesarchiv [*Schreiben an den Bundesminister für wirtschaftliche Zusammenarbeit: Mittel für Forschung auf dem Gebiet der Entwicklungshilfe; hier: Finanzierung eines Forschungsprojektes*].

Rau, Walter (1963b). Report on the Period from 06 December 1962 to 28 February 1963. 28 February, File Number: B 213/11968, Koblenz: Bundesarchiv [*Bericht für die Zeit vom 06.12.1962 zum 28.02.1963*].

Rau, Walter (1963c). Report on the Period from 01 March to 31 May 1963. 07 June, File Number: B 213/11968, Koblenz: Bundesarchiv [*Bericht für die Zeit vom 01.03. bis zum 31.05.1963*].

Rau, Walter (1963d). Report on the Period from 01 September to 30 November 1963. 04 December, File Number: B 213/11968, Koblenz: Bundesarchiv [*Bericht für die Zeit vom 01.09. bis zum 30.11.1963*].

Rau, Walter (1963e). Event Report on the Departmental Meeting on 12 December 1963 concerning the Complaints of the Head of DVB for South Korea. 12 December, File Number: B 213/11968, Koblenz: Bundesarchiv [*Ereignisbericht über die Ressortbesprechung am 12.12.1963 betreffend die Beschwerden des Leiters der DVB für Südkorea*].

Rau, Walter (1965). Note on the Establishment of an International Consultative Group. 13 October, File Number: B 213/11968, Koblenz: Bundesarchiv [*Vermerk zur Frage der Gründung einer internationalen Beratungsgruppe*].

Rau, Walter (1966b). Report on the Business Trip to Washington from 05 to 15 May 1966 to attend the Meeting of the Council of the International Secretariat for Volunteer Services (ISVS). 22 June, File Number: B 213/11968, Koblenz: Bundesarchiv [*Bericht über die Dienstreise nach Washington in der Zeit vom 5.-15. Mai 1966 zur Teilnahme an der Sitzung des ,Council'des ,International Secretariat for Volunteer Services (ISVS)'*].

Ulshöfer, Otfried (1965). Note on a Meeting at the BMZ on 21 June 1965 with the Deputy Head of USOM Korea, Mr. Brown. 29 June, File Number: B 213/11968, Koblenz: Bundesarchiv [*Vermerk über eine Besprechung im BMZ am 21.06.1965 mit dem stellvertretenden Leiter der USOM Korea, Mr. Brown*].

US Comptroller General (1973). Report to the US Congress: US Assistance for the Economic Development of the Republic of Korea. 12 July, Digitalized by Google via: https://www.gao.gov/assets/b-164264-096144.pdf [last accessed 15 March 2024].

Villeroy & Boch (1965). Memorandum. 13 September, File Number: B 213/11969, Koblenz: Bundesarchiv [*Memorandum*].

Wichelmann, Gerd (1966). Visit by the Acting Head of DVB in Korea, Mr. Wilhelm Boucherie, to Min. Dirig. I A on 20. October 1966. 21 October, File Number: B 213/11968, Koblenz: Bundesarchiv [*Besuch des kommissarischen Leiters der DVB in Korea, Herrn Wilhelm Boucherie bei Herrn Dirig. I A am 20.10.1966*].

3 Towards Global Cooperation and Justice

Korean Aid and Beyond

Jae-Eun Noh

Introduction

Discussion on aid has been centred around state actors and their commitment to developing countries. The focus then shifted to global partnership, as highlighted in the Busan High-level Forum in 2011 and as articulated as Goal 17 of the United Nations (UN) Sustainable Development Goals (SDGs). Multi-actors in global cooperation include intergovernmental organisations (IGOs), multinational corporations (MNCs), and the global civil society (GCS), which encompasses non-governmental organisations (NGOs), networks, and individuals operating beyond national borders (Pierobon, 2020). Aid and development should be integrated into broader efforts to facilitate global cooperation within a multi-faceted process of 'addressing challenges that are of universal concerns' (Janus, Klingebiel and Paulo, 2015: 164).

The COVID-19 pandemic presented a pressing need for global cooperation to meet common challenges, which included but were not limited to global health injustice. However, global communities' responses to the pandemic turned out to be a failure. For example, vaccine inequity was not resolved through the global governance system and aid mechanisms. With this in mind, among many intertwined reasons behind this failure, this chapter focuses on the securitisation and politicisation of aid (Brown, 2021) and its connection to broader foreign policies, including issues of trade, security, and international relations (Chen, Faure and Gulrajani, 2023). Many donor countries started phrasing national interests as a precondition of aid rather than a secondary result (Gulrajani and Silcock, 2020). Among them, South Korea (hereinafter, Korea) also joined them by explicitly seeking national economic interests such as market expansion and job creation through aid and development cooperation, as suggested in the latest 'Mid-term Strategy for Development Cooperation (2021–2025)' (Noh, 2022b). The COVID-19 pandemic has triggered a reversal of Korea's gradually becoming more accountable to global society (Noh, 2022a).

In other words, this chapter aims to explore the roles of Korean aid in global cooperation and justice in order to respond to global challenges. Firstly, it outlines the changes in aid in terms of approaches and modalities. It examines the current state of Korean aid based on the identified aid trends. Then, it discusses the theoretical

DOI: 10.4324/9781003497035-3

foundations of global justice to situate aid in a broader discussion about global inequalities. Different frames and stakeholder interests are examined with an example of global health injustice. Finally, it suggests how Korean aid can promote its human rights-based approaches (HRBAs) to global cooperation.

The Trends in Aid

Securitisation and Politicisation of Aid

Securitisation of aid has been suggested as a shift from duty-based ethics to consequentialism in development discourses (Duffield, 2014). Securitisation of aid is often called the three Ds, meaning development, diplomacy, and defence, and has been noticeable in some countries, including Australia, the United States (US) and the United Kingdom (UK) (Zwi, 2011). Such a change is not new, as aid has been an instrument for donor countries to gain influence (Chen et al., 2023). The promotion of national interests has always been one of the key drivers of decisions on aid (Gulrajani and Swiss, 2019). However, the COVID-19 pandemic accelerated aid to become more self-interested and politicised to serve the donor countries' interests (Brown, 2021). The health security and economic crisis concerns led donor countries to emphasise securing national interests through aid (Gulrajani and Silcock, 2020). Most traditional donor countries cut the aid budgets and made aid decisions in considering returns.

Changes in Aid Modalities

Self-interested and politicised aid can be observed in changes in aid modalities. Aid modalities comprise bilateral, multilateral, and multi-bi or interchangeably earmarked aid with a specific purpose. The flow of bilateral aid has been greatly influenced by donor countries' strategies to maximise the national benefits, as studied extensively about both traditional and emerging donors (for example, Semrau and Thiele, 2017; Tomlinson, 2016). Donors have increased earmarked funding for multilateral organisations under the umbrella of multilateralism (Eichenauer and Reinsberg, 2017). However, earmarked aid has complemented or reinforced bilateral aid for specific countries or themes of strategic importance, diverting resources away from multilateral organisations' original mandates to serve the global community (OECD, 2020). This explains why earmarked contributions to multilateral organisations are counted as bilateral official development assistance (ODA). A high portion of earmarked funding can hinder flexibility and harmonisation in multilateral organisations (OECD, 2020).

Other aid modalities, such as triangular and multilateral cooperation, have been in demand for effective global cooperation. Triangular cooperation that involves three or more states as partners has been promoted as a 'transformative development modality' (OECD, 2019: 7) and a 'horizontal partnership' (Anderson and Swanepoel, 2022: 47). Triangular cooperation can change the unilateral aid flow from the global North to the global South, promoting more respectful relationships. Triangular cooperation is expected to improve aid effectiveness by drawing on each state's different strengths and skills. It can also benefit development policies and practices to be culturally and regionally appropriate (UN, 2023). The Second High-Level UN Conference on South-South Cooperation outcome document, also known as 'BAPA+40' marking the Buenos Aires Plan of Action in 1978, recognised that triangular cooperation could add value to South-South cooperation and the accomplishment of the SDGs (UN, 2019). Despite these claimed features, triangular cooperation's transformability has been questioned due to the homogenising effects of non-traditional donors, in addition to practical challenges such as transaction and coordination costs and partner countries' different orientations (Friesen and Janauschek, 2021; Lim, 2019; McEwan and Mawdsley, 2012). Existing studies on triangular cooperation, for instance, among the EU, China, and Africa (Armel, 2020), or the US, Indonesia, and Fiji (Alta and Mukhtarov, 2022), suggest the importance of relationality.

There is an increasing need for multilateralism to respond to a myriad of complex global issues. The 2022 Effective Development Cooperation Summit reconfirmed the importance of reinvigorating a 'multilateral system to provide transformative, holistic, and integrated solution' to global challenges (GPEDC, 2022: 41). Multilateralism is believed to legitimise and facilitate global cooperation, particularly when the US-China superpower rivalry and regional mini-laterals grow (Jaldi, 2023; Woods, 2023). However, multilateral institutions have not been very successful in representing the voices of low-income countries (OECD, 2023a). Furthermore, multilateralism was questioned about its capability to tackle health disparities and social inequalities across regions and countries, particularly during the COVID-19 pandemic (Singh, Kaur and Chattu, 2022). Regarding aid modalities, aid through multilateral organisations does not guarantee pooling resources for global development. OECD donors' data between 1977 and 2008 shows that states make strategic decisions about aid allocations to multilateral aid institutions in line with their national preferences (Schneider and Tobin, 2011). Despite these shortcomings, multilateral institutions are expected to play a significant role in boosting global cooperation, as they are 'response-able' with their power, resources, and legitimacy (McNeill and StClair, 2009: 32).

Korean Aid

South Korea was the 15th largest donor country in its aid volume and the 28th largest in relative terms—0.17 per cent of its gross national income (GNI)—on the Organisation for Economic Co-operation and Development (OECD) Development Assistance Committee (DAC) in 2022. South Korea has prioritised channelling its aid through its bilateral agencies, the Korea International Cooperation Agency (KOICA) and the Export-Import Bank of Korea (KEXIM Bank), totalling 80.5 per cent (USD 1.9 billion), which is significantly higher than the DAC average of 58 per cent (OECD, 2022). Korean bilateral aid has strongly focused on Asia by region and economic infrastructure by sector, in line with Korea's economic and diplomatic initiatives (Hill, 2023). Aid policy documents, such as the third Mid-Term Strategy for Development Cooperation (2021–2025) published in 2021, reflect Korea's drives to enhance national interests and security concerns (Noh, 2022b).

Korea's commitment to triangular cooperation has been much lower than other donor countries (Lim, 2019). Some studies noted the potential role of Korea and the benefits for Korea in this triangular cooperation (Lim, 2019; McEwan and Mawdsley, 2012). As Korea has highlighted its bridge role as a country with a history of experiencing colonial exploitation and poverty like other low-income countries (Noh, 2022b), it can enhance reciprocity beyond the simple North-South binary (Mawdsley, 2012).

As for Korea, multilateral aid in the form of core contributions to multilateral organisations, without specifying which projects are to be funded, has been relatively consistent, as 20–25 per cent of the total ODA. In comparison, earmarked non-core contributions have increased from 3.7 per cent in 2010 to 16.7 per cent in 2021 (OECD, 2022). Korea has not prioritised core funding to multilateral organisations, as demonstrated in Figure 3.1, as of 22.3 per cent, which is much lower than the DAC average of 42 per cent.

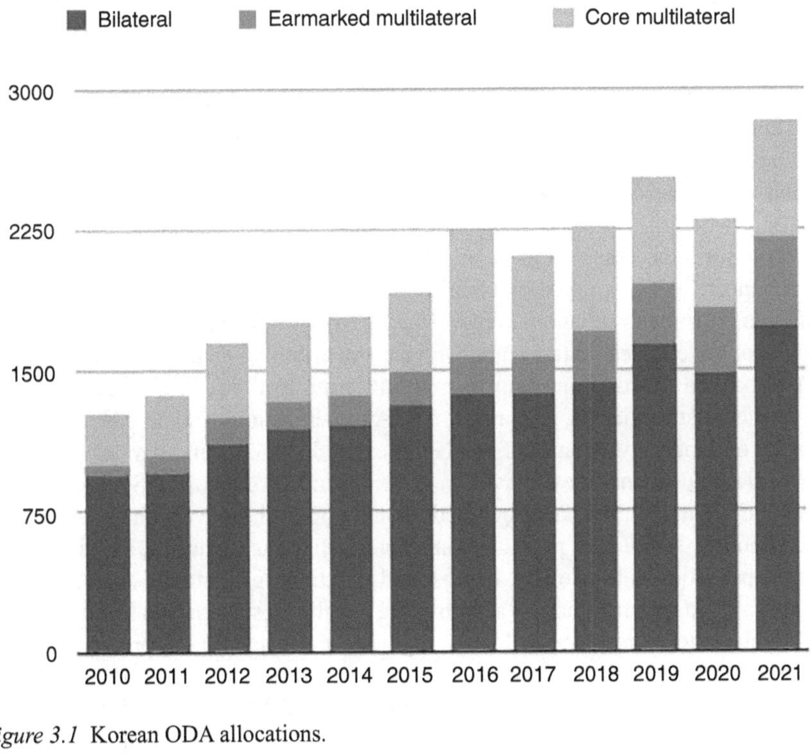

Figure 3.1 Korean ODA allocations.

Source: Revised from OECD (2022).

However, Korea's COVID-19 response included increasing multilateral spending, particularly on global health. As a result, 49.6 per cent of Korean aid to multilateral organisations, including both core and earmarked contributions, was allocated to the UN system, such as health-specialised agencies such as the World Health Organization (WHO) and United Nations Children's Fund (UNICEF) (OECD, 2022). In 2023, Korea announced that it would increase the 2024 aid budget by 43.2 per cent to amplify its presence and influence in global governance (Donor Tracker, 2023). With Korea's rising commitment to aid through and with multilateral organisations, it is getting more important to examine what informs the direction of global cooperation.

Why Global Justice?

In Search of Justice

Despite mixed evaluations, aid is often regarded as a redistribution mechanism to address global inequality (Collier, 2007). However, the current aid system has failed this mission. Reasons behind the failure include the increasing level of bilateral and multi-bi aid that serve national interests and the need for a fair and effective global governance system for multilateralism, as discussed in the earlier section. According to Ruggie (1992: 567), multilateralism is: 'not merely that it coordinates national policies in groups of three or more states…but that it does so on the basis of certain principles of ordering relations among those states'. This section focuses on exploring 'the principles' that should underpin global cooperation, and it suggests global justice as an essential principle to be highly considered.

Understandings of global justice vary. John Rawls' (1971) justice is grounded in fairness, and his principle of distributive justice states that inequalities can be justified only when they provide the greatest benefits to the least advantaged. Rawls' notion of justice is confined to the national border. However, the increasing global interconnectedness, as noted by Charles Beitz (1999), called for global ethics that can extend justice to the global level (Moyn, 2018). Beitz (1999) later argued that the global governance system should advance distributive justice to ensure fairness in a globalised world, promoting cosmopolitanism. Both Rawls and Beitz focused on the just distribution of primary goods. Another notion of justice is around the concept of capability. Amartya Sen (1999) expanded the meaning of poverty from economic status to include deprivation of opportunities and power. Sen's capability approach highlights the extent of freedom and opportunities, which are shaped by the economic, social, and political contexts. Martha Nussbaum (2011) also elaborated capabilities as the doings, beings, and functionings that people can achieve, promoting a just distribution of a set of core capabilities. Both Sen and Nussbaum highlighted the importance of human rights to the capability approaches (Nussbaum, 1997).

Earlier than Sen and Nussbaum, Henry Shue (1980) promoted the concept of basic rights. According to Shue (1980), basic rights suggested that states and non-state actors are duty bearers. His emphasis on basic rights built a consensus about social rights but also led to minimalist approaches to human rights by focusing on the protection of basic rights (Moyn, 2018). However, human rights have been widely embraced as a key principle to guide justice discourses with their normativity and legitimacy (Cornwall, 2007). Furthermore, human rights perspectives clarify that inter-state inequality is a matter of global justice, resulting from historical and structural disadvantages of low-income countries and that high-income countries bear primary responsibility for global inequalities (Beall, 2022; Pogge, 2008).

Human Rights for Aid and Beyond Aid

Human rights have been prominent in the international development community's recent initiatives for fair and just development. In particular, its universality provides a strong foundation for global justice (Taket, 2023). Human rights could be embraced in the SDGs with a greater focus than the Millennium Development Goals (MDGs) (Nelson, 2021). The SDGs' slogan, 'Leave No One Behind and Reaching the Furthest Behind First', emphasises universality, focusing on principles of equality and non-discrimination (Noh, 2023). The close connection between human rights and the SDGs presents that 92 per cent of the 169 SDG targets are linked to international human rights principles and standards (The Danish Institute for Human Rights, 2018). In the wake of the COVID-19 pandemic, the significance of human rights was highlighted to be the guiding principle of the new global order, as articulated in the UN's Call to Action for Human Rights in 2020 and the Sustainable Recovery Pledge in 2021 (Noh, 2023).

This pandemic raised fundamental questions that challenge the current political and economic order (Green, 2020). This is related to the call for 'beyond aid'. 'Beyond aid' implies questioning the current aid system and promoting transformation in development (Janus et al., 2015). Transformation involves rethinking development and reconstructing the global order. Therefore, 'beyond aid' also expands the discussion to the broader system that includes some connected but somewhat competing issues such as trade and security (Chen, Faure and Gulrajani, 2023). Human rights' indivisibility and interdependence highlight the equal importance and inter-relatedness of different rights. Such a nature of human rights leads to taking a holistic approach to development and justice (Hickey and Mitlin, 2009), offering principles for both aid and beyond aid. Human rights have been incorporated in aid since the 1990s in the name of human rights mainstreaming, a HRBA to development, human rights dialogue, human rights projects, and implicit human rights work (World Bank and OECD, 2016: 52). When it comes to 'beyond aid', a growing number of development actors strive to make trade rules fairer, given their significant influence on the rights to food, health, and participation of those living in low-income countries (Aaronson and Zimmerman, 2006). Although security has been usually regarded as separate from human rights, there is an increasing recognition of the correlation between the two (Burke-White, 2004; Goold and Lazarus, 2019). Human rights can adapt and guide security issues as safeguarding principles for those who are vulnerable (Goold and Lazarus, 2019), and improvement in human rights can reduce the likelihood of putting global security under threat (Burke-White, 2004). In short, human rights have the potential to make global cooperation work for global justice (McNeill and StClair, 2009). The following demonstrates the multi-layered complexities of global cooperation with an example of global health issues.

Global Health Justice

Global Governance for Health

Similarly to the definition of 'global cooperation', 'global health' entails 'issues that directly and indirectly affect health but that can transcend national boundaries' that require 'interdisciplinary and multidisciplinary approaches' to seek health equity (Koplan et al., 2009: 1993–1994). In global health, priorities have been shaped by different frames. Shffman and Shawar (2022) suggest three frames: technification; securitisation; and moralisation. Technification emphasises investment in medical science to assist experts in solving health issues, while securitisation highlights existential threats, which should be dealt with by powerful regulations. Moralisation places high emphasis on ethical imperatives such as human rights and social justice to address health inequities, often involving transnational advocacy campaigns (Shiffman and Shawar, 2022). In times of crisis, security tends to be more highlighted (Duffield, 2014), as observed in other practices invoked by fear during the COVID-19 pandemic (Noh, 2022a). However, the demands for human rights-guided responses to the health crisis have also been high. The Access to Essential Medicine Campaign, particularly for HIV/AIDS treatment, is an example of HRBAs (Shiffman and Shawar, 2022; Taket, 2023). The campaign for equal access was reignited in the wake of the COVID-19 pandemic to grapple with vaccine injustice and health inequity.

In line with the importance of global cooperation, the health sector has used the concept of Global Health Diplomacy (GHD), which means multi-level and multi-actor interactions and negotiations to deal with global health issues (Labonté and Ruckert, 2019). The term GHD also shows that health has gained significance in the global governance agenda and each state's foreign policies (Labonté and Ruckert, 2019). During this pandemic, GHD has facilitated formal and informal collaborations among multiple stakeholders but has also revealed its limitation of being dominated by the powerful (Singh, Kaur and Chattu, 2022). Despite a high hope for multilateralism in the name of a responsibility to protect (R2P) that highlights the international community's shared accountability for global health justice (Jecker, Atuire and Bull, 2022), multilateral organisations, including WHO, revealed its inherent problems of needing more low-income countries' participation and equity (Jaldi, 2023; Syam, 2022). In addition, the US-China rivalry hindered the functioning of multilateral organisations, as seen in that the US has withdrawn from the WHO and both the US and China actively used vaccines to leverage global hegemony (Jaldi, 2023; People's Health Institute, 2021). As a result, the lack of effective global governance resulted in delayed and unequal access to vaccines, treatments, and technologies. Furthermore, vaccine purchase and distribution through the COVID-19 Vaccines Global Access (COVAX) Facility did not work well as designed for pooled procurement due to vaccine nationalism and pharmaceutical companies' monopolies (Peacock, 2022). It is noteworthy that the unequal accessibility and affordability of vaccines are attributed to the long-lasting injustice in health infrastructure, research and development, and trade (Tosam et al., 2018).

Equal access to essential medicines has been delayed due to the intellectual property regime, the Trade-Related Intellectual Property Rights (TRIPs) agreement, established by the World Trade Organization (WTO) in 1995. Global campaigns for patent rule changes have promoted this access issue as a fundamental human right (Nelson, 2021; Pogge, 2008). In the vein of human rights and health justice, the GCS, including some development NGOs such as Oxfam, ActionAid, and Save the Children, has carried out TRIPs waiver campaigns since 2020 (The People's Vaccine, n.d.). The TRIPS waiver was finally agreed upon in 2022, but with a narrower scope than the original proposal for comprehensive access to vaccines, therapeutics, and technology. Global health inequality can be worsened by high-income countries administering booster shots and oral therapeutics (People's Health Movement Korea, 2022). As demonstrated in the history and outcome of the Access Campaigns for affordable and patent-free treatment, existing obstacles to providing access to medicines and medical technologies are deeply related to other policy domains such as trade, security, and international relations. This presents why global cooperation beyond aid is needed. The aid sector or state actors cannot ensure global health justice alone.

The role of aid in this health crisis was limited. Regarding research for vaccine development and production, the investments made primarily for domestic benefits are not counted as ODA according to the DAC guidelines (OECD, 2023b: 2). Although public funding and data enabled vaccine research and development (Mantilla and Barona, 2022), pharmaceutical companies have made huge profits through patent monopolies (Peacock, 2022). The politics of vaccine diplomacy influenced the aid-based distribution of COVID-19 vaccines (People's Health Institute, 2021). As donor countries provided vaccines mainly through bilateral agencies and COVAX with country-earmarking donations (Fang et al., 2023), vaccine donations mirrored donor countries' national interests. Later, their donations became recognised as an aid in kind by the OECD DAC's decision on a valuation of USD 6.72 per dose to discourage countries from selling their excess vaccines (OECD, 2023b: 1). Civil society has voiced concerns that counting unwanted vaccines as aid can lead to ODA inflation and other undesirable consequences (BOND, 2023; Oxfam, 2022a). They have also raised broader issues of regulating corporations' profit-driven practices through progressive taxation and challenging the neoliberal global order, which shapes an understanding of aid and health justice (Oxfam, 2022b; Szent-Iványi, 2022).

Korea's Position in Global Health Justice

Korea's bilateral ODA has strongly focused on health, as seen in the spending of USD 780.4 million in 2020 (OECD, 2022). Korea was ranked as the seventh largest DAC donor by the total bilateral and multilateral disbursements to the health

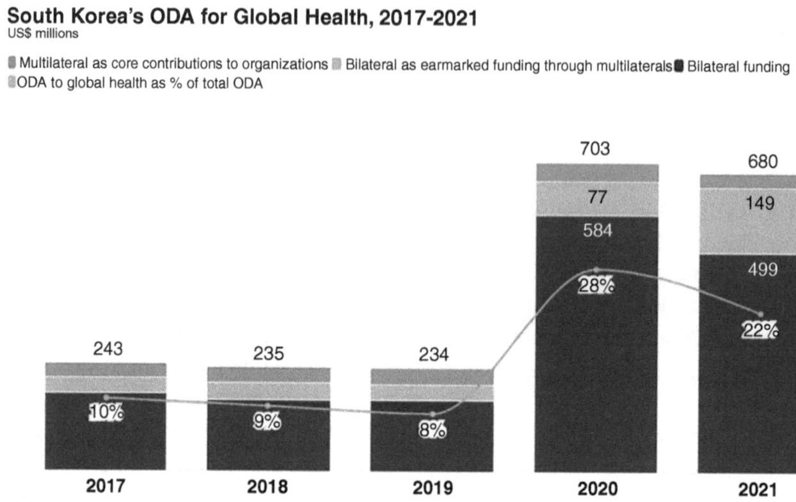

Figure 3.2 Korean ODA for global health.

Source: Revised from Donor Tracker (2023).

sector in 2020, largely due to the sharp increase in funding for global health (from 8 per cent in 2019 to 28 per cent of total ODA in 2020) as its COVID-19 response (Donor Tracker, 2023). Korea's spending on global health remains high despite a decline to 22 per cent of its ODA in 2021 (73 per cent as bilateral aid, 22 per cent as earmarked funding through multilateral organisations, and 5 per cent as core funding to multilateral organisations) (Donor Tracker, 2023) (Figure 3.2).

As for health, KOICA states its vision as ensuring health rights for all. KOICA launched the 'Agenda for Building resilience against COVID-19 through development cooperation (ABC)' programme as its core response to the COVID pandemic in 2020 as part of Korea's broader strategies for 'Building TRUST (Transparency, Resilience, Unity, and Safety Together)', addressed by the former President Moon Jae-in at the 73rd World Health Assembly (KOICA, 2020). These initiatives have highlighted the importance of 'comprehensive cooperation' based on the sense of 'global solidarity' (KOICA, 2020: 4).

Korea significantly increased its multilateral commitments to global health by fulfilling its pledge of USD 200 million to the COVAX Advance Market Commitment (AMC) and funding global health organisations such as the Global Alliance for Vaccines and Immunization (Gavi), the Global Fund, and the Coalition for Epidemic Preparedness Innovations (CEPI) that consist of the Access to COVID-19 Tools Accelerator (ACT-A) (see WHO official website). Korea also strengthened support for the production and distribution of COVID-19 vaccines by joining the ACT-A Facilitation Council with seven other countries—the US, China, India, Russia, Brazil, Indonesia, South Africa, and Mexico. Korea's enhanced multilateral engagement is suggested to be a strategic move to cultivate the power to influence global health policies (Attias, 2020).

Korea's increased commitment to global health can also be partly related to collective beliefs in its capacity to deal with the health crisis, as evidenced in Korea's successful response to the COVID-19 pandemic (Noh, 2022b). However, the most significant driver would be the government's will to make Korea a bio-health powerhouse by establishing a global vaccine hub and expanding investment in biomedical technology (People's Health Movement Korea, 2022). This initiative for a global vaccine hub was mainly to support Korean companies' vaccine production and exportation in the name of the public-private partnership (PPP) (People's Health Institute, 2021). GCS, including Korean actors such as the People's Health Institute and the Korean Federation Medical Activist Groups for Health Rights, has urged the necessity of the TRIPS waiver to allow generic production and affordable prices. Korea's opposition to the TRIPS waiver means putting national and corporate interests before global vaccine justice. Instead of pushing for vaccine development, the global community expected Korea to provide affordable biopharmaceuticals with the world's second-largest production facility and to transfer technology to low-income countries (People's Health Movement Korea, 2022). In 2022, WHO selected Korea as the global biomanufacturing training hub with South Africa. This would allow Korea to strengthen its role in global cooperation by supporting low-income countries' pharmaceutical production (WHO, 2022).

Directions for Korea's Global Cooperation

Whether by necessity or choice, Korea has strengthened its accountability for global cooperation. Korea has facilitated multi-actor dialogues by hosting a series of Busan Global Partnership Forums since 2014, tracking progress against principles agreed upon at the Busan High-level Forum in 2011. Korea has also advocated the importance of global partnership for development effectiveness as a steering committee member of the Global Partnership for Effective Development Cooperation (GPEDC). Despite the increased tensions between global responsibility and national interests over the course of the COVID-19 pandemic, Korea has taken up greater global responsibility by increasing its ODA, particularly on global health, even when many traditional donors cut aid budgets. However, as discussed earlier, some moves have been primarily driven by national economic interests and security concerns, conflicting with the foundational values of global justice. This final section suggests how Korea should enhance its role in global cooperation and its contribution towards global justice.

Collaboration with Global Civil Society

GCS has played a significant role in facilitating global cooperation and demanding global justice. As demonstrated in the Access to Essential Medicines Campaign, GCS has actively advocated for global health justice (Anaf et al., 2020). Noticeable changes in transnational corporations have also occurred due to pressure from GCS and local communities (O'Faircheallaigh and Ali, 2008). Korean civil society, including Korea-based development NGOs, has joined forces with GCS to make the

Korean government and companies accountable for those who experience global inequality.

In Korean aid, the critical role of civil society was acknowledged in the 'International Development Cooperation Government-Civil Society Partnership Basic Plan' announced in 2019 (ODA Korea, 2020). The development of this plan was initiated as a follow-up of the 2017 DAC peer review that Korea's government should clarify and deepen the partnership it seeks with civil society through a normative framework (ODA Korea, 2020: 44). The 2021 DAC recommendation on Enabling Civil Society in Development Cooperation and Humanitarian Assistance also suggests expanding civic space and empowering civil society (OECD, 2024). However, Korea's support for civil society has not been strong. Figure 3.3 below shows a gradual increase to 2.8 per cent of bilateral ODA in 2020, then a drop to 1.8 per cent in 2021, with a focus on supporting Korea-based NGOs (80.1 per cent). Increasing support for civil society organisations (CSOs), in particular locally based ones, will enhance the effectiveness and legitimacy of global cooperation.

In addition, the scope of cooperation should be beyond the aid sector. This chapter highlights that aid should embrace broader global challenges for greater global justice (Janus et al., 2015). Renowned development NGOs, such as ActionAid and Oxfam, have joined other civil society groups working in global movements to challenge unfair trade rules and medical monopolies (Noh, 2024). During the pandemic, European development NGOs have also advocated for debt cancellation and the transformation of the neoliberal system (Szent-Iványi, 2022). The pursuit of global justice should include questioning structural issues that have perpetuated

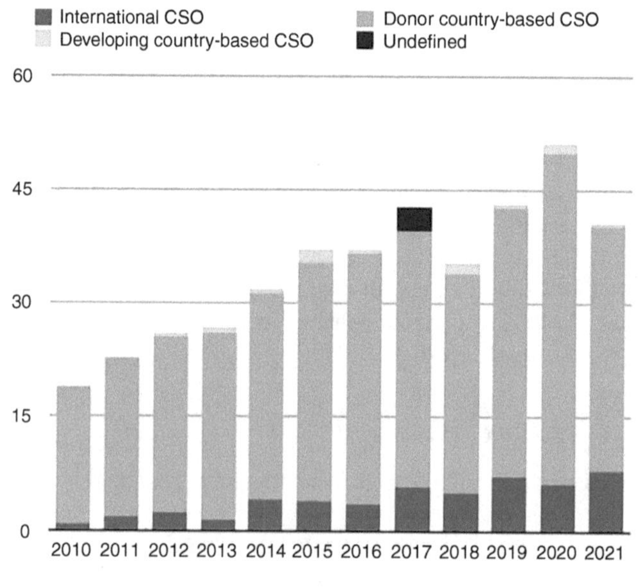

Figure 3.3 Korean aid to civil society.

Source: Revised from OECD (2022).

global inequality and injustice. These structural issues require concerted actions of various civil society groups, including human rights organisations, labour unions, and community-based organisations.

Commitment to Human Rights and Global Justice

Global cooperation should be strongly anchored in the norms and principles of human rights. KOICA introduced its 'Human Rights Management Charter' in 2018, following the suggestion of the National Human Rights Plans of Action (KOICA, 2021: 5). Korean aid has pursued a HRBA by incorporating human rights norms and principles in the whole process and developed targeted programmes for specific human rights through a two-track approach (Noh, 2023). Contribution of human rights includes highlighting duty-bearers' obligations, enabling multi-sector and multi-player cooperation for common goals of human rights realisation, and locating aid and development in a broader fight for global justice (Hickey and Mitlin, 2009). Global justice discussions have been around distribution and fairness, as discussed earlier in the sections on literature and health-related issues. As emphasised in the HRBA's principles of participation, accountability, non-discrimination, empowerment, and linkage to the human rights framework, human rights can offer insights into the development process as well as problems and solutions (Jonsson, 2003). This suggests that human rights-guided aid and development cooperation can strengthen the inclusion of the most marginalised for distributive justice.

The COVID-19 pandemic has reshaped Korea's global cooperation. Korea's COVID-19 response included more substantial support for global cooperation, as evidenced by increased funding to multilateral organisations. However, Korea's normative foundations for global cooperation and justice have weakened since the pandemic began (Noh, 2022a). It is noteworthy that the COVID-19 pandemic has also provided opportunities for change. Global injustice observed throughout the pandemic reveals that the current political and economic system has kept people from enjoying their human rights. This realisation has resulted in calls for urgent actions and new strategies (People's Health Movement Korea, 2022). The Sustainable Recovery Pledge launched by 48 states, including Korea, and 28 supporting organisations in 2021 affirmed the value of human rights for 'building forward better' (OHCHR, 2022). It is imperative to place human rights at the centre of global cooperation beyond aid.

Conclusion

This chapter has outlined the significance of global cooperation for global justice. Global cooperation involves the complexity of mediating norms and interests held by multiple actors and multiple sectors beyond aid. As an example, global health issues show how decisions for global cooperation are made and influenced by the frames (technical interventions, security, and moral imperative), a wide range of policies (aid, trade, and investment), and actors (multilateral institutions, states, GCS groups, and corporations). Aid and beyond aid are part of global cooperation that Korea should strengthen as a responsible member of the global community. This chapter argues that Korea needs to strengthen its role in global development cooperation to tackle global inequalities and achieve global justice. Aid and development actors in Korea should urge the Korean government to promote its global cooperation through CSOs and multilateral intuitions that nurture local agencies in line with the norms and principles of human rights and global justice.

References

Aaronson, Susan Ariel, and Jamie M. Zimmerman, 2006. Fair trade? How Oxfam presented a systematic approach to poverty, development, human rights, and trade. *Human Rights Quarterly, 28*, pp. 998–1030.

Alta, Aditya and Farhad Mukhtarov, 2022. Relationality as a lens for policy analysis: Preserving harmony in a triangular cooperation project to strengthen gender mainstreaming in Fiji. *Administration & Society, 54*(7), pp. 1283–1304.

Anaf, Julia, Fran Baum, Matthew Fisher, and Sharon Friel. 2020. Civil society action against transnational corporations: Implications for health promotion. *Health Promotion International, 35*(4), pp. 877–887.

Anderson, Courtney, and Libby Swanepoel. 2022. Rethinking Australia's role in international co-operation for the sustainable development goals: Towards transformative horizontal partnerships through triangular co-operation. *World Nutrition, 13*, pp. 46–53.

Armel, Kaze, 2020. Trilateral cooperation: China's and the EU's foreign assistance in Africa. *China Quarterly of International Strategic Studies, 6*(03), pp. 311–332.

Attias, Shay, 2020. Asian soft power grows in the coronavirus era. *BESA Center Perspectives, no. 1520.*

Beall, Katherine M., 2022. The global south and global human rights: International responsibility for the right to development. *Third World Quarterly, 43*(10), pp. 2337–2356.

Beitz, Charles R., 1999. *Political Theory and International Relations*. Princeton, NJ: Princeton University Press.

BOND (2023). Counting excess vaccine donations as ODA inflated aid in 2021. Available at: https://www.bond.org.uk/news/2023/02/counting-excess-vaccine-donations-as-oda-inflated-aid-in-2021-heres-why-they-still-shouldnt-count/ (Accessed on 24 February 2023).

Brown, Stephen, 2021. The impact of COVID-19 on development assistance. *International Journal, 76*(1), pp. 42–54.

Burke-White, William W., 2004. Human rights and national security: The strategic correlation. *Harvard Human Rights Journal, 17*, pp. 249–280.

Chen, Yunnan, Raphaëlle Faure, and Nilima Gulrajani, 2023. *Crafting Development Power: Evolving European Approaches in an Age of Polycrisis*. London: ODI.

Collier, Paul, 2007. *The Bottom Billion: Why the Poorest Countries Are Failing and What Can Be Done About It*. New York: Oxford University Press.

Cornwall, Andrea, 2007. Buzzwords and fuzzwords: Deconstructing development discourse. *Development in Practice, 17*(4–5), pp. 471–484.

Donor tracker (2023). Donor profile_South Korea. Available at: https://donortracker.org/donor_profiles/south-korea#oda-spending (Accessed on 20 February 2023).

Duffield, Mark, 2014. *Global Governance and the New Wars: The Merging of Development and Security* (2nd ed.). London: Zed Books.

Eichenauer, Vera Z., and Bernhard Reinsberg, 2017. What determines earmarked funding to international development organizations? Evidence from the new multi-bi aid data. *The Review of International Organizations, 12*, pp. 171–197.

Fang, Yian, Tianyue Ma, Ming Wu, and Sian Hsiang-Te Tsuei, 2023. Mitigating donor interests in the case of COVID-19 vaccine: The implication of COVAX and DAC membership. *BMJ Global Health*, *8*(1), p. e010188.

Friesen, Ina, and Leon Janauschek, 2021. EU-China engagement in humanitarian aid: Different approaches, shared interests? *Briefing Paper. No. 11/2021*. Deutsches Institut für Entwicklungspolitik (DIE), Bonn.

Global Partnership for Effective Development Co-operation (GPEDC), 2022. Rebuilding trust through effective development co-operation. Available at: https://www.effectiveco-operation.org/SummitReport (Accessed on 21 February 2023).

Goold, Benjamin J., and Liora Lazarus, 2019. *Security and Human Rights*. London: Bloomsbury Publishing.

Green, Duncan, 2020. Covid-19 as a critical juncture and the implications for advocacy. *Global Policy*, *23*(April), pp. 1–16.

Gulrajani, Nilima, and Emily Silcock, 2020. *Principled Aid in Divided Times*. London: ODI.

Gulrajani, Nilima, and Liam Swiss, 2019. Donor proliferation to what ends? New donor countries and the search for legitimacy. *Canadian Journal of Development Studies/Revue canadienne d'études du développement*, *40*(3), pp. 348–368.

Hickey, Samuel, and Diana Mitlin, 2009. *Rights-Based Approaches to Development: Exploring the Potential and Pitfalls*. Sterling: Kumarian Press.

Hill, Cameron, (2023). Aiming for the top ten: Korea's aid, DevPolicy Blog. Available at: https://devpolicy.org/aiming-for-the-top-ten-koreas-aid-20230601/ (Accessed on 19 June 2023).

Jaldi, Abdessalam, 2023. *The Crisis of Multilateralism Viewed from the Global South, Policy Paper April*. Mohammed VI Polytechnic University: Policy Center for the New South, Rabat. https://www.policycenter.ma/about-policy-center-new-south

Janus, Heiner, Stephan Klingebiel, and Sebastian Paulo, 2015. Beyond aid: A conceptual perspective on the transformation of development cooperation. *Journal of International Development*, *27*(2), pp. 155–169.

Jecker, Nancy S., Caesar A. Atuire, and Susan D. Bull, 2022. Towards a new model of global health justice: The case of COVID-19 vaccines. *Journal of Medical Ethics, 49*(5), pp. 367–374.

Jonsson, Urban, 2003. *Human Rights Approach to Development Programming*. Nairobi: UNCEF ESARO.

KOICA (Korea International Cooperation Agency), 2020. KOICA's COVID-19 response. Available at: https://www.unescap.org/sites/default/files/02_KOICA.pdf (Accessed on 11 July 2023).

KOICA (Korea International Cooperation Agency), 2021. KOICA human rights mid-term strategy (2021–2025).

Koplan, Jeffrey P., T. Christopher Bond, Michael H. Merson, K. Srinath Reddy, Mario Henry Rodriguez, Nelson K. Sewankambo, and Judith N. Wasserheit, 2009. Towards a common definition of global health. *The Lancet, 373*(9679), pp. 1993–1995.

Labonté, Ronald and Arne Ruckert, 2019. *Health Equity in a Globalizing Era: Past Challenges, Future Prospects*. Oxford: Oxford University Press.

Lim, Sojin, 2019. Determinants of aid modalities. *North Korean Review*, *15*(1), pp. 73–93.

Mantilla, Katiuska King, and César Carranza Barona, 2022. COVID-19 vaccines as global public goods: Between life and profit. *South Centre Research Paper,* 154.

Mawdsley, Emma, 2012. The changing geographies of foreign aid and development co-operation: Contributions from gift theory. *Transactions of the Institute of British Geographers*, *37*(2), pp. 256–272.

McEwan, Cheryl, and Emma Mawdsley, 2012. Trilateral development cooperation: Power and politics in emerging aid relationships. *Development and Change*, *43*(6), pp. 1185–1209.

McNeill, Desmond, and Asunción Lera StClair, 2009. *Global Poverty, Ethics and Human Rights: The Role of Multilateral Organisations*. London: Routledge.

Moyn, Samuel, 2018. *Not Enough: Human Rights in an Unequal World*. Cambridge, MA: Harvard University Press.

Nelson, Paul, 2021. *Global Development and Human Rights: The Sustainable Development Goals and Beyond*. Toronto: University of Toronto Press.

Noh, Jae-Eun, 2022a. Constructing 'others' and a wider 'we' as emotional processes: A case of South Korea in times of crisis. *Thesis Eleven*, *170*(1), pp. 43–57.

Noh, Jae-Eun, 2022b. The emotional underpinning of norms and identities in framing Korean aid. *Development in Practice*, *33*(3), pp. 361–372.

Noh, Jae-Eun, 2023. Human rights. In: KOICA (eds) *International Development Cooperation: Advanced Edition*. Sungnam: KOICA ODA Education Center, pp. 578–652.

Noh, Jae-Eun, 2024. The fight for global health justice: The advocacy of international humanitarian development NGOs during the COVID-19 pandemic. *VOLUNTAS: International Journal of Voluntary and Nonprofit Organizations*, *35*, pp. 661–675.

Nussbaum, Martha C., 1997. Capabilities and human rights. *Fordham Law Review*, *66*(2), pp. 273–303.

Nussbaum, Martha C., 2011. *Creating Capabilities: The Human Development Approach*. Cambridge, MA: Belknap Press of Harvard.

ODA Korea, 2020. 2020 Korea official development assistance whitepaper. Available at www.odakorea.go.kr (Accessed on 19 June 2023).

OECD, 2019. Enabling effective triangular co-operation. Available at: https://www.oecd-ilibrary.org/docserver/5fc4501e-en.pdf?expires=1688163278&id=id&accname=guest&checksum=CD58DB071FFAFCDFE8A753032E556A31 (Accessed on 1 July 2023).

OECD, 2020. Earmarked funding to multilateral organisations: How is it used and what constitutes good practice? Available at: https://www.oecd.org/dac/financing-sustainable-development/development-finance-topics/Multilateral-development-finance-brief-2020.pdf (Accessed on 1 July 2023).

OECD, 2022. Development cooperation profiles. Available at: https://www.oecd-ilibrary.org/sites/d919ff1a-en/index.html?itemId=/content/component/d919ff1a-en#fnotea26z2 (Accessed on 7 January 2023).

OECD, 2023a. Development cooperation report 2023: Debating the aid system. Available at: https://www.oecd.org/dac/development-co-operation-report-20747721.htm (Accessed on 07 January 2023).

OECD, 2023b. Frequently asked questions on the ODA eligibility of COVID-19 related activities. Available at: https://www.oecd.org/dac/financing-sustainable-development/faqs-oda-eligibility-of-covid-19-related-activities.pdf. (Accessed on 9 April 2024).

OECD, 2024. DAC recommendation on enabling civil society in development co-operation and humanitarian assistance. Available at: https://legalinstruments.oecd.org/api/print?ids=666&lang=en (Accessed on 15 July 2024).

O'Faircheallaigh, Ciaran, and Saleem Ali, 2008. *Earth Matters: Indigenous Peoples, the Extractive Industries and Corporate Social Responsibility*. Sheffield: Greenleaf.

OHCHR (Office of the High Commissioner for Human Rights), 2022. Building forward better: Reaffirming the sustainable recovery pledge and taking stock of commitments. Available at: https://www.ohchr.org/en/2022/01/building-forward-better-reaffirming-sustainable-recovery-pledge-and-taking-stock (Accessed on 7 January 2023).

Oxfam, 2022a. Donating unwanted vaccine does should not be part of already stretched aid budgets. Available at: https://www.oxfam.org/en/press-releases/donating-unwanted-vaccine-doses-should-not-be-part-already-stretched-aid-budgets (Accessed on 24 February 2023).

Oxfam, 2022b. Profiting from pain. Available at: https://www.oxfam.org/en/research/profiting-pain (Accessed on 27 February 2023).

Peacock, Stuart J., 2022. Vaccine nationalism will persist: Global public goods need effective engagement of global citizens. *Globalization and Health*, *18*(1), pp. 1–11.

People's Health Institute, 2021. *COVID-19 Vaccinations and People's Rights*. Seoul: People's Health Institute.

People's Health Movement Korea, 2022. Changing political economy of pharmaceutical production in post-COVID-19 era and civil society movement strategy in South Korea. Issue paper. Available at: http://health.re.kr/?p=9237 (Accessed on 27 February 2023).

Pierobon, Chiara, 2020. Global governance, multi-actor cooperation, and civil society. In: Leal Filho, W., Azul, A., Brandli, L., Özuyar, P., Wall, T. (eds) *Peace, Justice and Strong Institutions*. Cham: Springer, pp. 317–327.

Pogge, Thomas, 2008. *World Poverty and Human Rights* (2nd ed.). Cambridge: Polity.

Rawls, John, 1971. *Theory of Justice*. Cambridge: Cambridge University Press.

Ruggie, John Gerard, 1992. Multilateralism: The anatomy of an institution. *International Organization*, *46*(3), pp. 561–598.

Schneider, Christina J., and Jennifer Tobin, 2011. Eenie, meenie, miney, moe? Institutional portfolios and delegation to multilateral aid institutions. *Available at SSRN 1949238*.

Semrau, Finn Ole, and Rainer Thiele, 2017. Brazil's development cooperation: Following in China's and India's footsteps? *Journal of International Development,* 29(3), pp. 287–307.

Sen, Amartya, 1999. *Development as Freedom*. Oxford: Oxford University Press.

Shiffman, Jeremy, and Yusra Ribhi Shawar, 2022. Framing and the formation of global health priorities. *The Lancet*, *399*(10339), pp. 1977–1990.

Shue, Henry, 1980. *Basic Rights*. Princeton, NJ: Princeton University Press Princeton.

Singh, Bawa, Jaspal Kaur, and Vijay Kumar Chattu, 2022. Global vaccine inequities and multilateralism amid COVID-19: Reconnaissance of Global Health Diplomacy as a panacea? *Health Promotion Perspectives*, *12*(4), pp. 315–324.

Syam, Nirmalya, 2022. Mainstreaming equity in the international health regulations and future WHO legal instruments on pandemic preparedness and response. *South Centre Policy Brief, 108*, pp. 1–7.

Szent-Iványi, Balázs, 2022. *European Civil Society and International Development Aid: Organisational Incentives and NGO Advocacy*. Oxon: Taylor & Francis.

Taket, Ann, 2023. Human rights and global public health. In: Liamputtong, P. (eds) *Handbook of Social Sciences and Global Public Health*. Cham: Springer, pp. 1–18.

The Danish Institute for Human Rights, 2018. *Human Rights and the 2030 Agenda for Sustainable Development*. Copenhagen: The Danish Institute for Human Rights.

The People's Vaccine, n.d. Who we are. Available at: https://peoplesvaccine.org/ (Accessed on 10 July 2023).

Tomlinson, Brian, 2016. *Reality of Aid 2016: An Independent Review of Poverty Reduction and Development Assistance*. Manilla: IBON.

Tosam, Mbih J., Primus Che Chi, Nchangwi Syntia Munung, Odile Ouwe Missi Oukem-Boyer, and Godfrey B. 2018. Global health inequalities and the need for solidarity: A view from the Global South. *Developing World Bioethics*, *18*(3), pp. 241–249.

United Nations (UN), 2019. Report of the second high-level United Nations conference on south-south cooperation. Available at: https://www.unsouthsouth.org/wp-content/uploads/2019/07/N1920949.pdf (Accessed on 1 July 2023).

United Nations (UN), 2023. United Nations system-wide strategy on South-South and triangular cooperation for sustainable development. Available at: https://policycommons.net/artifacts/8936304/united-nations-system-wide-strategy-on-south-south-and-triangular-cooperation-for-sustainable-development/9747920/ (Accessed on 4 July 2023).

WHO, 2022. Moving forward on goal to boost local pharmaceutical production, WHO establishes global biomanufacturing training hub in Republic of Korea. Available at: https://www.who.int/news/item/23-02-2022-moving-forward-on-goal-to-boost-local-pharmaceutical-production-who-establishes-global-biomanufacturing-training-hub-in-republic-of-korea (Accessed on 5 July 2023).

Woods, Ngaire, 2023. Multilateralism in the twenty-first century. *Global Perspectives, 4*(1), 68310.

World Bank and OECD, 2016. *Integrating Human Rights into Development: Donor approaches, Experiences, and Challenges* (3rd ed.). Washington, DC: World Bank; OECD, Organisation for Economic Co-operation and Development. DOI: 10.1596/978-0-8213-9621-6.

Zwi, Anthony B., 2011. International aid and global health. In: Benatar, S., Brock, G. (eds) *Global Health and Global Health Ethics*. Leiden: Cambridge University Press, pp. 184–197.

4 Analysis of KOICA under Gender Mainstreaming Approach[1]

A Case Study in Darkhan, Mongolia

Patricia Chica-Morales and Antonio J. Doménech

Introduction

Before 1995, discussions on women and their role in society were based mainly on welfare and analytical approaches (Plattner, 1996). It was not until the Beijing Declaration and Platform for Action that a global consensus was reached, at least in theory, on the importance of women as drivers of human, social, economic, and sustainable development (Chen, 1995; Plattner, 1996). Gender mainstreaming (GM) is an agreed strategy of the governments and official institutions to achieve gender equality in development policies. According to the definition of the Council of Europe (2018: 9), GM means 'integrating a gender perspective at all stages and levels of policies, programmes and projects'. It recognises that GM is a 'dual approach' or twin-track strategy that not only works on women-focused policies but also works on gender inequality in all policies, strategies, and activities carried out (Council of Europe, 2018: 9). Applying GM also means analysing and working with the structural roots of inequalities faced by women in all parts of the world (Engeli and Mazur, 2018; True, 2003).

As recognised by the Organisation for Economic Co-operation and Development (OECD) Development Assistance Committee (DAC), the official development assistance (ODA) agencies are supposed to apply this twin-track approach (Grown, Addison and Tarp, 2016). However, academics point out that there is a gap between the theoretical approach and the operational approach when applying GM in institutions such as donor agencies (Barnett, 2018; Bustelo, 2017; Engeli and Mazur, 2018; Espinosa, 2013; Lee-Gosselin, Briere and Ann, 2013). Among OECD DAC donor countries, the government of South Korea (or Korea hereinafter) has also introduced the GM approach in its aid policies. For example, the Korea International Cooperation Agency (KOICA), as a main grant aid implementation agency, has established guidelines to promote gender equality and contribute to women's empowerment in the context of sustainable development (Kim, Kang and Kim, 2018). 'Gender equality' is, for example, one of the cross-cutting sectors of the Mid-Term Strategy (2021–2025) of the KOICA, with targets for its achievement associated with projects in rural development, science and technology, governance, education, and climate change, among others (KOICA, 2021: 11). However, the OECD DAC

DOI: 10.4324/9781003497035-4

peer review reports and academics in the field criticise that the Korean ODA system has a major shortcoming in the application of GM (for example, see Kim and Shim, 2018; Nam, 2018; OECD, 2018; OECD DAC, 2022).

With this in mind, this chapter aims to analyse how the government of Korea has promoted GM policy in its aid provisions, while the country has experienced turmoil in promoting gender equality in the institutional system. In doing so, this chapter focuses on the case of KOICA with its GM application and discusses how KOICA could improve its GM approach in line with international standards. In particular, this chapter explores the case of KOICA's 'Green Ger Village Master Plan' in Mongolia. The Green Ger Village Master Plan is not targeted at women; however, this chapter intends to examine whether the GM approach has been applied in all KOICA projects as a cross-cutting issue, and thus, the case project does not need to focus on women. This chapter has employed three main tools: the Gender Mainstreaming Toolkit for Cooperation Projects (Council of Europe, 2018); the Gender Mainstreaming Toolkit (European Institute for Gender Equality, 2016); and the Spanish Agency for International Cooperation (AECID) Guide for Gender Mainstreaming (AECID, 2015). These tools offer so-called checklists and guidelines for GM that can examine whether the GM approach has been implemented in the project at all phases.

Gender Mainstreaming in ODA

Since the Beijing Declaration of 1995, there has been an evolution in promoting gender equality. For example, the Women in Development (WID) approach focused on education and family planning, and the elimination of women's poverty was developed between the 1950s and 1970s. The Woman and Development (WAD) approach was followed, working towards increasing women's economic and political capacity, during the 1970s. Then, in the late 1980s, the Gender and Development (GAD) approach was introduced, focusing on gender rather than women in patriarchy and the structures that create social, economic, political, and cultural inequality (Espinosa, 2016: 155 & 157; Moser, 1993: 2).

Among those, the GAD approach has been widely used by the OECD DAC and most of the governmental institutions of the European Union (Espinosa, 2016). Accordingly, the GM as specified in the GAD approach is supposed to be included in the OECD DAC member countries' policies towards the creation of gender equality (Engeli and Mazur, 2018; Espinosa, 2016; Kantola and Lombardo, 2017; True, 2003). It is noteworthy that the GAD and GM cross-cutting approach results in the closer proximity of feminist movements. Based on the GAD and GM approaches, it has been considered that institutional and organisational changes are essential for achieving gender equality. According to feminist academics, if institutions are not feminist and their personnel are not trained to integrate the approach, it would be hard for them to implement public policies that break the structural inequality of each context (Espinosa, 2013; Mukhopadhyay, Steehouwer and Wong, 2006).

However, within the field of development studies, there has also been discussion about this approach and the challenges it presents. As advocated by feminist development studies scholars, the promotion of egalitarian development goes through the incorporation of a gender perspective in all development policies and interventions in a cross-cutting manner to break with the patriarchal structures of our institutions and social systems (Engeli and Mazur, 2018; Espinosa, 2016; Kantola and Lombardo, 2017; Mukhopadhyay, Steehouwer and Wong, 2006; Singh, 2007; True, 2003). For example, the GM has a risk of Westernisation in favour of Western feminist ideals, ignoring the local identities of each context (Singh, 2007). At the same time, there can be resistance to the GM process at the actual implementation level (Jaquette, 2017). Kantola and Lombardo (2017) identify that GM requires intensive work at the institutional level because it can create actual changes in policies and strategies that lead to greater gender equality. However, if there is political resistance and organisational and social difficulties, there would be no changes at the institutions, and thus, there would be no actual implementation of the approach (Espinosa, 2016).

Moser and Moser (2005) further point out the importance of staffing and training in the gender approach. In reality, the GM implementation and evaluation process is particularly neglected, and bilateral donor agencies tend to focus almost exclusively on quantitative data and the volume of funding they allocate to the issue rather than monitoring actual changes in terms of gender equality (Espinosa, 2016). Often, projects make broad references to the approach by lacking GAD analysis in context. Also, in many cases, there is a lack of qualified personnel for its design and evaluation in implementing the GM approach at aid agencies (Espinosa, 2013: 179; Song and Kim, 2013: 80). In light of this, an increasing number of documents and toolkits have been introduced for more effective application in the practice of GM in recent years (Council of Europe, 2018). For instance, the OECD DAC has published official documents and tools to improve gender equality support in aid practice, such as the DAC gender equality policy marker (OECD DAC, 2016). The DAC gender equality policy marker proposes a 'three-point scoring system' to determine if projects and policies apply GM or not (OECD DAC, 2016). According to this marker, if an aid project does not target women, it has a score of 0. If gender equality is important but is not the project's main objective, its score becomes 1. If gender equality is the main objective of the project, then it is scored 2 (OECD DAC, 2016: 2). However, this is more an evaluative tool for quantitative analysis than a tool for the effective application of GM.

Thus, some researchers have proposed a practical approach to the implementation of GM. For example, the Gender Equality Policy in Practice Approach developed by Engeli and Mazur (2018) suggests more in-depth examination during the implementation stage as it often undergoes modifications of the initial design (usually the phase on which policymakers focus the most). This approach consists of addressing three components when implementing aid policies with GM: the mix of implementation instruments for policy action; the process of inclusive policy empowerment in practice; and gender transformation as the outcome (Engeli and Mazur, 2018: 114).

Gender Mainstreaming in ODA in South Korea

Background Understanding of the Development of Gender Equality in South Korea

South Korea has a long tradition of women's movements in favour of gender equality in the country. Since the first women's movements at the beginning of the 20th century, women have organised themselves to protest against gender inequality. Accordingly, women's associations mobilised to stand up for egalitarian education rights and free love (Choi, 2016). During the early Korean economic development period (1960–1980), strong labour movements emerged to denounce discrimination in women's wages and conditions and favour democracy (Ching and Yoon, 1995). In the 1990s, protests for a more egalitarian role in the family became important, starting with the abolition of the *hoju* system (호주제 in Korean) (Nam, 2010). The *hoju* system established the patrilineality of the family, the existence of a head of the family with decision-making power over the rest of the family, and greater economic power (Yang, 2006: 13–15). The ending of this system in 2005 (with final entry into force in 2008) legally eliminated all privileges of the firstborn son (at least in law) and allowed inheritance for women (Yang, 2006: 13).

Apart from this, other protests during this period took place to recognise the situation of the 'comfort women' (Korean women who were sexually enslaved during Japanese imperialism) against domestic violence and sexual exploitation of women in the country. In the 2000s, the main demands of such protests moved to the inequality of opportunities in the world of work and the strong gender gap (Jung, 2013). South Korean feminist movements also challenged the weaknesses of the country's feminist policies. They have claimed that, for more than 20 years, the country's different governments have implemented volatile policies that have been poorly communicated and scantly adapted by society, with little application of the GM approach (Kim, 2019).

According to many feminist scholars, Korean feminist activism has gained a further boost since 2015 (Jeong and Lee, 2018). In terms of their scope, reach, and variety of targets, the movements against the gender gap, sexualised bodies, spy cameras, or the criminalisation of abortion (regulated in 2021) maintained a high presence in these past years (Kim, 2021: 75–76). In 2015, thousands of hashtags #나는페미니스트입니다 ('I am a feminist' in Korean) were circulated on Twitter, collectively claiming feminist identity in the face of anti-feminist sentiment rising in Korea (Kim, 2021). This was also observed during the #metoo campaign in 2018. This movement provided public space for many South Korean women to talk about situations of gender-based violence in a work environment (Kim, 2021: 93).

Feminist movements have achieved cooperation and participation in the South Korean government through the promotion of institutional feminism (Kim and Kim, 2011). It was South Korea's adherence to the Beijing Pact in 1995 that triggered the emergence of institutional feminism in Korea (Kim and Kim, 2011; Lee, 2020). Another significant attributing factor for this change can come from the pro-woman administrations of former Presidents of South Korea, Kim Dae-jung (1997–2003), Roh Moo-hyun (2003–2007), and Moon Jae-in (2017–2022) that allowed coordinated work with women's movements in policy design (Kim and Kim, 2011; Lee and Chang, 2021). Korean Women's Associations United (KWAU) also played a remarkable role in revising laws to promote gender equality in the first decade of 2000 (Kim and Kim, 2011; 392–393). The President's Special Committee on Women's Affairs was then created, which gave rise to the Ministry of Gender Equality in 2001 (Kim and Kim, 2011: 392). As a result of this, the Women's Development Act was enacted in 1995, the Gender Discrimination Prevention and Relief Act was established in 1999, and the Head of Household System was abolished, culminating with a revision of the Civil Law in 2003 (Kim, 2007: 114).

However, despite the achievements of the South Korean gender movements, it remains a country with a very wide gender gap. This is visible in the underrepresentation of women in positions of power (only 18.6 per cent of the seats in the National Assembly in 2022 and only 8.7 per cent of private sector management positions) (OECD Stat, 2022; Statista, 2022), the gender pay gap (the biggest of OECD countries), the difficult return to work of women after motherhood (Lee, 2020: 385; OECD, 2019: 75), the number of cases of gender-based violence and abuses in the labour environment, and the unequal division of tasks in the household (KDWI, 2021: 37; Tsuya, Bumpass and Choe, 2000: 195). Moreover, a strong negative perception of feminism in the country persists (Jeong and Lee, 2018). There has been an increase in anti-feminism, which does not support gender policies and thus considers them to be unnecessary (Kim, 2019). Questioning gender policies was highlighted in the 2022 presidential election campaign (in terms of benefits, budget, and results), challenging the legitimacy of gender policies with broad societal support (Chica-Morales and Casares, 2022).

KOICA and Gender Mainstreaming in Its Aid Policy

In line with the United Nations (UN) Sustainable Development Goals (SDGs) Goal 5 (Gender Equality), the government of Korea promotes the 'Better Life for Girls' programme as a strand of the 'Better Life for All programme', with a strong emphasis on inclusive education, in its aid policies (GoK, 2022). Since 1995, gender equality has been one of KOICA's main objectives in its Framework Act on International Development Cooperation, as well as in the agency's strategies (Song and Kim, 2013: 81). For example, KOICA introduced the Gender Equality Development Cooperation Strategy and the KOICA Gender Mainstreaming Guideline in 2011 (KOICA, 2014: 5). KOICA also developed project assessment methodology in 2018 and included the so-called 'gender perspective' (KOICA, 2018).

KOICA has made more efforts to improve its GM process. For instance, in coordination with UN Women and KWAU and the German Cooperation Agency GIZ, KOICA developed the 'Gender Mainstreaming in Development Programming Collection' which includes concrete aspects such as 'Gender Toolkit: integrating

Table 4.1 KOICA's Gender Equality Mid-Term Strategy (2021–2025)

Strategic Objectives 1	– Support women's economic empowerment to achieve gender equality – Key sectors: Rural development, ICT, energy, and vocational training – Programmes: Establish an equal distribution system and ensure access to resources, and provide vocational education and training for women
Strategic Objectives 2	– Improve the social status of women – Key sectors: Governance, peace, and education – Programmes: Promote women's participation in decision-making, strengthen gender perspectives in public and private governance, and raise gender awareness.
Strategic Objectives 3	– Ensure the protection of the rights of women and girls – Key sectors: Public health – Programmes: Ensure sexual and reproductive health and rights, eradicate gender-based violence, climate action, and disaster risk reduction.

Source: Authors' own compilation, based on KOICA (2021).

gender in programming for every child in South Asia' and 'Gender-responsive Project Management: a practical guide' in 2021 (UN WOMEN, KOICA and KWAU, 2021), in line with its Gender Equality Mid-Term Strategy (2021–2025).

KOICA's Gender Equality Mid-Term Strategy (2021–2025) sets the Strategic Objectives (SO) for key sectors and programmes for promoting gender equality (KOICA, 2021: 11), which focus on education and economic empowerment to achieve gender equality. Following Table 4.1 shows KOICA's three SOs as appeared in its Gender Equality Mid-Term Strategy.

KOICA's mission in this strategy is to contribute 'to achieving the global goal of gender equality (SDG5) and integrating a gender perspective in all development projects and processes' (KOICA, 2021: 11). The objectives and programmes tend to focus on education and economic empowerment to achieve gender equality (see Table 4.1). The Gender Equality Mid-Term Strategy shows that there is a commitment to gender equality in KOICA's programmes and projects, at least in its policy (KOICA, 2021).

Reports on KOICA gender projects show most of them tend to be channelled by multilateral aid (in collaboration with international agencies such as UN WOMEN) and as public-private alliances (KIEP, 2017; KOICA, 2022; UNFPA, 2019). Also, programmes such as 'Ewha-KOICA Master's Programme in International Studies: Capacity Development of Women Leaders', 'Fill the GAP' initiative, as a knowledge platform dedicated to gender equality and women's empowerment, and 'Mid-term Plan (2019–2021) for Capacity Building on Gender Equality and Empowerment of Women and Girls' have been designed with a central objective in training and awareness for gender equality (KOICA, 2019: 24).

However, the OECD DAC recommends that, despite progress in the integration of goals to achieve gender equality, more attention to gender equality needs to be paid and, especially, the budget for gender equality-related projects needs to be increased (OECD, 2018: 20, 52). The 2020 OECD Report on Development Finance for Gender stated that Korea was the fourth country with the lowest share of ODA in terms of gender equality (OECD DAC, 2022: 3). Even though the OECD DAC recommends the adoption of GM tools and guidelines in donor aid policies, it does not seem to be sufficient in implementing it in projects.

In other words, there seems to be a lack of guidelines and tools to apply and evaluate GM and a lack of awareness and training of KOICA staff (KOICA, 2021; Nam, 2018; OECD, 2018). The 'twin-track' GM approach has not been fully adopted either at the institutional or operational level. That is, even though there have been an increasing number of projects focusing on women, GM has not been included in other sectors (Kim and Shim, 2018). KOICA staff members also expressed their difficulties in the GM approach, including a lack of understanding of gender projects among Korean ODA experts or project participants, the Korean government's lack of comprehension of gender projects, a top-down approach, an insufficient number of Korean gender projects, and a need for a higher level of awareness and training on GM among staff (Kim and Shim, 2018: 120, 142 Nam, 2018: 465).

Gender Mainstreaming in ODA: A Case Study of KOICA in Mongolia

Understanding Gender Equality in Mongolia

Mongolia is a country that has undergone profound social, cultural, and environmental changes in a short period (Sarlagtay, 2004). After the fall of the Soviet bloc in 1990, the country went from a nomadic social structure based on grazing and the relationship with its community to living in impoverished neighbourhoods due to the massive settlement process (Ole and Li, 2006). In this, the settlement processes were key to the traditional yurts, or *ger*, with which families moved to the city as their only housing solution. The accelerated concentration of these families gave rise to slums and marginal districts established without urban planning in cities such as Darkhan (Sarlagtay, 2004).

Ger housing districts are far from government development plans, with difficult access to basic services and serious public health situations. Furthermore, there are high levels of outdoor air pollution from factories and the mining industry, and the population is exposed to high levels of small particles suspended in the air (particulate matter PM 2.5) from coal stoves in the *ger* houses (Lim et al., 2018). Lack of sanitation facilities combined with poor waste treatment prevents access to running and drinking water, causing a large number of gastrointestinal infections and affecting agriculture and crops (Sigel, Altantuul and Basandorj, 2012; WHO, 2019).

The nomadic society and the Soviet period have strongly influenced the construction of gender relationships, in which women have had significant power in society, family, and decision-making (Benwell, 2006). Socially, contrary to other developing countries, Mongolia has a reverse gender gap in many aspects of society, which creates an interesting scenario in which to design policies as it is qualitatively different from the rest of the countries. Mongolian women maintain a major representation in tertiary education (including rural areas), in tourism, education, health, commerce, financial institutions, and public administration (Benwell, 2006; Mongolian Statistical Information Service, 2018). The male population, on the other hand, is under-represented in schools and educational centres, worsening in the last levels of education (Mongolian Statistical Information Service, 2018). Men generally hold jobs in the military, industry, mining, and transport and turn out to be the majority in management positions (Mongolian Statistical Information Service, 2018).

However, this reverse gap in education and jobs does not imply that there is gender equality in other aspects of society. Women tend to bear the economic and family burden, and domestic violence figures have risen since the economic crisis that hit the country after the fall of the Soviet bloc in 1991 (Lacaze, 2013; Maškarinec, 2019). Moreover, the representation of women in positions of power (40 per cent compared to men) or parliament (around 17 per cent) is discouraging given that they are generally highly qualified (NSOM, 2022). Mongolian women's empowerment is also attributed to a reaction to Mongolian men's masculinity crisis and their passive role in society as a result (Benwell, 2006). The lack of employment in the country since the mid-1990s has removed men from their role as 'head of the family' leading to a less active role in society and/or serious alcoholism problems. (Benwell, 2006: 130).

Faced with this situation, the 'matriarchal' civil society seems to be actively working to defend women's rights and break with the systemic, elite patriarchal structure (Fish, 1998; Undarya, 2013). Since the fall of the Soviet bloc, women's movements in Mongolia have played an essential role in the fight for climate change and human rights in the country and are currently the driving force for sustainable development and gender equality. The report on associations led by women in Mongolia confirms that women have a pioneering role in promoting equal education, human rights, and the environment (Mongolian Women's Fund, 2009).

While not all of these associations are established as 'feminist', the majority of them are women-led associations. Institutions, such as the Mongolia Women Funds (MONES), the National Network of Mongolian Women's NGOs, and associations like Breath Mongolia, which leads the fight for the improvement of the country's environment, are key to women's empowerment in Mongolia (Undarya, 2013). Mongolia is also a female country in quantitative terms, with a female population approaching 62 per cent due to emigration and the lower life expectancy of men than women (NSOM, 2023).

KOICA in Mongolia

Mongolia has been one of Asia's major recipients of ODA since 1991 (Rossabi, 2005: 9). South Korea, after Japan and the United States, was Mongolia's third-largest donor of the ODA (OECD DAC, n.d.). While the government of Korea has provided its aid to Mongolia since 1991, it was not until 2016 that Korea decided to incorporate Mongolia among its list of priority countries within the Asian region. It did so by increasing the volume of ODA and enhancing the strategy with the Mongolian country. Quantitatively, Mongolia was the sixth largest recipient of KOICA, with a total amount allocated of USD 9,821 million in 2021 (KOICA, 2022: 45).

The policy framework regulating the strategic partnership between the government of Mongolia and the government of Korea in terms of ODA is the Country Cooperation Strategy (CPS) 2021–2024 (Government of Korea, 2021). This strategy is aligned with the 'Vision 2030 for Mongolia's Sustainable Development' national development strategy and the Government of Mongolia's Program of Action 2021–2023. Particularly, it refers to the importance of working with *ger* districts to improve water management and health programs (Government of Korea, 2021: 6). In line with Korea's aid programmes, a Mongolia Saemaul Center has existed since 2004, oriented towards sustainable development through citizen empowerment and public participation. These projects include activities such as the construction of 'Saemaul streets' by residents, the maintenance of cattle benches, the construction of small neighbourhood gardens, and reforestation, among others (Korea Saemaul Undong Center, n.d.; Lee and Lee, 2017: 387).

Regarding projects with a gender approach, 'Promoting gender equality in public decision-making and women's empowerment in Mongolia (2021–2024)' was created by KOICA, together with the United Nations Development Programme (UNDP) (KOICA, 2022), in line with the KOICA Gender Equality Mid-Term Strategy (KOICA, 2021). This project aims to overcome the gap between the high representation of women in civil society and the low representation of women in politics and parliament (UNDP, 2021). Although during the communist era, the participation of women in this sphere was practically equal, in the later period they lost their position in this sphere of society (UN Women, 2019).

The project focuses on six key areas: strengthening the legal environment for gender equality; consolidating support networks for women aspiring to political office; increasing the number of women eligible for decision-making positions; improving gender awareness among voters, political parties, and the media; sensitising potential female candidates in political parties; and improving gender awareness in the media (UNDP, 2021). The main activities of the project include the elaboration of draft legislation to strengthen the legal framework for gender equality, the creation of support networks for female candidates for political office, and the sensitisation of voters, parties, and the media on gender equality. The project has allocated USD 2.32 million with its 97 per cent budget funded by KOICA (UNDP, 2021).

Green Ger Village Master Plan and Gender Mainstreaming of KOICA

Darkhan is a city of around 105,000 inhabitants located in the central region of Mongolia belonging to the *aimag* Darkhan-Uul (NSOM, n.d.). Darkhan has a strong female context, as 80 per cent of women oversee housing management and administration (NSOM, n.d.). In Darkhan, districts are not only made up of yurts but are also mixed with prefabricated dwellings that suffer from the absence of basic characteristics of decent housing (Sigel, Altantuul and Basandorj, 2012). As in the capital Ulan Baatar, the shaping of these districts has taken place far from urban planning and central government response, giving rise to improvised, impoverished neighbourhoods (Erdenebayar et al., 2019). Consequently, the lack of social infrastructure has made these districts one of the main causes of air, soil, and water pollution in the city, leading to a detrimental effect on the health and quality of life of the region's population (Chica-Morales, Muñoz and Domenech, 2021; Erdenebayar et al., 2019; Puntsagnamjil, 2020).

Among these districts, KOICA has implemented a plan for the improvement of urban and environmental conditions since 2018, focusing on District 15. The so-called Green Ger Village Master Plan is led by KOICA through the KOICA Incheon Development Cooperation Center (IC-IDCC) and the local university, MULS. This project aims to create a sustainable *ger* (traditional housing of Mongolian nomads) housing district that betters the environmental quality and public health of the local population (KOICA, 2017). The main funding comes from KOICA's Development Experience Exchange Program (DEEP). The below information about this plan has been drawn upon the interim document 'Report on the results of the 2017 academic incubation programme', which details the identification and formulation phase of the Green Ger Village Master Plan (KOICA, 2017).

A variety of local agents, such as Citizens' Initiative-Development Drivers, national agents, including the University of Malaga in Spain, and international and private agents engaged in the project, contributing mainly with human resources, thus enriching the formulation, implementation, and evaluation of the plan. The plan includes an exchange of researchers and student volunteers in the field. The general objective of the Green Ger Village Master Plan is to improve environmental conditions in Darkhan District 15 through environmental education and public participation. The plan is in line with the Mongolia-South Korea CPS, as mentioned above, and the SDGs 6 (Clean Water and Sanitation), 7 (Affordable and Clean Energy), and 11 (Sustainable Cities and Communities). There have been three areas to focus on, as below:

A Community work for the improvement of environmental living conditions in the district. This includes activities to build up paving and street repair, reforestation works, urban vegetable gardens, and sealing of toilets attached to homes, among others. It also includes initiatives that encourage public participation;

B Environmental education through awareness-raising actions in collaboration with citizens;

C Implementation of a sustainable urban plan. It covers the improvement of public infrastructure such as sewage systems, water supply, power lines, schools, public transportation, parks, and the promotion of the use of renewable energy sources as a method of obtaining electricity (KOICA, 2017: 87–92).

As mentioned above, this chapter intends to analyse its case study against the three main tools: the Gender Mainstreaming Toolkit for Cooperation Projects; the Gender Mainstreaming Toolkit; and the AECID Guide for Gender Mainstreaming. In doing so, a checklist combining these three tools is presented in Table 4.2.

Table 4.2 Checklist for Gender Mainstreaming in the Green Ger Village Master Plan

Stage	*Y/N*	*Comments*
Identification		
SWOT analysis: Has gender analysis been incorporated?	No	There is no reference to gender, the role of women in communities, or the differences in opportunities between women and men.
Context analysis: Are authorities receptive to including gender equality in their agenda?	Yes	The government includes gender equality as a goal in its Vision 2030 and has various tools for the promotion of gender equality in the country. However, it is not that clear in the local context.
Use of National Systems: Are sex-disaggregated data (mainly official statistics) available?	Yes	The government has a gender-specific statistical database in English and Mongolian: National Statistic Office of Mongolia.
Have consultations with women's associations or feminist associations been included in the identification process?	Yes/No	The high participation of women in the local NGO Citizens' Initiative—Development Drivers suggests that women have been part of the consultation process. However, this NGO is not by its definition a "feminist NGO' or an NGO for women.
Is GM considered one of the strategic orientations?	No	Not mentioned.
Has GM been included in the definition of indicators and guidelines?	No	No. SDG 5 appears in general terms but has no targets or indicators to achieve it.
Have actions been designed (for men and women) to generate changes in traditional gender roles, thus preventing their perpetuation?	No	The actions are designed to work with communities regardless of the gender of the participants.
Are sex-disaggregated data and an adequate gender analysis available to show the contribution to gender equality?	No	We have access to disaggregated data, but these have not been used for the formulation phase and therefore do not show whether they contribute to gender equality.
Do gender organisations in the partner country participate in the plan?	No	—
Implementation and monitoring		
Were the causes that limit women's participation in different decision-making spaces analysed?	No	Although in Mongolia women participate in many areas, this situation has not been taken into consideration.
Have sex-disaggregated data been analysed?	No	—

(*Continued*)

Table 4.2 (Continued)

Stage	*Y/N*	*Comments*
Are gender indicators linked to the project considered?	No	No. SDG 5 appears in general terms but has no targets or indicators to achieve it.
Has a monitoring system been established to verify the achievement of results in reducing gender inequality gaps?	No	—
Is gender impact assessment foreseen in the planned evaluations?	No	—
Project logic		
Objectives: Are there any gender-specific objectives?	Yes/No	SDG 5 Gender is mentioned only once without indicating the goals and targets to achieve them.
Main activities and their scheduling. Are gender roles and the sexual division of labour considered when planning activities?	No	Not mentioned specifically.
Main activities and their programming: Are there specific actions aimed at modifying these roles and promoting women's participation?	No	—
Do the objectives promote equal opportunities in access to project services (credit, employment, training, etc.)?	Yes	The high degree of empowerment and active nature of Darkhan women suggests that the objectives promote their access; however, it is unclear whether men would be willing to participate in project services.
Budget and financing schedule		
Is it clear what percentage of the total budget will directly benefit women and men?	No	—
Have specific actions been budgeted to favour women's participation and their equal access to project benefits?	No	—

Source: Authors' own compilation, based on Council of Europe (2018), European Institute for Gender Equality (2016), and AECID (2015).

Since the evaluation is carried out at a very early stage of the project, the following aspects have been evaluated: project identification; implementation; and monitoring, project logic, budget, and financing schedule. The evaluation of KOICA GM status in the Green Ger Village Master Plan against the checklist in Table 4.2 can be summarised as below:

- There are local and governmental institutions with experience in the field of gender equality promotion, but they are not included as part of the intervention's coordination group;
- SDG 5 is included among the intervention's objectives, but no targets, indicators, or actions are established to help achieve them, nor is GM considered. On the other hand, the definition is vague and general;
- There is no system for inclusion or monitoring of the promotion of gender equality; and
- There is no analysis of the causes that lead to the different participation of men and women or the impact by gender.

Therefore, it can be concluded that there is no integration of GM in this project at either the design or implementation phase. This does not mean that the presence of women is not considered, but rather that guidelines or policies to achieve greater gender equality in a population with a high female representation have not been consciously included. This is a transcendent statement since this plan does not correctly describe the context and the beneficiaries, who, in a representative and socially committed majority, are women. This may be due to two reasons: KOICA's difficulties in integrating GM broadly in all its projects; and the emerging feminist movement in Mongolia is not yet widely represented in society (Mongolian Women's Fund, 2009; Nielsen, 2012). Given the assessment described above, the implementation of GM in the Green Ger Village Master Plan is required. This, in turn, will require providing it with tools for its monitoring and subsequent evaluation.

Conclusion

This chapter has explored the Green Ger Village Master Plan of KOICA in Mongolia in order to examine whether Korean aid policy (and practice) has been gender mainstreamed. In Mongolia, the KOICA projects have not fully incorporated with the GM as a 'twin-track' approach. The focus of Korean ODA is still heavily based on WAD. In other words, KOICA projects that are part of the Gender Equality Mid-Term Strategy are highly women focused but not gender focused; therefore, they still tend to employ the WAD approach, not GAD. The WAD approach understands women as subjects but not the evolution of gender roles and relations, which implies fundamental differences in the whole process of development aid. WAD was previously used; however, GM strategy had developed the concept further as part of the GAD approach. The conceptual shift from women to gender was a breakthrough in development policies in main donor countries.

The cause of these shortcomings in applying the GM approach in Korean ODA could lie precisely in what was discussed at the beginning of this chapter. Social awareness is still low to some extent despite the existence of gender movements in Korea. This makes it difficult for the institutional level to understand the need to apply the GM approach transversally to all public policies (whether national or international). Within the ODA policies and practices, this is followed by a lack of suitable indicators for the systematic monitoring and evaluation of plans and projects. They tend to be mostly quantitative and generalist indicators that go little beyond the usual gender segregation of the population or results lacking actual gender perspective.

From the findings of this research, KOICA, as a public institution working on ODA, does not seem to have reached a gender mainstream stage yet. For example, in the case study in Mongolia, the main objective is not to break the oppressive gender hierarchy for women but merely to improve this region's social and environmental development. It can be argued that KOICA, like other international donor agencies, does not apply GM due to a lack of institutional and social awareness at a broad level and also because of the difficulties in applying and evaluating it. This reality is also identified in the country's institutional feminism, where the GM approach is being applied as a strategy for promoting gender equality, but with difficulties still.

Note

1 This research work was supported by the Seed Program for Korean Studies of the Ministry of Education of the Republic of Korea and the Korean Studies Promotion Service at the Academy of Korean Studies (AKS-2021-INC-2250002). We appreciate the time of the people interviewed and consulted in South Korea and Mongolia from KOICA and the Green Ger Village Master Plan.

References

AECID. (2015). *Guía de la AECID para la transversalización del enfoque de género. Manuales de cooperación española.*

Barnett, M. (2018). Gender equality, norms and practices: Post-script to special issue on new actors, old donors and gender equality norms in international development cooperation. *Progress in Development Studies*, *18*(3), 208–213. https://doi.org/10.1177/1464993418766588

Benwell, A. F. (2006). Facing Gender Challenges in Post-Socialist Mongolia. In B. Ole & N. Li (Eds.), *Mongols: from country to cities* (pp. 110–139). Nordic Institute of Asian Studies.

Bustelo, M. (2017). Evaluation from a gender + perspective as a key element for (re)gendering the policymaking process. *Journal of Women, Politics & Policy*, *38*, 84–101.

Chen, M. A. (1995). Engendering world conferences: The international women's movement and the United Nations. *Third World Quarterly*, *16*(3), 477–494. https://doi.org/10.1080/01436599550036013

Chica-Morales, P., & Martín Casares, A. (2022). El discurso neomachista de la fundación 신 남성연대 (Solidaridad de Nuevos Hombres) en el ciberespacio: su difusión entre los jóvenes y su impacto en las políticas contemporáneas en Corea del Sur.

Dilemata, *38*, 193–208. https://www.dilemata.net/revista/index.php/dilemata/article/view/412000486/823

Chica-Morales, P., Muñoz, V. F., & Domenech, A. J. (2021). System dynamics as ex ante impact assessment tool in international development cooperation: Study case of urban sustainability policies in Darkhan, Mongolia. *Sustainability*, *13*(8), 4595. https://doi.org/10.3390/su13084595

Ching, M., & Yoon, L. (1995). Minjung feminism: Korean Women's movement for gender and class liberation. *Women's Studies International Forum*, *18*(4), 417–430.

Choi, H. (2016). Women's literacy and new womanhood in late Choson Korea. *Asian Journal of Women's Studies*, *6*(1), 88–115.

Council of Europe. (2018). *Gender Mainstreaming Toolkit for Cooperation Projects*. Council of Europe is the Publisher. https://www.un.org/sexualviolenceinconflict/wp-content/uploads/2020/01/report/gender-mainstreaming-toolkit-for-co-operation-projects/Final_Gender-Mainstreaming-Toolkit_February_2019.pdf.pdf

Engeli, I., & Mazur, A. (2018). Taking implementation seriously in assessing success: The politics of gender equality policy. *European Journal of Politics and Gender*, *1*(1), 111–129. https://doi.org/10.1332/251510818x15282097548558

Erdenebayar, E., Santos, K. D., Edwards, A., Dugersuren, N. O., Ochir, C., & Nriagu, J. (2019). Environmental injustice and childhood lead exposure in peri-urban (ger) areas of Darkhan and Erdenet, Mongolia. *BMC Public Health*, *19*(1), 1–11. https://doi.org/10.1186/s12889-019-6486-x

Espinosa, J. (2013). Moving towards gender-sensitive evaluation? Practices and challenges in international-development evaluation. *Evaluation*, *19*(2), 171–182. https://doi.org/10.1177/1356389013485195

Espinosa Fajardo, J. (2016). La evaporación de los compromisos de género en la práctica del desarrollo. In C. Magallón Portolés, K. Unceta, P. J. Martínez Osés, J. M. Medina Rey, G. González-Bueno Uribe, J. M. Moreno Domínguez, J. Espinosa Fajardo, & A. Acosta Espinosa (Eds.), El mundo que queremos. La agenda 2030 (pp. 151–189). Mira Editorial.

European Institute for Gender Equality. (2016). *Gender Equality Training: Gender Mainstreaming Toolkit*. European Institute for Gender Equality. https://doi.org/10.2839/638858. https://eige.europa.eu/sites/default/files/documents/mh0716093enn.pdf

Fish, M. S. (1998). Mongolia: Democracy without prerequisites. *Journal of Democracy*, *9*(3), 127–141. https://doi.org/10.1353/JOD.1998.0044

Government of Korea. (2021). *The Republic of Korea's Country Partnership Strategy for Mongolia the Government of the Republic of Korea*. https://www.odakorea.go.kr/fileDownLoad.xdo?f_id=1655770618116N5NMA2GGUZECNTNPAYFPJ1BU90

Government of Korea. (2022). *KOREA ODA White Paper 2020*. https://www.odakorea.go.kr/SynapDocViewServer/viewer/doc.html?key=484bc815828743b18259f56a0514b581&convType=img&convLocale=en_US&contextPath=/SynapDocViewServer

*CPS*Grown, C., Addison, T., & Tarp, F. (2016). Aid for gender equality and development: Lessons and challenges. *Journal of International Development*, *28*(3), 311–319. https://doi.org/10.1002/JID.3211

Jaquette, J. S. (2017). Women/gender and development: The growing gap between theory and practice. *Studies in Comparative International Development*, *52*(2), 242–260. https://doi.org/10.1007/s12116-017-9248-8

Jeong, E., & Lee, J. (2018). We take the red pill, we confront the DickTrix: Online feminist activism and the augmentation of gendered realities in South Korea. *Feminist Media Studies*, *18*(4), 705–717. https://doi.org/10.1080/14680777.2018.1447354

Jung, K. (2013). Practicing Feminism in South Korea: The Women's Movement Against Sexual Violence. In K. Jung (Ed.), *Practicing Feminism in South Korea: The Women's Movement against Sexual Violence* (pp. 1–147). Milton Park: Routledge. https://doi.org/10.4324/9781315887289

Kantola, J., & Lombardo, E. (2017). Feminist Political Analysis: Five Approaches. In *Gender and Political Analysis* (pp. 20–48). Palgrave Macmillan. Publication series. ISBN: 978-0-230-21418-7.

KDWI, Korea Development Women Institute. (2021). 장진희, 박건, & 이동선. (2021). 코로나 19 가 여성노동자에게 미친 영향: 자녀돌봄공백과 직장 내 불이익을 중심으로. *월간 한국노총*, *581*, 31–31.

KIEP, Korea Institute for International Economic Policy. (2017). *Study on Development Cooperation Strategies for Gender Equality in Cambodia*. 김은경, 오은진, 김영택, 김복태, 김혜영, 조영숙, & 심예리. (2017). 캄보디아 성평등을 위한 개발협력 방안 연구. ODA 정책연구, 17(03).

Kim, B. (2019). 젠더 갈등과 반페미니즘의 문법. Gender conflict and anti-feminism grammar. *Cross-Cultural Studies*, *56*, 1–25. https://kiss.kstudy.com/Detail/Ar?key=3706115

Kim, E. K., & Shim, Y. (2018). A critical analysis of South Korea's ODA projects for gender equality. *Asian Women*, *34*(3), 119–147. https://doi.org/10.14431/aw.2018.09.34.3.119

Kim, J. (2021). The resurgence and popularization of feminism in South Korea: Key issues and challenges for contemporary feminist activism. *Korea Journal*, *61*(4), 75–101.

Kim, S. K., & Kim, K. (2011). Gender mainstreaming and the institutionalization of the women's movement in South Korea. *Women's Studies International Forum*, *34*(5), 390–400. https://doi.org/10.1016/j.wsif.2011.05.004

Kim, S. U. (2007). Gender equality legislation in Korea. *Asian Journal of Women's Studies*, *13*(3), 109–131. https://doi.org/10.1080/12259276.2007.11666031

Kim, S. Y., Kang, S., & Kim, J. H. (2018). The impact of KOICA's projects on gender equality: How to strengthen project implementation. KOICA, 한국국제협력단 *연구보고서*, 1–20. https://www.dbpia.co.kr/Journal/articleDetail?nodeId=NODE07534040

KOICA. (2014). *KOICA Gender Strategy & Activity*. https://www.oda.go.kr/opo/cmcd/comm/downloadFile.do?P_STRE_FILE_NM=kms1531609331360648663.pdf

KOICA (2017). Report on the Results of the 2017 Academic Incubation Programme. Seongnam, KOICA. [한국국제협력단 (2017). 2017년 제2기인큐베이팅프로그램 결과 보고서. 성남, 한국국제협력단].

KOICA (2018). 김선영, 강승헌, 김진화, 송민재, & 최민호. KOICA 사업의 성평등 실행 강화 방안 연구. 연구보고서, 1–193. The Impact of KOICA's Projects on Gender Equality: How to Strengthen Project Implementation.

KOICA. (2019). *KOICA 2018 Annual Report*. https://www.oda.go.kr/opo/cmcd/comm/downloadFile.do?P_STRE_FILE_NM=FCB206AC-0983-C457-D28A-AF411597E6F2.pdf

KOICA. (2021). *KOICA'sMid-term Sectoral Strategy (2021–2025)*. https://www.koica.go.kr/koica_en/3491/subview.do

KOICA. (2022). *2021 KOICA Annual Report*. https://www.koica.go.kr/koica_en/3492/subview.do#none

Korea Saemaul Undong Center. (n.d.). *Definition, goals and step Saemaul Undong*. Retrieved June 16, 2020, from https://www.saemaul.or.kr/eng/sub/whatSMU/definition.php

Lacaze, G. (2013). Crisis in masculinity versus the flight of women: The gender-based dynamics of post-socialist Mongolia. *L'Homme et La Société*, *189–1*(3), 107–122.

Lee, E., & Lee, S. C. (2017). Examining the internal features of Korea's Green Commitment in Mongolia. *International Review of Public Administration*, *22*(4), 380–404. https://doi.org/10.1080/12294659.2017.1412045

Lee, H.-R., & Chang, J. (2021). From the front line of contemporary South Korean feminist criticism. *Azalea: Journal of Korean Literature & Culture*, *14*(14), 215–241. https://doi.org/10.1353/aza.2021.0014

Lee, S. H. (2020). Beyond the policy rhetoric: The limitations of gender mainstreaming in South Korea relating to women and childcare. *Social Policy and Society*, *19*(3), 379–395. https://doi.org/10.1017/S1474746419000484

Lee-Gosselin, H., Briere, S., & Ann, H. (2013). Resistances to gender mainstreaming in organisations: Toward a new approach. *Gender in Management*, *28*(8), 468–485. https://doi.org/10.1108/GM-10-2012-0081

Lim, M., Myagmarchuluun, S., Ban, H., Hwang, Y., Ochir, C., Lodoisamba, D., & Lee, K. (2018). Characteristics of indoor pm2.5 concentration in gers using coal stoves in ulaanbaatar, mongolia. *International Journal of Environmental Research and Public Health*, *15*(11). https://doi.org/10.3390/ijerph15112524

Maškarinec, P., S. Franceschet, M. L. Krook and N. Tan (Eds). (2019). Mongolia: Transformation of Women's Representation. In *The Palgrave Handbook of Women's Political Rights (Gender and politics)* (pp. 713–727). Palgrave Macmillan. https://link.springer.com/book/10.1057/978-1-137-59074-9

Mongolian Statistical Information Service. (2018). *Gender Statistics*. https://www.1212.mn/Stat.aspx?LIST_ID=976_L03_976_L33

Mongolian Women's Fund. (2009). *The Field of Women's Organizing in Mongolia: Possibilities of a Feminist Movement*. Global Fund for Women.

Moser, C. (1993). *Gender Planning and Development: Theory, Practice and Training*. Routledge.

Moser, C., & Moser, A. (2005). Gender mainstreaming since Beijing: A review of success and limitations in international institutions. *Gender & Development*, *13*(2), 11–22.

Mukhopadhyay, M., Steehouwer, G., & Wong, F. (2006). *Politics of the Possible: Gender Mainstreaming and Organisational Change* (pp. 1–168). KIT-Royal Tropical Institute.

Nam, S. (2010). The women's movement and the transformation of the family law in South Korea. Interactions between local, national and global structures. *European Journal of East Asian Studies*, *9*(1), 67–86. https://doi.org/10.1163/156805810X517670

Nam, S. (2018). Toward everyday practices of gender: Implications of feminist political ecology for gender mainstreaming in Korean ODA. *Asian Journal of Women's Studies*, *24*(4), 463–488. https://doi.org/10.1080/12259276.2018.1531812

Nielsen, A. S. (2012). Globalised Feminism Mongolia. *Global Society*. https://doi.org/10.14361/9783839412732-toc

NSOM. (2022). *Proportion of women in managerial positions percent (SDG 5.5.2)*. National Statistics Office of Mongolia. https://www.1212.mn/en/statistic/statcate/573055/table-view/DT_NSO_0400_046V1

NSOM. (2023). *Population of Mongolia, by Single Age, Sex and by Age Group*. https://www.1212.mn/tables.aspx?tbl_id=DT_NSO_0300_071V3&Group_select_all=0&GroupSingleSelect=_1&Sex_select_all=0&SexSingleSelect=_11_12_1&YearY_select_all=0&YearYSingleSelect=_2018&viewtype=table

NSOM. (n.d.). *Head of Household Person, by Region*. https://www.1212.mn/en/statistic/statcate/573051/table-view/DT_NSO_3300_044V1

OECD. (2018). *OECD Development Cooperation Peer Reviews: Korea 2018*. OECD Publishing. https://doi.org/10.1787/9789264288829-en

OECD. (2019). *Rejuvenating Korea: Policies for a Changing Society, Gender Equality at Work*. OECD Publishing. https://doi.org/10.1787/c5eed747-en.

OECD DAC. (n.d.) *Aid at a Glance Charts*. Mongolia. https://www.oecd.org/dac/financing-sustainable-development/development-finance-data/aid-at-a-glance.htm

OECD DAC. (2016). *Handbook on the OECD-DAC Gender Equality Policy Marker*. https://www.oecd.org/dac/gender-development/dac-gender-equality-marker.htm

OECD DAC. (2022). *Development Finance for Gender Equality and Women's Empowerment: A Snapshot*. https://one.oecd.org/document/DCD(2022)20/en/pdf

OECD Stat. (2022). *Female Share of Seats on Boards of the Largest Publicly Listed Companies, by Country*. https://stats.oecd.org/index.aspx?queryid=54760#

Ole, B., & Li, N. (2006). A New Moment in Mongol history: The Rise of the Cosmopolitan City. In Nordic Institute of Asian Studies (Ed.), *Mongols: From Country to Cities* (pp. 1–21). NIAS Press.

Plattner, M. (1996). The status of women under international human rights law and the 1995 UN World Conference on Women, Beijing, China. *Kentucky Law Journal, 84*, 1996. https://uknowledge.uky.edu/klj/vol84/iss4/17

Puntsagnamjil, M.-A. (2020). *Study on the Driving Mechanism of Residential Waste Separation Behavioral Intention (Ph.D. Thesis)*. Incheon National University, Rep. South Korea.

Rossabi, M. (2005). *Modern Mongolia from Khans to Commissars to Capitalists*. University of California Press.

Sarlagtay, M. O. (2004). Mongolia: Managing the transition from nomadic to settled culture. In F. Rolfe (ed). *The Asia Pacific: A Region in Transition*. Asia-Pacific Center for Security Studies. (pp. 323–334). https://dkiapcss.edu/wp-content/uploads/2010/PDFs/Edited%20Volumes/RegionalFinal%20chapters/Chapter19Sarlagtay.pdf

Sigel, K., Altantuul, K., & Basandorj, D. (2012). Household needs and demand for improved water supply and sanitation in peri-urban ger areas: The case of Darkhan, Mongolia. *Environmental Earth Sciences*, *65*(5), 1561–1566. https://doi.org/10.1007/s12665-011-1221-7

Singh, S. (2007). Deconstructing "gender and development" for "identities of women." *International Journal of Social Welfare*, *16*(2), 100–109. https://doi.org/10.1111/j.1468-2397.2006.00454.x

Song, J., & Kim, E. M. (2013). A critical review of gender in South Korea's official development assistance. *Asian Journal of Women's Studies*, *19*(3), 72–96. https://doi.org/10.1080/12259276.2013.11666157

Statista. (2022). *Share of Women in the National Assembly in South Korea from 2005 to 2022*. https://www.statista.com/statistics/641688/south-korea-female-national-assembly-member/

True, J. (2003). Mainstreaming gender in global public policy. *International Feminist Journal of Politics*, *5*(3), 368–396. https://doi.org/10.1080/1461674032000122740

Tsuya, N. O., Bumpass, L. L., & Choe, M. K. (2000). Gender, employment, and housework in Japan, South Korea, and the United States. *Review of Population and Social Policy*, *9*, 195–220.

UNDP (2021). *Promoting gender equality in public decision-making and women's empowerment in Mongolia*. https://www.undp.org/mongolia/projects/promoting-gender-equality-public-decision-making-and-womens-empowerment-mongolia

Undarya, T. (2013). State of Civil Society Development in Mongolia. *The Mongolian Journal of International Affairs*, *18*. https://cswatch.org/

UNFPA, V. (2019). *Launch of the KOICA Funded Project on Building a Model to Respond to Violence Against Women and Girls in Vietnam*. https://vietnam.unfpa.org/en/news/launch-koica-funded-project-building-model-respond-violence-against-women-and-girls-viet-nam

UN Women. (2019). *Report of Mongolia on the Implementation of the Unga Resolution (Entitled "Improvement of the Situation of Women and Girls in Rural Areas."* https://www.unwomen.org/sites/default/files/Headquarters/Attachments/Sections/Library/Publications/2019/A-74-224-Submission-Mongolia-en.pdf

UN WOMEN, KOICA & KWAU. (2021). *Gender Mainstreaming in Development Programming*. publisher 한국여성단체연합. https://women21.or.kr/overseas/18197?ckattempt=1. *젠더와 개발 분야 최신 정책문서 자료집*.

WHO. (2019). *Drinking-water*. https://www.who.int/news-room/fact-sheets/detail/drinking-water

Yang, H. (2006). Vision of postcolonial feminist jurisprudence in Korea: Seen from the family-head system in family law. *Journal of Korean Law*, *5*, 12.

5 Implementing the Han River Miracle in the Mekong Basin? South Korea's Economic Development Policies towards the Mekong River Basin Nations

Juhee Jeong

Introduction

Due to their geopolitical importance and significant potential for economic growth, the countries of the Mekong River Basin (MRBs) have emerged as a competitive arena for the execution of development strategies. The Mekong region comprises six East Asian countries: China; Myanmar; Thailand; Lao People's Democratic Republic (PDR); Cambodia; and Vietnam. The upper basin includes the Tibetan Plateau, the three-river area, and the Lancang Basin in China and Myanmar. The lower basin, covering Thailand, Lao PDR, Cambodia, and Vietnam, consists of the Northern Highlands, the Khorat Plateau, the Tonle Sap Basin, and the Mekong Delta (MRC, 2022a). China's expanding economic power and political influence, most profoundly felt in Southeast Asia, have stirred global attention (Yoshimatsu, 2015). Amid ongoing tensions in the South China Sea, China's diplomatic power and economic sway have incited concerns in the United States (US) regarding its leadership of the international order and its influence in both Southeast and East Asia. Within this, the Mekong region has risen as a key player in the political economy of Southeast Asia, which, despite being largely economically underdeveloped, boasts an abundance of natural resources. Furthermore, the region holds geostrategic importance as China's southern 'backyard' and a critical link between South and Northeast Asia (Yoshimatsu, 2015: 174, Strangio, 2020). Therefore, the Mekong countries, which constitute half of the Association of Southeast Asian Nations (ASEAN) membership, play an increasingly significant role in this vital regional organisation in the Indo-Pacific.

The Republic of Korea (ROK, South Korea, or Korea) is also deeply involved in the development of the Mekong Basin. Since 2011, the ROK has undertaken various initiatives to foster Korea-Mekong relations, including annual Korea-Mekong Foreign Ministers meetings. South Korea's previous President Lee Myung-bak, who championed the enhancement of Korea's role as a middle power through his 'New Asia Initiative' in 2009, played a pivotal role in this development (Watson and Schwak, 2019: 154–155 & 166). At the inaugural Korea-Mekong Foreign Ministers' meeting on 28 October 2011, in Seoul, the 'Han River Declaration' was adopted, which sought to establish a comprehensive partnership between Korea

DOI: 10.4324/9781003497035-5

and the Mekong countries for mutual prosperity (Kim et al., 2013). Korea aimed to replicate its 'Miracle of the Han River' in the Mekong region, using increased official development assistance (ODA) for infrastructure and water resource development as the primary tool. This ambition aligns with the 'New Southern Policy' introduced by former South Korean President Moon Jae-in, who came to power in 2017 (Hahnkyu, 2023: 59–76). During his 2019 visit to Laos, President Moon, alongside Laotian President Bounnhang Vorachith, unveiled the 'Korea-Mekong Vision' at the 'Mekong River Basin Comprehensive Management Project' site in Vientiane (MOFA, 2019). This demonstrated Korea's emphasis on the Southeast Asia region and highlighted the interest of beyond major powers but regional countries in the Mekong region. Within a competitive landscape of development policies that each country has crafted for the Mekong region Korea has continued its cooperation despite the perception that Korea's foreign policy is subject to change every five years.

However, despite Korea's cooperation with the Mekong Basin countries, it is unclear whether Korea's diplomatic positioning has correspondingly improved. In 2020, the total trade volume between the Mekong region and South Korea reached USD 83.2 billion with investments amounting to USD 4.4 billion, and infrastructure cooperation of USD 3.3 billion (MOFA, 2020). The Institute of Southeast Asian Studies (ISEAS) 2022 survey revealed that only 6.8 per cent of respondents selected Korea when asked, 'if ASEAN were to seek out "third parties" to hedge against the uncertainties of the US-China Strategic rivalry, who is your most preferred and trusted strategic partner for ASEAN?' (Seah et al., 2022: 33). This is relatively low compared to Japan's 29.2 per cent, Australia's 10.3 per cent, and the United Kingdom's 8.4 per cent (Seah et al., 2022: 33). Existing studies, such as Kim (2018b) and Snyder (2018), often attribute this discrepancy to the five-year single-term system of Korea's presidency, causing policy discontinuity, or to a perceived lack of credibility. However, these studies often overlook a thorough analysis of the specific context or content of the strategies at play.

Accordingly, this chapter employs the role theory to analyse ongoing policies towards the Mekong region by countries such as the US, China, and Japan and the competition among their respective approaches in economic development. This chapter aims to clarify why Korea's position in the Mekong region remains relatively tenuous and limited compared to other major players despite its significant investment in this region and ODA. A key issue identified in this chapter is the mismatch between Korea's self-perception, rooted in the narrative of propagating its 'miracle' economic development model, and the role that Mekong countries expect Korea to play. This discrepancy is further examined through the concept of role conflict. By dissecting the differences between the Korea-Mekong vision—continuously propagated from the tenure of President Lee Myung-bak to President Moon Jae-in—and the development vision of the Mekong countries' union, the Mekong River Commission (MRC), this chapter seeks to elucidate the differences between Korea's self-perceived role and the role expectation from Mekong countries.

Background Understanding of the Rivalries in Mekong River Basins

China

China grapples with significant freshwater scarcity. This is primarily due to a vast north-south divide in water availability (Wang et al., 2012: 926). While the south enjoys relative abundance, the north, which accounts for 60 per cent of the country's cultivated land and houses 45 per cent of the population, has access to a mere 13.8 per cent of China's freshwater resources (Sebastian, 2012: 624). About 380 million people in the north, constituting one-third of the country's population, live in conditions of 'absolute water scarcity' (McCormack, 2001: 9). Coupled with its massive population and rapidly expanding economy, China also has an immense demand for electricity (Smil, 1988). In light of this, the Mekong's resources have become of immense value to China (Liebman, 2005). Consequently, 11 massive dams dot the mighty Mekong River before it exits China and traverses Myanmar, Laos, Thailand, Cambodia, and Vietnam (Osborne 2009). There has been widespread criticism alleging that these dams negatively impact the lives of people in the lower-basin Mekong countries (Kuenzer et al., 2013; Goh, 2017). China, considering water management data a state secret, has not been forthcoming about these impacts (Eyler, 2020). The construction of these dams has led to a reduction in crop yield due to the release of nutrient-deficient water and is a contributing factor to the occurrence of floods and droughts. Critics argue that by unilaterally accumulating political power through the exploitation of geography and the manipulation of natural waterways, China seems determined to set regional water management rules to suit its interests (Thitinan, 2016).

In response to these criticisms, Chinese Vice Foreign Minister Luo Zhaohui attended and addressed the inauguration ceremony of the Lancang-Mekong Water Resources Cooperation Information Sharing Platform's website, hosted by the Ministry of Water Resources on 30 November 2020 (Luo, 2020). He expressed his 'concern' that China and Mekong countries should 'eliminate' external interruptions because '…"some" countries outside the region have repeatedly used the issue of Mekong Water Resources to spread rumours and amplify the so-called "Chinese threat" for political purposes, in order to sow discord among countries and sabotaging sub-regional cooperation' (ibid.). Furthermore, China's establishment of the Lancang-Mekong Cooperation (LMC) signifies its strategic effort to create its own rules and institutions. This strategy is based on a fivefold summit agenda encompassing connectivity, industrialisation, border trade, water resource management, agricultural cooperation, and poverty reduction (Thitinan, 2016).

United States

The US government introduced new initiatives, the Lower Mekong Initiative (LMI) in 2009, by recognising the geopolitical significance of the Mekong region, and the Friends of the Lower Mekong (FLM) in 2011 as key institutions to provide comprehensive support for the region (Yoshimatsu, 2015: 176). Washington extends development aid to Mekong countries, focusing on sustainability and human security as objectives and emphasising transparency and accountability in management. This policy approach was intended to improve overall living conditions and bolster government capacity for effective administration in the Mekong countries (Yoshimatsu, 2015). Particularly concerning the Mekong River's 'water' data, the Eyes on Earth, an environmental watchdog based in the US, published their findings in a report titled 'Quantity of Water Flowing Through the Upper Mekong Basin Under Natural (Unimpeded) Conditions' (Basist and Williams, 2020: 7–19). Their study devised a model that predicts the natural flow of the Upper Mekong and then uses this prediction to discern how the series of dams built across the Upper Mekong is modifying the river's natural flow (Basist and Williams, 2020: 4). In addition, the US, in collaboration with the five MRB countries, has worked to strengthen its engagement in infrastructure and energy investment, water security and transboundary river management, and human capital investments through the Mekong-US Partnership (Charoensri, 2022: 26–45). The Sister Rivers Exchange Programme, an element of this partnership, pairs the Mekong and Mississippi rivers (Chheang, 2010). This programme was managed by the US Army Corps of Engineers (USACE) and aimed to share best practices in water and river management (Lee, 2024).

Japan

Japan has refined its approach to the Mekong region, tying its ODA to the trading and investment activities of Japanese private companies in this region (Ogasawara, 2015). In 2009, the inaugural Mekong-Japan Summit took place in Tokyo, where the Tokyo Declaration of the First Meeting between the Heads of Government of Japan and the Countries of the Mekong Region and the Mekong-Japan Action Plan 63 were adopted (MOFAJ, 2009). At the 10th Mekong-Japan Summit in 2018, the Tokyo Strategy was accepted, reaffirming their determination to collaborate in achieving the United Nations (UN) Sustainable Development Goals (SDGs) in the Mekong region to fully implement the 2030 Agenda for Sustainable Development. This document delineated areas of cooperation between the Mekong countries and Japan (Dung and Phuong, 2023). The chief goal of this initiative was to support Mekong countries in achieving the SDGs by 2030, which was deemed crucial '... not [just] for "us" but also for future generations in both the Mekong countries and Japan' (MOFAJ, 2019: 1). Considering the various challenges faced by the Mekong region, such as tackling pollution and climate change, ensuring sustainable and efficient use of resources, and fostering inclusive growth, priority areas for cooperation have been established. These include environmental and urban issues, waste management, disaster risk reduction and disaster management, reducing greenhouse gas emissions and building climate resilience, as well as water and forest management (MOFAJ, 2019: 1–9). These goals are seen as vital to fostering inclusive growth. Moreover, in 2019, Japan and the US launched the Japan-US-Mekong Power Partnership (JUMPP) to promote a sustainable energy sector and quality energy infrastructure development (Koga, 2022: 31).

South Korea

South Korea's engagement with the Mekong region began with its participation in the Mekong Committee donor conference in December 1992 (MOFA, 2021). After the inauguration of President Lee Myung-bak, the first South Korea-Mekong Foreign Ministers' Meeting was held in 2011, at which the Han River Declaration was adopted. Subsequent annual Foreign Ministers' Meetings led to the establishment of the South Korea-Mekong Cooperation Fund, and its operation rules based on the terms of reference (TOR) were successively adopted. In 2013, the first South Korea-Mekong Business Forum was held, emphasising the strengthening of economic cooperation (Lee, 2019). Following this, the Year of South Korea-Mekong Exchange was selected, the South Korea-Mekong Action Plan (2014–2017) was adopted, and the Mekong Institute (MI) was designated as the office for the South Korea-Mekong Cooperation Fund (Kwak, 2022: 36). Concurrently, the fund's TOR was adopted. Furthermore, President Moon Jae-in, who took office in 2017, continued to strengthen relations with the MRB countries based on his New Southern Policy, as previously mentioned in this chapter. Notably, at the 7th South Korea-Mekong Foreign Ministers' Meeting, the South Korea-Mekong Action Plan (2017–2020) was adopted, and for the first time in 2019, the foreign ministers' meeting was elevated to a summit level (Panda, 2020; Ping, 2020: 7).

The South Korea-Mekong Summit, along with the South Korea-ASEAN Special Summit, became a key part of multilateral and bilateral cooperation, striving to further strengthen South Korea-Mekong cooperation by reviewing and evaluating the results of the cooperation through the Han River-Mekong River Declaration and presenting a future vision (Kim, 2022: 251–269). While the priority areas of cooperation in 2011, when the first South Korea-Mekong Foreign Ministers' Meeting was held, focused on infrastructure, information and communication technology (ICT), green growth, water resources development, agriculture and rural development, and human resources development, based on ASEAN connectivity, President Moon Jae-in's 'South Korea-Mekong Vision' proposed more specific plans and prosperity measures with the goal of shared prosperity and peace in East Asia, based on sharing existing experiences and aiming for sustainable prosperity (Ping, 2020). For instance, it supported rural development projects for the economic development of Mekong countries based on the experience of rural development, linked Mekong's biological resources to green growth such as bio and medical, and proposed a vision for becoming a partner for peace and prosperity beyond economic cooperation, based on infrastructure, agriculture, ICT, human resources development, and cultural tourism cooperation to enhance mutual understanding and expand cooperation for ASEAN peace (Lee, 2019).

Theoretical Framework and Methodology

Building upon Holsti's (1970) study of national role conception, role theory, which has roots in sociology, psychology, and anthropological studies, has found application in foreign policy analysis (Harnisch, 2011b). This approach underscores the concept of the 'self', largely predicated on the state leaders, to elucidate various beliefs or images concerning the state's identity (Thies, 2017: 2). National role conceptions are described as the way states behave within the international system, focusing primarily on a state's internal dimensions and disregarding interactions with other states (Wish, 1980; Shih, 1988). Wish (1980: 532) defines national role conceptions as 'foreign policymakers' perceptions of their nations' standing in the international system'. These perceptions encompass the broad types of decisions, regulations, obligations, and enduring responsibilities associated with these international roles (Wish, 1980).

When applying this role theory approach to foreign policy analysis, it is critical to consider the 'expectations of significant others', a factor that influences a state's role behaviour (Biddle, 1986: 67–92). A state's role does not align with these 'expectations', and therefore no interaction occurs between actors; the state's behaviour is not seen as a role being assumed but as self-assertive or self-centred behaviour that is not accepted by others (Holsti, 1970; Walker, 1987). Kaarbo and Cantir (2013: 465–483) present the phenomenon of disagreement between two roles regarding the same situation, or between external role expectations and internal role conceptions for the same issue, as 'role conflict'. This arises because states often harbour more than one national role conception, and other entities hold role expectations for these states that might not be congruous with self-definitions (Jönsson and Westerlund, 1982).

The external role expectation is critical to the role conception of a state, as it is crucial for the interaction between self-conception and the perceptions of others. Here, the external role expectation is understood as the expectations that another party (alter) ascribes to and expects the self (ego) to enact (Kirste and Maull, 1996: 289; Wehner, 2015). Harnisch, Frank and Maull (2011) further explain that role expectations are different according to corporate actors, depending on which states or international organisations. They typically comprise ego, for example, domestic and/or individual expectations (internal role expectation) about what the appropriate role is and what it entails, and alter expectations, for instance, implicit or explicit demands by others, such as counter or complementary roles, and audience cues (Harnisch, 2011b: 7–15).

The role expectations can vary in terms of their scope, specificity, communality, and thus their obligation. As a result, the possibility of role conflicts arises within both individual roles and role sets, such as conflicts between ego and alter expectations within a single role (intra-role conflicts), or between different roles (inter-role conflicts) (Harnisch, 2011b: 7–15). Role conflict is commonly defined in a few ways: as a conflict between nationally defined role conceptions within a state and externally defined role expectations. For instance, a mismatch between ego and alter expectations, a conflict between two or multiple roles addressing the same situation, or a conflict within elements of the same role (Bengtsson and Elgström, 2012: 93–108; Harnisch et al., 2011: 76 & 256–258). Regarding role conflict, Biddle (1986: 82) explains that when others do not hold consensus expectations for an individual's behaviour, these 'others' may form groups with distinctive and incompatible expectations. In such cases, the person is subjected to conflicting pressures, experiences stress, and must resolve by 'learning' or 'copying' behaviour. As a result, role conflict can be defined as the simultaneous emergence of two or more incompatible expectations for an individual's behaviour. However, not much literature has addressed the process of role conflict so far (Kaarbo and Cantir, 2013).

In light of this, this chapter approaches the idea that Mekong nations may harbour divergent role expectations for South Korea, each shaped by their distinct domestic contexts. Also, given their historical experiences with foreign powers, they could be wary of external influences and might prefer South Korea to assume a less dominant role. Alternatively, they may harbour suspicions regarding South Korea's intent, potentially perceiving it as using the Mekong countries as a temporal strategic counterbalance in its diplomacy between the great powers, namely, the US and China. This potential mismatch in role expectations and role conception could manifest as questions about the feasibility or consistency of South Korea's development projects, indicative of a role conflict. The interplay between South Korea's national role conception and the role expectations of Mekong countries can thus significantly impact diplomatic relations and the efficacy of foreign policies. Consequently, this research delves into this potential role conflict, examining how it moulds the interactions between South Korea and Mekong countries and influences South Korea's diplomatic sway in the region.

At the same time, the crux of this research is the assumption that a discrepancy between South Korea's role conception and the Mekong countries' role expectations for South Korea culminates in a role conflict. This is ostensibly manifested in the diminished levels of trust and diplomatic influence in the Mekong region, notwithstanding South Korea's concerted efforts to broaden its diplomatic footprint. With this in mind, this chapter has analysed South Korea's national role conceptions and the Mekong countries' role expectations by the qualitative content analysis of their respective development strategies and policy visions to discern the existence of role conflict.

South Korea in the Mekong River Basins: A Case Study

In the endeavour to foster regional integration and cooperation within the MRB, both the ROK and the MRC have put forth noteworthy strategies: the Korea-Mekong Vision initiated in 2019 and the MRC's Strategy spanning 2016–2020, respectively. Although these strategies converge on a shared objective, their respective ODA tactics and prioritisation of social and environmental issues diverge markedly. In this, this chapter analyses these two cases in comparison by highlighting their similarities and differences and the potential ramifications their implementation may hold for the future development of the MRB.

South Korea's 'Republic of Korea-Mekong Vision'

Hae-yoon Park, the Director of Southeast Asia and the Pacific at the former Ministry of Foreign Affairs and Trade (the Ministry is now the Ministry of Foreign Affairs) during the Lee administration, described the 2011 adoption of the 'Comprehensive

Partnership for Mutual Prosperity between Korea and the Mekong' (known as the 'Han River Declaration') as a concept linking the 'Miracle of the Han River' to a 'Miracle of the Mekong River' (Sohn, 2011: 28). In October 2010, in line with the comprehensive relationship enhancement that had progressed through the establishment of a 'Korea-ASEAN Strategic Partnership', the relationship between Korea and the Mekong region nations also developed mutually beneficially in various cooperation fields such as politics, economics, and socio-culture (Hahnkyu, 2023: 59–76). Both sides recognised that the development of the Mekong region, with its enormous economic growth and development potential, is not only essential for accelerating ASEAN integration and increasing connectivity but also for the formation of the ASEAN Community in 2015. It also aims to promote regional cooperation and community formation in East Asia while respecting ASEAN's centrality (Teo, 2023; Kwak, 2022).

Both South Korea and the Mekong region nations sought mutually beneficial bilateral relationships. They pursued complementary development alongside other cooperation bodies in the Mekong region. Public and private sector dialogues on socio-economic development were supported, and private sector participation in relevant areas was encouraged. Finally, they committed to development cooperation in line with international aid principles. These principles include the Paris Declaration of the Organisation for Economic Co-operation and Development (OECD), the Development Assistance Committee (DAC), the High-Level Forum series, and the G20 Seoul Development Consensus, aimed at enhancing aid effectiveness (Watson and Schwak, 2019: 159). The priority cooperation areas for ODA provision were established around three pillars, considering the needs of the Mekong region, Korea's strengths, and aid capabilities. These include ASEAN connectivity, sustainable development, and people-centred development. Infrastructure and information and communication technologies fall under the ASEAN connectivity category, green growth and water resource development under sustainable development, and agriculture and rural development, and human resource development under people-centred development (MOFA, 2021: 48).

The Han River Declaration of the Lee Myung-bak administration has significance, in that it concretises cooperation between Korea and the Mekong countries, and it uniquely contributed to regularising the Korea-Mekong Foreign Ministers' Meeting concurrently with the announcement of the declaration (Watson and Schwak, 2019). However, there were limitations, including vague boundaries in the cooperation area, Korea's attempt to clearly define its role in the ASEAN cooperation body through cooperation with Mekong countries, and the lack of concrete direction and plan setting in encouraging private sector participation (Kwak, 2022). It was not until three years after the 2011 declaration that a cooperation action plan was adopted in 2014. Although it was described as a mutually beneficial bilateral relationship, the methods proposed by Korea mostly had the direction of 'transferring' Korea's advanced technology and information without a long-term vision (Kwak, 2022: 36–37). Considering these aspects, along with the known part where former Minister of Foreign Affairs Byung-se Yoon mentioned the North Korean issue at the 4th Korea-Mekong Foreign Ministers' Meeting and asked for their cooperation on the Korean Peninsula issue, Korea-Mekong cooperation could be perceived as a temporary diplomatic strategy, largely influenced by Korea's stance (MOFA, 2014; Kwak, 2022: 38).

In November 2019, the Moon administration hosted the first Mekong-ROK summit to discuss the ROK-Mekong vision. This summit coincided with the 30th anniversary of ASEAN-ROK dialogue relations and resulted in the adoption of the Mekong-Han River Declaration for establishing partnership for People Prosperity, and Peace (3Ps) (Hahnkyu, 2023). These three pillars align with the Moon administration's New Southern Policy, demonstrating the administration's commitment to Mekong cooperation and underscoring the feasibility of its regional initiative. According to President Moon, the declaration elevates the Mekong-ROK cooperation to the summit level and places a higher priority on deepening the relationship (Watson and Schwak, 2019: 175). As a result of the expansion of the Mekong-ROK Cooperation Fund, the trade volume between Korea and Mekong countries increased to over USD 84.5 billion, with mutual people-to-people exchanges tripling to reach nearly 7 million (Kwak, 2022: 36). President Moon outlined three paths to advance the Mekong-ROK partnership to the next level. Firstly, he emphasised the significance of 'sharing experiences and moving towards mutual prosperity' and agreed to establish a public research institute in the Mekong region modelled after Korea's research institutions, the Korea Development Institute (KDI) and the Korea Institute of Science and Technology (KIST) (MOFA, 2021: 41, 63). Secondly, he highlighted the importance of ICT-based cooperation projects, including education, new growth industries, forest preservation, and nurturing individuals with a future-oriented capacity for innovation (Hahnkyu, 2023: 59–76). Thirdly, he explained his plans for rural development projects, which would disseminate Korea's Saemaul Undong to enhance the capabilities of the next generation (Kim, 2018a: 491). To promote sustainable prosperity, the ROK-Mekong Biological Diversity Center and the Korea-Mekong Water Resources Joint Research Center have been established to address transnational threats to the MRB and ensure the safe and efficient utilisation of its water resources. Furthermore, the Korea-Mekong Future Peace Community project and the Peace Forest Initiative, through the Korea-Mekong Forest Cooperation Center and the Asian Forest Cooperation Organization, have been proposed.

The first year of the new Korea-Mekong cooperation resulted in the adoption of the Mekong-Han River Declaration for establishing partnership for People, Prosperity, and Peace. The people sector of the partnership aims to achieve a People for Inclusive Society. According to the Mekong-Han River Declaration, the partnership's shared vision is to achieve a community that is 'people-centred and people-oriented' with a focus on cooperation that ensures economic, financial, and social inclusiveness (Mekong-Han River Declaration, 2019: 3). Collaborative projects such as the preservation and restoration of cultural heritage towards sustainable and smart development of culture and tourism in the Mekong region promote culture and tourism cooperation. The sector also includes promoting vocational education and training, capacity-building in higher education, improvement of e-learning resources, and Korean language education to advance human resources development (Mekong-Han River Declaration, 2019). Healthcare cooperation is also a key aspect of the sector to achieve Universal Health Coverage (UHC) (Hahnkyu, 2023: 59–76). The prosperity sector is based on sharing experience and includes ten action plans that are closely related to the Miracle of the Han River, the rapid economic development that the ROK has experienced (Mekong-Han River Declaration, 2019). The commitment to collaboration involves partnerships between various South Korean and Mekong country agencies, including the Korea Trade-Investment Promotion Agency (KOTRA) and the Myanmar Trade Promotion Organization (MYANTRADE), the KIST, and the Vietnam-KIST (V-KIST), as well as the KDI and the Myanmar Development Institute (MDI) (MOFA, 2021: 63).

Agriculture and rural development are considered the foundation for development, and cooperative projects such as the Integrated Rural Development Projects, Saemaul Undong, and Energy Independent Energy Town Projects have been designed to improve productivity in rural areas (Hong, 2021: 16, Yonhap News Agency, 2019). Infrastructure construction is also a priority through the ROK's Economic Development Cooperation Fund (EDCF), a loan aid mechanism (Ahn, 2019). ICT-driven projects, including smart cities, and the encouragement of private sector investment in micro, small, and medium-sized enterprises (MSMEs) and start-ups in the Mekong countries and the ROK have also been encouraged (Hahnkyu, 2023: 59–76). The Mekong-ROK Business Council has been established, and the ROK's business community benefits from reduced production costs and signing the Double Taxation Avoidance Agreement (Mekong-Han River Declaration, 2019).

The Peace sector of the ROK-Mekong vision is dedicated to the protection and preservation of the environment in the Mekong sub-region. This is achieved through collaborative efforts in managing water resources, conserving biodiversity, overseeing forest management, and developing environmental infrastructure. According to the Mekong-Han River Declaration (2019), the sector aims to achieve green growth and sustainable development, and the establishment of centres such as the Mekong-ROK Biodiversity Center and the Mekong-ROK Water Resources Joint Research Center has been planned (Mekong-Han River Declaration, 2019). Non-traditional action plans have also been put in place to address issues such as climate change, natural disasters, support for victims, and the clearance of explosive remnants of war (ERW) (Kim and Kim, 2022). The Mekong countries have expressed their support for complete denuclearisation and for the United Nations Convention on the Law of the Sea (UNCLOS) to enhance maritime security and freedom of navigation in regional and global issues (Mekong-Han River Declaration, 2019).

In summary, the ROK-Mekong vision aims to achieve sustainable prosperity and peace in East Asia through sharing experiences, promoting sustainable prosperity, and strengthening connectivity for common prosperity. The Mekong-Han River Declaration prioritises deepening the relationship between ROK and the Mekong region and outlines a framework for cooperation in seven priority areas: cultural and tourism; human resources development; agriculture and rural development; infrastructure, information, and communication technology; environment; and non-traditional security challenges (Mekong-Han River Declaration, 2019: 1–7). While there are overall differences, cooperation between Korea and the Mekong region has consistently taken the form of an approach based on the 'Miracle on the Han River', and it appears that there is a commitment to transferring Korean success cases.

The Mekong River Commission's 'Strategic Plan 2016–2020'

Established on 5 April 1995, the MRC is the sole river basin organisation in the region and plays a pivotal role in water diplomacy through the Mekong Agreement by Cambodia, Lao PDR, Thailand, and Vietnam. It excels in facilitating cooperation, building networks, and disseminating information about the Mekong River (Keskinen et al., 2021: 1). Since its inception, the MRC has committed to enhancing cooperation among the four lower Mekong countries by promoting sustainable development initiatives (Campbell, 2016). The organisation particularly focuses on hydropower development, addressing energy cooperation and investment issues tailored to the diverse needs of the Mekong Basin countries. While some countries face power shortages, others aim to export electricity through hydropower dam development (Lee, 2023). Although physical conflicts and ideological confrontations among the Mekong Basin countries have subsided, differing national perspectives on the Mekong River's water resources, divided by borders, persistently generate new competition and tensions (Lee, 2023). Consequently, the MRC has recognised the importance of effective collaboration and coordination among diverse stakeholders to maximise the benefits of the basin. To enhance basin management and development, the commission actively strengthens its cooperation through the dialogue partners scheme with China and Myanmar, through regular meetings and technical exchanges to address transboundary water management issues (Feng et al., 2019). The Mekong Agreement has established a legal framework that promotes cooperation principles among member countries for the sustainable development and management of the MRB, thus playing a crucial role in supporting the social and economic welfare of the countries and communities reliant on the MRB (Feng et al., 2019; Ha, 2011).

Especially the strategic plan of the MRC for 2016–2020 demonstrates an overall blueprint for the organisation's vision to facilitate the sustainable development of the MRB over the subsequent five years. The plan seeks to bolster collaboration among the MRC, its member countries' implementation agencies, dialogue partners, development partners, and other stakeholders (Budryte, Heldt and Denecke, 2018: 349–361). Moreover, this plan addresses formidable challenges posed to the MRB, which include water resources management, climate change, and sustainable development. This plan lays out four strategic priorities: Basin Development Strategy (BDS); Data, Information, and Knowledge; Dialogue and Cooperation; and Institutional Strengthening (MRC, 2016: 8–23). To achieve its goals, the MRC emphasises the importance of engaging stakeholders, sharing knowledge, and utilising evidence-based decision-making (Sok, Meas and Nguonphan, 2023).

According to the plan, the MRC has designated the enhancement of national plans, projects, and resources from a basin-wide perspective as its foremost key result area. The MRC aims to play a pivotal role in shaping the plans and initiatives of its member countries, particularly those impacting the management of the Mekong Basin (Ha, 2011). The plan has been designed to accomplish three strategic outcomes: increased comprehension and application of evidence-based knowledge; optimised environmental management and sustainable water resource development; and provision of guidance for the development and management of water and related projects and resources (Sok et al., 2023: 80–98). Each of these outcomes is associated with specific approaches, outputs, necessary resources, and monitoring indicators. Therefore, this strategic plan demonstrates its guiding direction in supporting sustainable development in MRB countries (Sok et al., 2023).

Also, by demonstrating its strategic plan, the MRC focuses primarily on basin planning and management to achieve three strategic outcomes: establishing a basin-wide, integrated planning framework; enhancing the management of MRC's knowledge, information, and data systems; and improving basin management effectiveness through effective stakeholder engagement (MRC, 2016: 9–23). This appears to account for the diverse perspectives of member countries on the current Mekong River cooperation system. For instance, upstream countries such as Thailand often exhibit a relatively passive stance towards other members' demands. This can be attributed to their relatively stable economic development and well-established legal and institutional frameworks, fostering a degree of scepticism regarding the MRC's role. Conversely, countries like Cambodia and Vietnam's southern regions, where residents heavily depend on the Mekong River fisheries, are directly impacted by unregulated basin development. Consequently, these nations advocate for a more robust cooperation framework within the MRC to address their specific needs (Ellen, 2007; Lee, 2015). In essence, the MRC's strategic plan can be understood as an effort to act as a unified community while recognising the diverse perspectives of the Mekong countries.

The accompanying Action Plan details specific activities and targets to fulfil the BDS goals (Campbell, 2016). To effectively manage its knowledge, information, and data systems, the MRC is committed to enhancing its monitoring and evaluation capabilities, improving data collection and management systems, and developing a knowledge management strategy to increase the accessibility and utilisation of MRC data and information by member countries and stakeholders (Campbell, 2011: 724–740). The State of Basin Report provided an update on the economic, social, environmental, climate, and cooperation conditions in the basin, guiding future basin management objectives using the MRC Indicator Framework (Ghosh and Modak, 2021). Together, the strategic plan and the BDS serve as the principal guiding documents for the sustainable development of the MRBs, which member countries are mandated to follow according to the Mekong Agreement (Budryte et al., 2018).

The commission also emphasises the significant role of a Regional Stakeholder Platform to facilitate a common understanding of evidence related to the basin and to provide a forum for significant stakeholder involvement in the assessment of scenarios and projects (Sok et al., 2019). This platform is expected to enable a diverse range of stakeholders to participate in MRC decision-making processes and allow the commission to respond more effectively to stakeholder needs and concerns. Moreover, the MRC highlights the value of cooperation among riparians by facilitating cost and benefit sharing in mutually beneficial basin-wide and joint projects between member countries (Lee and Lee, 2015).

Lastly, the MRC focuses on its capacity to engage political decision-makers through targeted initiatives such as the annual MRC Summit and specific outreach activities. It also includes amplifying its collaboration with other regional organisations to boost collective efforts towards sustainable development and management of the MRB (Ha, 2011). However, cooperation with external entities raises questions about whether the Mekong Basin countries can advance towards sustainable development in the face of various external challenges under the current Mekong River cooperation system (Lee, 2016). For example, the MRC operates Stakeholder Regional Forums with the participation of the US, Japan, Australia, the European Union, and the World Bank. However, the fact that it relies primarily on external funding from member countries demonstrates a structural weakness, as it cannot ignore the expectations and interests of these contributors until it achieves financial independence (Bajorinas, 2021: 28; Lee, 2023: 61; Soulito, 2019: 14).

In summary, the MRC plays a crucial role in water diplomacy and regional cooperation by providing a platform for member countries to engage in dialogue, collaborate on transboundary water management, and jointly tackle the basin's challenges. Its strategic plan for 2016–2020 highlights its commitment to sustainable development, focusing on key areas such as the basin development strategy, data management, and institutional strengthening to enhance cooperation and implement effective water management practices. This plan is instrumental in addressing the diverse needs of the basin's countries, dealing with challenges like water resource management, climate change, and the need for sustainable development. Through initiatives aimed at improving stakeholder engagement and enhancing the management of the basin's resources, the MRC aims to align the various interests of its member countries and external partners, navigating complex geopolitical landscapes to ensure the Mekong's role in the socioeconomic welfare of the region. Therefore, this section has illustrated how the MRC's efforts not only contribute to regional stability and development but also embody a strategic approach to harmonising differing national perspectives on river development, positioning the MRC as a central institution in achieving long-term sustainability in the MRB.

Discussion and Analysis: South Korea in Mekong River Basins

Economic Development Strategies of the Republic of Korea and the Mekong River Commission

The ROK and the MRC have each proposed individual plans for economic cooperation with the MRB countries. The ROK has unveiled the 'Mekong-ROK Vision', detailing its strategy for economic cooperation with the MRC member countries

(Hahnkyu, 2023: 59–76; MOFA, 2019). This vision aligns with the Mekong region's development priorities, aiming to promote economic growth, alleviate poverty, and foster social and environmental sustainability. Five key cooperation areas underscore this vision: infrastructure development; ICT; water management; agriculture and rural development; and education and capacity building (Hahnkyu, 2023; MOFA, 2019). Drawing inspiration from its own 'Miracle of the Han River'—a transformative journey that propelled the ROK from a war-devastated, poverty-ridden nation into a global economic powerhouse (Jang, 2020)—the ROK aims to apply these lessons to the Mekong region and catalyse a similar transformation. Infrastructure development is emphasised as a principal driver of economic growth, and private sector involvement is a key element in this vision (Jang, 2020).

Contrastingly, the MRC, through its Strategic Plan 2016–2020, seeks to advance sustainable development in the MRB (MRC, 2016.). This plan focuses on three key areas: the development of sustainable hydropower; adaptation to climate change; and integrated management of water resources (Sok et al., 2023: 81–82). The goal is to achieve a balance between economic growth, environmental sustainability, and social equity while promoting collaboration and coordination between member countries (MRC, 2021). The MRC employs a comprehensive approach to development in the MRB. It highlights the need to balance economic growth with environmental conservation and social development. The MRC's strategy accentuates the importance of local community and stakeholder participation in decision-making processes, acknowledging their crucial role in sustainable development. It also emphasises the value of regional cooperation, outlining measures to bolster collaboration among member countries (Schmeier, 2009).

As provided in the previous section, both the Mekong-ROK Vision and the MRC's Strategic Plan 2016–2020 have aimed for sustainable development in the MRB, albeit through differing approaches. The ROK's vision leans towards infrastructure development, capacity building, and human resource development, while the MRC's strategy prioritises environmental conservation and resource management. Each plan emphasises regional cooperation and proposes measures to boost collaboration among member countries. The ROK's vision suggests creating a Mekong-ROK Business Council, whereas the MRC's strategy accentuates the necessity for coordinated water resource management in the region.

As Table 5.1 demonstrates, while sharing a common goal of promoting sustainable development in the MRB, the 'ROK-Mekong Vision' and the 'MRC's Strategic Plan 2016–2020' embody significantly different strategies. The ROK's vision underscores economic development and investment, focusing on infrastructure development and capacity building. It also recognises the essential role of the private sector in propelling economic growth. The ROK intends to transfer its 'Miracle of the Han River' developmental lessons to the Mekong region. Conversely, the MRC's strategy places emphasis on environmental conservation and resource management, identifying public sector investment as vital to sustainable development. The plan adopts a participatory approach to development, acknowledging the importance of local community and stakeholder involvement in decision-making processes. Its three focal areas are sustainable hydropower development, climate

Table 5.1 Comparative Approaches in ROK-Mekong Vision and MRC Strategic Plan 2016–2020

	ROK-Mekong Vision	*MRC Strategic Plan 2016–2020*
Aim	• Economic growth (Alleviate poverty) • Foster social and environmental sustainability • Strengthen South Korea's ties with Mekong	• Sustainable development • Balancing economic development, environmental sustainability, and social equity • Enhancing water security
Objective	• Transfer developmental experience (Miracle of the Han River) • Prioritise infra development, capacity building, and private sector involvement	• Ensuring sustainable management of water resources • Foster regional cooperation • Prioritise environmental conservation and public sector engagement
Sector	• Infrastructure development • Information and communication technology • Water management • Agriculture and rural development • Education and capacity building	• Sustainable hydropower development • Climate change adaptation • Integrated water resources management
Approaches	• Engage with private sector investments and international stakeholders	• Emphasises the involvement of local communities and stakeholders

Source: Author's own compilation, based on Cheongwadae (2019a), (2019b), (2019c), MRC (2016), South Korea Ministry of Foreign Affairs (2021)

change adaptation, and integrated water resources management. These measures aspire to balance economic development, environmental sustainability, and social equity while fostering cooperation and coordination among member countries.

The ROK's vision delineates five cooperation areas, as explored above. Among these, its emphasis on infrastructure development reflects the ROK's perception of its role as a primary driver of economic growth. In comparison, the MRC's strategic plan gives precedence to hydropower development as a clean energy source to meet the region's growing energy needs. It also highlights the need for integrated water resource management as a mechanism to harmonise competing demands and ensure water security for all users. This involves encouraging local community and stakeholder participation in water resource management, promoting transboundary cooperation, and strengthening regional governance frameworks. Those gaps demonstrate two different approaches to economic development, one positioning itself as a role model for developing countries based on its model and the other emphasising the need for cooperation among member states.

Therefore, this research argues that the ROK's vision draws from its own development experience, intending to translate its successful model to the Mekong region. In the case of MRC, its strategic plan employs a participatory approach to development, underlining the importance of stakeholder involvement and collaboration. The plan also advocates for a balanced approach to development, acknowledging the interrelation of economic, social, and environmental sustainability. While both plans stress the significance of regional cooperation, they diverge in their specific focus areas and development approaches. These differences imply that a comprehensive and coordinated approach to MRB's development might necessitate the integration of both plans, capitalising on their respective strengths and expertise to achieve sustainable and inclusive growth (Kim et al., 2013).

Concerning progress, the South Korean government issued the 2021 'Report on South Korea-Mekong Cooperation' to evaluate its cooperation progress with Mekong countries (Cambodia, Laos, Myanmar, Thailand, and Vietnam) across various sectors, including trade, investment, development, and culture (Song, 2024: 1–27). The report underscores the accomplishments of South Korea's engagement with the Mekong region, such as increased trade and investment flows, expanded cultural exchanges, and fortified development cooperation. However, the report also recognises the challenges facing South Korea-Mekong cooperation, including disparities between South Korea's and the Mekong countries' development strategies, limited participation of local communities in cooperation projects, and issues regarding transparency, governance, and capacity-building.

In conclusion, while the Mekong-ROK Vision and MRC's Strategic Plan 2016–2020 share common objectives such as promoting sustainable development and enhancing regional cooperation, they differ in their development approaches and priorities for the MRB. In addition to challenges related to implementation rates, significant obstacles include limited local community participation and discrepancies between development strategies. An integrated approach that harnesses the strengths of both plans and addresses these challenges is vital for realising sustainable and equitable development in the region.

Role Theory and the Republic of Korea's Engagement with the Mekong River Basins

Based on the above analysis, the following discussion has been drawn about the national role conceptions of South Korea and the role expectations of the Mekong countries: South Korea's collaboration with the Mekong region, largely facilitated through its ODA, is deeply intertwined with its perceived roles. Firstly, South Korea differentiates itself from the powerful nations that historically invaded Southeast Asia (Teo, Singh and Tan, 2013). It identifies itself as a middle-power country, distinct from these contentious nations. Secondly, South Korea builds its sense of community on the shared colonial experiences of invasion that it has with most Southeast Asian nations, emphasising that it was not a colonial power (MOFA, 2019). Thirdly, it emphasises its successful navigation through these historical adversities to achieve economic growth, transforming its identity from an emerging state to a responsible regional power (Kwak, 2022). This positioning highlights more of a 'helping' role, positioning itself as a role model for emerging countries, questioning cooperation on equal footing (Lee, 2019: 1–4). This perspective is reinforced by South Korea's narrative of transitioning from an aid-receiving to an aid-giving country, often symbolised by the 'Miracle of the Han River' in its cooperation with Mekong countries (Kim and Kalinowski, 2020). Thus, South Korea's national role conception is largely seen as a role model, a leader for emerging countries, and a rightful 'middle power' available to 'help' emerging countries (Hermanns, 2013: 55–82; Shin, 2016: 195). This self-oriented perception, however, could be critiqued for promoting a Korea-centric role in interactions with not only Mekong countries but also other developing countries. The strategy of cooperation, rather than acknowledging the uniqueness of the partner countries, appears more as an attempt to replicate South Korea's development model (Domjahn, 2013).

South Korea's approach to development diverges from the orientation preferred by the Mekong countries. As analysed previously, the MRC lays out the developmental stages, status analysis, and future development direction set by the Mekong countries in the short and long term. This highlights a stark contrast between South Korea's self-imposed role and the role Mekong countries anticipate from South Korea. In this sense, this chapter points out the inherent limitations of South Korea's 'one size fits all' approach. While elements of South Korea's economic development model can inspire other countries, it is challenging to understand the outcomes without factoring in Korea's unique temporal and situational attributes (Kim, 1993; Minns, 2001). Similarly, the Mekong countries, situated upstream and downstream of the river, confront unique circumstances and diverse cultural and economic development priorities. When examining individual countries, each one's political, economic, and social situations vary and possess their own distinct characteristics. Consequently, overemphasising the Korean model without considering the local context could result in mismatches between Korea's overall strategy and regional vision and the actual expectations of these countries (Chun, Munyi and Lee, 2010).

Secondly, with the transition from President Moon Jae-in's regime to Yoon Seok-yeol's and the shift from the New Southern Policy to the Korea-style Indo-Pacific strategy, questions have arisen about the future of Korea-Mekong cooperation (John, 2023). Inconsistent levels of engagement might hinder South Korea's positioning as a dependable, long-term partner (Koga, 2023). In other words, frequent changes in the degree of engagement could lead to discrepancies in expectations of South Korea being a 'responsible partner country', particularly if its involvement in the Mekong region is seen as sporadic or inconsistent (Koga, 2023: 73–74).

Thirdly, questions have arisen as to whether South Korea and the Mekong countries can establish a shared approach to environmental conservation and sustainable agricultural development, both priorities for the Mekong region. South Korea's strategy towards the MRB countries leans heavily towards its economic development model, focusing on industrial development via infrastructure expansion and the transfer of cutting-edge technologies. This approach could lead to potential discrepancies in the prioritisation of sectors or issues (Lee, 2022). In particular, South Korea's economic development model, famously known as the 'Miracle of the Han River', shifted focus from agriculture to industrial development. This shift can pose a problem for the Mekong countries, where agriculture is a major industry.

It also highlights potential challenges the South Korean model might bring in this context (Grabowski, 2019).

Lastly, it is worth noting that Southeast Asia, including the MRB countries and ASEAN, is currently navigating a significant power rivalry, often seen as a battleground for US-China tensions (Khan, 2012; Park, 2020). Unlike the previous Moon Jae-in administration, which aimed to carve out South Korea's independent diplomatic route between the US and China via the 'New Southern Region' initiative, the current Yoon Seok-yeol government's 'Free and Open Indo-Pacific' (FOIP) strategy might raise concerns about South Korea favouring one side in the US-China diplomatic tussle (Panwar, 2022: 51–57).

Particularly, ASEAN countries are making significant efforts to maintain their neutrality, often referred to as ASEAN centrality, without picking sides (Heydarian, 2020; Yoneji, 2018). Consequently, South Korea should exhibit greater sensitivity when formulating and implementing strategies aimed at Southeast Asian countries (Jamil, 2023). When South Korea cooperates with countries that also have dealings with North Korea, there may be calls to declare or support statements condemning North Korea's actions, in line with South Korea's stance on North Korean issues. Undoubtedly, it is essential to acknowledge that North Korea's nuclear issue poses a threat not only to South Korea but to the entire security landscape of East Asia (Chang and Lee, 2018). Simultaneously, it is important to respect the unique qualities of ASEAN member states, which typically emphasise a 'non-intervention' approach, and often refrain from meddling in the internal affairs of other nations with respect to their sovereignty (Ramcharan, 2000: 60–88). Particularly when South Korea primarily conveys its stance by extending support and funds through its ODA, the positive aspects of the 'Miracle of the Han River' could be overlooked (Er, 2023; Watson and Schwak, 2019). If South Korea's strategy in the Mekong region is perceived as an attempt to offset the influence of other significant powers in the area, it may not meet the expectations of the Mekong countries for an independent partnership that respects their sovereignty and agency.

Conclusion

This chapter has employed the core concepts of role theory to elucidate South Korea's collaborative efforts in the MRB. The commitments made by Presidents Lee and Moon towards cooperation with the Mekong countries indicate South Korea's ambition to fortify its role as a critical partner and extend its influence in the Southeast Asian region. However, the analysis of distinct development policy directions reveals discord between South Korea's domestic role conceptions and the expectations of the Mekong countries. South Korea perceives itself as a middle power and a model of economic growth for emerging nations, shaping its engagement with the Mekong region. However, its 'one size fits all' approach, grounded in its own development narrative, might not resonate with the unique contexts and needs of the Mekong countries. The shift from President Moon Jae-in's New Southern Policy to Yoon Seok-yeol's Korean version of Indo-Pacific strategy further brings into question South Korea's consistency of its diplomatic priority, and its economically centred approach may clash with the Mekong countries' environmental and agricultural priorities.

As South Korea finds itself amid a power rivalry in Southeast Asia, it needs to tactfully navigate its position to avoid appearing biased towards either the US or China. This necessitates a heightened sensitivity in its strategy, taking into account the 'non-intervention' stance of ASEAN member states (Rubiolo and Aguirre, 2023: 461–468). Fundamentally, South Korea's engagement in the Mekong region should balance its global aspirations with respect for the Mekong countries' sovereignty, specific circumstances, and expectations, thereby fostering a partnership that values independence and mutual respect. While this chapter examines the issue from the perspective of role conflict, it opens the door for further exploration, particularly regarding South Korea's directionality problem, implying that the Mekong countries might not necessarily be the significant others. Hence, future research needs to delve into identifying the key factors influencing the cooperation between South Korea and the MRB countries and their interplay. Such in-depth studies will be crucial to better understand and enhance this cooperative relationship.

References

Ahn, S. H. (2019). Anatomy of the Republic of Koreas Niche strategic engagement in the Greater Mekong sub-region (GMS): ROKs tailor-made strategy and its security policy implication. *Korean Journal of Policy Studies*, *34*(3), 97–121.

Bajorinas, K. (2021). *Power Relations in the Mekong River Basin: A Look into the Discourse of the Mekong River Commission*. LUNDS Universitet. Department of Human Geography.

Basist, A., & Williams, C. (2020). Monitoring the Quantity of Water Flowing Through the Mekong Basin Through Natural (Unimpeded) Conditions, Sustainable Infrastructure Partnership, Bangkok.

Bengtsson, R., & Elgström, O. (2012). Conflicting role conceptions? The European Union in global politics. *Foreign Policy Analysis*, *8*(1), 93–108.

Biba, S. (2012) .China's continuous dam-building on the Mekong River. *Journal of Contemporary Asia*, *42*(4), 603–628. doi: 10.1080/00472336.2012.712257.

Biddle, B. J. (1986). Recent developments in role theory. *Annual Review of Sociology*, *12*(1), 67–92.

Bruzelius Backer, E. (2007). The Mekong River Commission: Does it work, and how does the Mekong basin's geography influence its effectiveness. *Journal of Current Southeast Asian Affairs*, *26*, 31–55.

Budryte, P., Heldt, S., & Denecke, M. (2018). Foundations of the participatory approach in the Mekong River basin management. *Science of the Total Environment*, *622*, 349–361.

Campbell, I. C. (2011). Managing international river basins: Successes and failures of the Mekong River Commission. In R. Quentin Grafton, & K. Hussey (Eds.), *Water Resources Planning and Management* (pp. 724–740). Cambridge University Press, Cambridge.

Campbell, I. C. (2016). Integrated management in the Mekong River basin. *Ecohydrology & Hydrobiology*, *16*(4), 255–262.

Chang, K., & Lee, C. (2018). North Korea and the East Asian Security order: Competing views on what South Korea ought to do. *The Pacific Review*, *31*(2), 245–255.

Charoensri, N. (2022). Changing regional dynamics in the greater Mekong subregion: The rivalry between Japan, China and the US and the impacts to regional connectivity. *Thammasat Review*, *25*(2), 26–45.

Cheongwadae. (2019a). 문 대통령 ‘한-메콩 비전’ 발표…”평화와 번영 동반자 관계로” [mun dae-tong-lyeong t-han-me-kong bi-jeon-t bal-pyo-tss-te-pyeong-hwa-wa beon-yeong dong-ban-ja gwan-gye-lo-te], Retrieved from https://www.korea.kr/news/policyNewsView.do?newsId=148864467.

Cheongwadae. (2019b). 문 대통령-메콩정상 ‘한강·메콩강 선언’…7대분야 협력 강화, [mun daetongryeong-mekongjeongsang ‘hangang·mekonggang seoneon’…7daebunya hyeopryeok ganghwa], Retrieved from https://www.korea.kr/news/policyNewsView.do?newsId=148866945.

Cheongwadae. (2019c). [전문] 사람·번영·평화의 동반자 관계 구축을 위한 한강-메콩강 선언 [[jeon-mun] sa-lam-tbs-beon-yeong-tbs-pyeong-hwa-ui dong-ban-ja gwan-gye gu-chug-eul wi-han han-gang-me-kong-gang seon-eon], Retrieved from https:// https://www.korea.kr/news/policyNewsView.do?newsId=148866946#policyNews.

Chheang, V. (2010). Environmental and economic cooperation in the Mekong region. *Asia Europe Journal*, *8*(3), 359–368.

Chun, H. M., Munyi, E. N., & Lee, H. (2010). South Korea as an emerging donor: Challenges and changes on its entering OECD/DAC. *Journal of International Development*, *22*(6), 788–802.

Domjahn, T. M. (2013). What (if anything) can developing countries learn from South Korea? *Asian Culture and History*, *5*(2), 16.

Dung, N. D., & Phuong, N. H. (2023, April). Strategic competition of China, Japan, and South Korea in the Mekong sub-region. In *East Asia in the 21st Century* (pp. 63–76). Nomos Verlagsgesellschaft mbH & Co. KG.

Er, L. P. (Ed.). (2023). *South Korea's New Southern Policy: A Middle Power's International Relations with Southeast Asia and India*. Taylor & Francis.

Eyler, B. (2020). Science shows Chinese dams are devastating the Mekong. *Foreign Policy*, 22, 1–8.

Feng, Y., Wang, W., Suman, D., Yu, S., & He, D. (2019). Water cooperation priorities in the Lancang-Mekong River basin based on cooperative events since the Mekong River Commission establishment. *Chinese Geographical Science*, *29*, 58–69.

Ghosh, N., & Modak, S. (2021). What governance lesson does Mekong bear for Ganges–Brahmaputra–Meghna (GBM) basin? *Journal of Asian Economic Integration*, *3*(2), 211–234.

Goh, E. (2017). China in the Mekong River basin: The regional security implications of resource development on the Lancang Jiang. In M. Caballero-Anthony, & A. D. B. Cook (Eds.), *Non-Traditional Security in Asia* (pp. 237–258). Routledge.

Grabowski, R. (2019). Structural change: Is South Korea a good model for developing countries? *Asian Development Perspectives*, *10*(1), 19–29.

Ha, M. L. (2011). The role of regional institutions in sustainable development: A review of the Mekong River Commission's first 15 years. *Consilience*, (5), 125–140.

Hahnkyu, P. (2023). Seoul's New Southern Policy Plus (NSPP) and the Mekong Region: Cooperation for sustainable development and inclusive growth. In Lam Peng Er (ed). *South Korea's New Southern Policy* (pp. 59–76). Routledge.

Harnisch, S. (2011b). Role theory: Operationalization of key concepts. In S. Harnisch, C. Frank, & H. Maull (Eds.), *Role Theory in International Relations* (pp. 7–15). Routledge.

Harnisch, S., Frank, C., & Maull, H. W. (Eds.). (2011). *Role Theory in International Relations* (Vol. 90). Taylor & Francis.
Hermanns, H. (2013). National role conceptions in the 'Global Korea'foreign policy strategy. *The Korean Journal of International Studies*, *11*(1), 55–82.
Heydarian, R. (2020). *At a Strategic Crossorads: ASEAN Centrality Amid Sino-American Rivalry in the Indo-Pacific*. Brookings Institution.
Holsti, K. J. (1970). National role conceptions in the study of foreign policy. *International Studies Quarterly*, *14*(3), 233–309.
Hong, C.-S. (2021). Strenthening Regional Energy Governance in the Mekong Subregion, Pacific Forum. *Issues and Insights Working Paper*, Vol. 21, WP12, July.
Jamil, N. S. (2023). ASEAN and the Republic of Korea as middle powers: ASEAN centrality and NSPP amid great power transition. In P. E. Lam (Eds.), *South Korea's New Southern Policy* (pp. 42–56). Routledge.
Jang, J. (2020). South Korea's 'new Mekong-Han river strategy' and the Korean wave diplomacy. *Journal of Contemporary East Asia Studies*, *9*(1), 89–106. doi: 10.1177/2476108820916224.
John, J. V. (2023). South Korea's new southern policy and the middle power quest: Implications for India-Korea relations. *Asian Affairs*, *54*(2), 327–341.
Jönsson, C., & Westerlund, U. (1982). Role theory in foreign policy analysis. In C. Jönsson (Ed.), *Cognitive Dynamics and International Politics* (pp. 122–157). St. Martin's Press.
Kaarbo, J., & Cantir, C. (2013). Role conflict in recent wars: Danish and Dutch debates over Iraq and Afghanistan. *Cooperation and Conflict*, *48*(4), 465–483.
Karim, M. F. (2023). Role conflict in international relations: The case of Indonesia's regional and global engagements. *International Relations*, *37*(1), 96–116.
Keskinen, M., Salmine, E., & Haapala, J. (2021). Water diplomacy paths: An approach to recognize water diplomacy actions in shared waters. *Journal of Hydrology*, 602, 1–13.
Khan, R. M. (2012). Sino-US rivalry in Southeast Asia. *Turkish Policy Quarterly*, *11*(3). doi: 10.25077/ajis.10.1.28-47.2022.
Kim, B. K., & Kim, T. (2022). Scaling-up Dynamics in KOICA's Peace-Development Nexus Projects in the Mekong Region: Cases of Lao PDR and Cambodia (No. 2022–6). *UNRISD Working Paper*.
Kim, D. Y. (2022). 한국의 새로운 對 아세안 (ASEAN) 협력 전략: 중견국 외교를 통한 소다자주의적 접근 [hangugui saeroun 對 asean (ASEAN) hyeopryeok jeonryak: junggyeonguk oegyoreul tonghan sodajajuuijeok jeopgeun.]. *아시아연구*, *25*(1), 251–269.
Kim, E. M. (1993). Contradictions and limits of a developmental state: With illustrations from the South Korean case. *Social Problems*, *40*(2), 228–249.
Kim, H. N., & Kalinowski, T. (2020). Only shallow? Public support for development cooperation in South Korea. *Asian International Studies Review*, *21*(2), 29–53.
Kim, H. S. (2018a). The political drivers of South Korea's official development assistance to Myanmar. *Contemporary Southeast Asia*, *40*(3), 475–502.
Kim, S. M. (2018b). Cursed by Geopolitics? South Korea's Place in asia's Changing Politics Of Space. *German Institute for International and Security Affairs,* https://www.swp-berlin.org/publications/products/projekt_papiere/Kim_BCAS_2018_South_Korea_geopolitics_9_.pdf
Kim, T., Cheong, J., Lee, J. H., Shin, M., & Park, N. R. (2013). Korea's Development Cooperation with the Mekong Region. *KIEP Research Paper No. World Economy Update-13–40*.
Kirste, K., & Maull, H. W. (1996). Zivilmacht und Rollentheorie. *Zeitschrift für internationale Beziehungen*, 283–312.

Koga, K. (2022). The emerging power play in the Mekong subregion: A Japanese perspective. *Asia Policy*, *17*(2), 28–34.

Koga, K. (2023). Struggle for coalition-building: Japan, South Korea, and the indo-Pacific. *Asian Politics & Policy*, *15*(1), 63–82.

Kuenzer, C., Campbell, I., Roch, M., Leinenkugel, P., Tuan, V. Q., & Dech, S. (2013). Understanding the impact of hydropower developments in the context of upstream–downstream relations in the Mekong river basin. *Sustainability Science*, *8*, 565–584.

Kwak, S. (2022). The future direction of Republic of Korea and Mekong cooperation in a climate of U.S.-China competition. *Asia Policy, 17*(2), 35–42. doi: 10.1353/asp.2022.0024.

Lee, S. (2024, January, 18), US Engineers, Scientists Continue Work with Mekong Partners on Water Security, U.S. Army, Retreived from 28th, April, 2024. https://www.army.mil/article/273067/us_engineers_scientists_continue_work_with_mekong_partners_on_water_security.

Lee, S., & Lee, S. (2015). Cooperation in the Mekong River basin through benefit sharing. *Proceedings of International Conference on Ecohydrology (ICE)* (p. 436). Asia Pacific Centre for Ecohydrology – UNESCO/Research Center for Limnology – LIPI. ISBN: 978-979-8163-22-7.

Lee, Y. H. (2019). 제 1차 한-메콩 정상회의의 주요 내용과 과제, [je 1cha han-mekong jeongsanghoeuiui juyo naeyonggwa gwaje] 대외경제정책연구원 (KIEP), Retrieved from https://www.kiep.go.kr/aif/issueDetail.es?brdctsNo=273025&mid=a30200000000&search_option=&search_keyword=&search_year=&search_month=&search_tagkeyword=&systemcode=03&search_region=03010100&search_area=&currentPage=4&pageCnt=10.

Lee, Y. H. (2022). 한국의 아세안 소지역 (sub-region) 협력 거버넌스: 메콩 유역을 중심으로. [hangugui asean sojiyeok (sub-region) hyeopryeok geobeoneonseu: mekong yuyeogeul jungsimeuro] *동남아연구, 32*(2), 31–58.

Lee, Y. H. (2023). Water diplomacy on transboudary dam development: Role and challenges of the Mekong River Commission (MRC). *동남아시아연구, 33*(3), 39–70.

Liebman, A. (2005). Trickle-down hegemony? China's "peaceful rise" and dam building on the Mekong. In Institute of Southeast Asian Studies (Ed.), *Contemporary Southeast Asia* (pp. 281–304). Singapore University Press.

Luo, Z. (2020). Ministry of Foreign Affairs of the People's Republic of China, Vice Foreign Minister Luo Zhaohui Attends 2020 Mekong-Lancang Cooperation Media Online Summit, Retrieved from https://www.fmprc.gov.cn/eng/wjb_663304/zygy_663314/gyhd_663338/202011/t20201126_493613.html (accessed on 28 April 2024).

McCormack, G. (2001). Water margins: Competing paradigms in China. *Critical Asian Studies*, *33*(1), 5–30.

Mekong-Han River Declaration. (2019, November 27). Mekong-Han River Declaration for Establishing Partnership for People, Prosperity, and Peace, Retrieved from https://overseas.mofa.go.kr/mr-en/brd/m_4208/view.do?seq=775752&srchFr=&srchTo=&srchWord=&srchTp=&multi_itm_seq=0&itm_seq_1=0&itm_seq_2=0&company_cd=&company_nm=&page=1.

Mekong River Commission (MRC). (2016). Strategic Plan 2016–2020, Retrieved from https://www.mrcmekong.org/wp-content/uploads/2024/08/Strategic-Plan-2016-2020-1.pdf.

Mekong River Commission (MRC). (2021). Strategic Plan 2021–2025, Retrieved from https://www.mrcmekong.org/wp-content/uploads/2024/08/BDS-2021-2030-and-MRC-SP-2021-2025.pdf.

Mekong River Commission (MRC). (2022a), Geography, Retrieved from https://www.mrcmekong.org/about/mekong-basin/geography/.

Ministry of Foreign Affairs (MOFA). (2019). Mekong-ROK Cooperation: Mekong-ROK Vision, Retrieved from https://www.mofa.go.kr/eng/brd/m_5678/view.do?seq=323013&srchFr=&srchTo=&srchWord=&srchTp=&multi_itm_seq=0&itm_seq_1=0&itm_seq_2=0&company_cd=&company_nm=&page=1&sort=oldest&list_typ=&v_ersn=&_Selec.

Ministry of Foreign Affairs of the People's Republic of China (PRC MOFA). (2020). Vice Foreign Minister Luo Zhaohui Attends the Inauguration Ceremony of the Lancang-Mekong Water Resources Cooperation Information Sharing Platform's Website, Retrieved from https://www.fmprc.gov.cn/mfa_eng/wjbxw/t1837496.shtml (accessed on 14 February 2021).

Minns, J. (2001). Of miracles and models: The rise and decline of the developmental state in South Korea. *Third World Quarterly*, *22*(6), 1025–1043.

MOFA. (2014). Retrieved from https://www.korea.kr/briefing/pressReleaseView.do?newsId=155982415#pressRelease.

MOFA. (2019). Retrieved from https://www.korea.kr/briefing/speechView.do?newsId=132031727#speech.

MOFA. (2021). 10. 메콩 개황, Retrieved from https://www.mofa.go.kr/www/brd/m_4099/down.do?brd_id=15388&seq=367668&data_tp=A&file_seq=1.

MOFAJ. (2009). The Tokyo Declaration of the First Meeting between the Heads of Government of Japan and the Mekong Region Countries, Ministry of Foreign Affairs, Tokyo, November 7, 2009.

MOFAJ. (2019). The Mekong-Japan Initiative for SDGs Toward 2030, Retreived from https://www.mofa.go.jp/files/000535957.pdf.

MOFA (2020) Overview of Mekong-ROK Cooperation. Retrieved from http://https://www.mofa.go.kr/eng/wpge/m_5466/contents.do.

Ogasawara, T. (2015). Development of the Mekong region as part of Japan's diplomatic strategy for East Asia. *Asia-Pacific Review*, 22(1), 34–45.

Osborne, M. (2009). *The Mekong: River under Threat*. Lowy Institute for International Policy.

Panda, J. P. (2020). Framing an Indo-Pacific Narrative in India-South Korea Ties. *Academic Paper Series of Korea Economic Institute of America. 2020a,* Retrieved from https://www.keia.org/sites/default/files/publications/kei_aps_panda_200106.pdf (accessed on 26 July 2021).

Panwar, Y. (2022). South Korea's approach to the Indo–Pacific. *Jindal Journal of International Affairs*, *10*(1), 51–57.

Park, Y. S. (2020). The escalating US-China hegemonic rivalry in Asia-Pacific and South Korea. *21 세기정치학회보, 30*(3), 123–144.

Ping, H. C. (2020). THE NEW SOUTHERN POLICY Institute of Strategic and International Studies (ISIS), Malaysia.

Ramcharan, R. (2000). ASEAN and non-interference: A principle maintained. *Contemporary Southeast Asia, 22*(1), 60–88. http://www.jstor.org/stable/25798479.

Rubiolo, F., & Aguirre, F. L. (2023). SOUTH KOREA AS A MIDDLE POWER IN EAST ASIA? National Interests and Regional Constraints toward ASEAN. *World Affairs*, *186*(2), 442–468.

Schmeier, S. (2009). Regional cooperation efforts in the Mekong river basin: Mitigating river-related security threats and promoting regional development. *Austrian Journal for Southeast Asian Studies*, *2*(2), 28–52.

Seah, S., et al. (2022). *The State of Southeast Asia: 2022.* Singapore: ISEAS-Yusof Ishak Institute, Retrieved from https://www.iseas.edu.sg/wp-content/uploads/2022/02/The-State-of-SEA-2022_FA_Digital_FINAL.pdf.

Soulito, J. (2019). The Mekong River: Geopolitics over development, hydropower and the environment. In Daniela Adorna Diaz, *European Parliament Study: Policy Department for External Relations* (pp. 1–55). Directorate General for External Policies of the Union.
Shih, C. Y. (1988). National role conception as foreign policy motivation: The psychocultural bases of Chinese diplomacy. *Political Psychology, 9*, 599–631.
Shin, S. O. (2016). South Korea's elusive middlepowermanship: Regional or global player? *The Pacific Review*, *29*(2), 187–209.
Smil, V. (1998). China's energy and resource uses: Continuity and change. *The China Quarterly*, *156*, 935–951.
Snyder, S. A. (2018). Revising South Korea's Constitution. In S. A. Snyder, G. Lee, & Y.-H. Kim (Eds.), *Domestic Constraints on South Korean Foreign Policy* (pp. 56–68). Council on Foreign Relations.
Snyder, S. A., Lee, G., Kim, Y. H., & Kim, J. (2018). *Domestic Constraints on South Korean Foreign Policy*. Council on Foreign Relations.
Sohn, J. M. (2011, October 28). Kyunghyang Shinmun. (2011, October 28). 한·메콩 외교장관회의 개막…'한강선언' 채택 [Title of the Article in English]. *Kyunghyang Shinmun*, Retrieved from https://m.khan.co.kr/politics/defense-diplomacy/article/201110281532121.
Sok, S., Meas, S., Chea, S., & Chhinh, N. (2019). Regional cooperation and benefit sharing for sustainable water resources management in the lower Mekong basin. *Lakes & Reservoirs: Research & Management*, *24*(3), 215–227.
Sok, S., Meas, S., & Nguonphan, P. (2023). The Mekong regional integration: What roles does the Mekong River Commission play? In C. Ploberger (Eds.), *River Basins and International Relations* (pp. 80–103). Routledge.
Song, J.S. (2024). 대 메콩지역 국가 개발협력: 현황 및 발전방안. [dae mekongjiyeok gukga gaebalhyeopryeok: hyeonhwang mit baljeonbangan] *주요국제문제분석, 2023*(52), 1–27.
South Korea Ministry of Foreign Affairs. (2021). Mekong-ROK Cooperation: Mekong-ROK Vision, Retrieved from https://www.mofa.go.kr/eng/brd/m_5678/view.do?seq=323013&srchFr=&srchTo=&srchWord=&srchTp=&multi_itm_seq=0&itm_seq_1=0&itm_seq_2=0&company_cd=&company_nm=&page=1&sort=oldest&list_typ=&v_ersn=&_Selec.
Strangio, S. (2020). *In the Dragon's Shadow: Southeast Asia in the Chinese Century*. Yale University Press.
Teo, S. (2023). South Korea in the ASEAN-centered regional network. *Asian Politics & Policy*, *15*(1), 98–112.
Teo, S., Bhubhindar Singh and S. S. Tan (2013). South Korea's middle-power engagement initiatives: perspectives from Southeast Asia. RSIS Working Paper, No. 265. Singapore: Nanyang Technological University.
Thies, C. (2017, December 22). Role Theory and Foreign Policy. In *Oxford Research Encyclopedia of International Studies* (pp. 1–44). Retrieved from 30 September, 2024: https://oxfordre.com/internationalstudies/view/10.1093/acrefore/9780190846626.001.0001/acrefore-9780190846626-e-291.
Thitinan, P. (2016). China's Alarming 'Water Diplomacy' on the Mekong, Nikkei Asia, Retrieved from https://asia.nikkei.com/Politics/Thitinan-Pongsudhirak-China-s-alarming-water-diplomacy-on-the-Mekong.
Watson, I., & Schwak, J. (2019). Water security, riparian identity and Korean nation branding in the Mekong subregion. *Pacific Focus*, *34*(2), 153–182.

Walker, Stephen (ed) (1987). *Role Theory and Foreign Policy Analysis*. Durham: Duke University Press.

Wehner, L. E. (2015). Role expectations as foreign policy: South American secondary powers' expectations of Brazil as a regional power. *Foreign Policy Analysis*, *11*(4), 435–455.

Wish, N. B. (1980). Foreign policy makers and their national role conceptions. *International Studies Quarterly*, *24*(4), 532–554.

Wang, X., Zhang, J., Shahid, S., ElMahdi, A., He, R., Bao, Z., & Ali, M. (2012). Water resources management strategy for adaptation to droughts in China. *Mitigation and Adaptation Strategies for Global Change*, *17*, 923–937.

Yoneji, K. (2018). The US-China-Japan triangle and the concept of "ASEAN Centrality": Myth or reality? In The Asan Forum, International Relations and Asia's Southern Tier: ASEAN, Australia, and India (pp. 143–157). The Asan Institute For Policy Studies.

Yonhap News Agency. (2019). Full text of a joint declaration adopted at Mekong-S. Korea summit. Yonhap News Agency. Retrieved from 27 November, 2019: https://en.yna.co.kr/view/AEN20191127004200315.

Yoshimatsu, H. (2015). The United States, China, and geopolitics in the Mekong region. *Asian Affairs: An American Review*, *42*(4), 173–194. doi: 10.1080/00927678.2015.1106757.

6 Altruism or Ulterior Motives? South Korean Aid towards North Korea's Sustainable Development

Queralt Boadella-Prunell and Lauren Eloise Robertson

Introduction

Following the OECD (2005) and the OECD (2008), the OECD (2011) was agreed by the member countries of the Organisation for Economic Co-operation and Development (OCED) Development Assistance Committee (DAC), as a result of the fourth High-Level Forum (HLF) on Aid Effectiveness (OECD, 2011). The forum brought together pundits from various fields to examine how aid effectiveness, and then effectiveness of development cooperation, can be communicated in current official development assistance (ODA) practices. South Korea, as the hosting nation of the fourth HLF, was at the forefront of the discourse surrounding the forum. Its focus was particularly placed on its transition from recipient to donor states, an ideal representation of the golden standard of a success story of developmental support (Kim and Garland, 2019: 1247–1248).

Since South Korea became an OECD DAC donor country in 2010, its development aid budget has continued to increase along with its aid programmes (OECD, 2022b). Given this, scholars tend to pay attention to how South Korea's experience has affected its behaviour as an emerging donor (for example, Kim, Choi and Chung, 2023; Lim, 2014). In 2019, Seoul provided approximately USD 2,898 million of ODA, making it one of the largest DAC donors in terms of ODA volume (Jung and Yoo, 2021: 1). Observing South Korea's direct ODA contributions, scholars have examined how aid projects and budget expenditure reflect its own development experience as well as solidifying its role as an emerging donor (Kim, Choi and Chung, 2023; Chun et al., 2010: 790).

Accordingly, there is a considerable body of literature regarding South Korea's aid to ODA recipient partners and its aid motivations (for example, see Kim, 2018, 2019; Kim and Gray, 2016; Lim, 2014; Patterson and Choi, 2019; Choi 2010). Yet inter-Korean support finds itself within a grey area as aid directed towards North Korea falls outside the category of ODA (Hur, Park and Kim, 2017; Lim, 2019). In 2014, it was estimated that as much as USD 13.3 million in aid that was provided to North Korea from South Korea would be ODA-eligible funding (UNESCAP, 2018: 14). Although being ODA eligible, this funding has been limited under the domestic legal ramifications and parameters of the South Korean constitution and the Inter-Korean Exchange and Cooperation Act Article 3 of the

DOI: 10.4324/9781003497035-6

constitution states that the territory of South Korea is the entirety of the peninsula and the surrounding islands (Republic of Korea, 1948), while Article 12 of the Inter-Korean Exchange and Cooperation Act states that 'transactions between South Korea and North Korea shall be deemed internal transactions between the same people, not those between nations' (Korea Law Translation Centre, 2019). Domestically, internal bodies such as the Korea International Cooperation Agency (KOICA) have suggested research into the possible benefits of streamlining aid to North Korea through ODA mechanisms (Ji, 2019). This suggestion was however met with backlash due to the assumption that this would fundamentally disregard the South Korean constitution and would acknowledge North Korea as a separate, recipient state (Jeon, 2019).

In place of ODA, the encompassing body of funding that the Ministry of Unification uses to direct aid and developmental support to North Korea is the Inter-Korean Cooperation Fund (IKCF). This fund is split into four categories to address inter-Korean concerns: humanitarian aid; support for social and cultural exchanges; support for the exchanges of separated families; and support for inter-Korean economic cooperation (MoU, 2023; Park and Lee, 2011: 7). The issue in the IKCF is that although unification policies state that environmental cooperation is a clear goal and motivation of support, it is unclear how this would be communicated transparently through this fund. Unlike ODA, which is subject to clear measurements and accountability mechanisms with the Paris Declaration on Aid Effectiveness, the Accra Agenda for Action, and the Busan Partnership for Development Cooperation (OECD, 2011), there are limitations to the monitoring of this inter-Korean support.

As the IKCF case has shown, the discourse surrounding inter-Korean relations suggests that several South Korean administrations consider inter-Korean aid to be key for peaceful unification (Lee, 2012; MoU, 2023; Park, 2011), but there are other motivations behind this aid. The concepts of altruism and good intentions are often tied to the premise of international aid, yet endogenous and exogenous factors about the donor's or the recipient's states can sway the motivations and trajectory of aid (Temple, 2014: 547). Development support beyond the scope of good intentions involves donor states pursuing aid projects while harbouring 'ulterior motives' insofar that the benefits they are set to receive exceed in importance and significance those of the recipient state (Wright et al., 2001). In this case, South Korea pursues peaceful unification while providing aid as part of their inter-Korean exchange and cooperation efforts (MoU, 2023), and the notion of cooperation implies mutual benefits for the involved parties. Hence, this chapter seeks to answer the following research questions: what motivation does South Korea have when engaging in aid cooperation with North Korea?; what is North Korea's motivation for engaging in inter-Korean exchange and cooperation?

This chapter analyses whether South Korean aid expenditure directed to North Korea falls under the aid-for-development premise often purported in inter-Korean activities or, rather, whether there are ulterior motives behind it, such as reflecting its commitment to international norms (Lim, 2014) and pursuing peace across the Peninsula. This chapter therefore aims to examine the influencing factors that shape how South Korea gives aid and for what reasons to North Korea. In doing so, the study conducts a literature review on aid motivations and behaviours of donors to identify which benefits, such as expanding spheres of influence, have driven them to provide aid to specific donors, focusing mostly on European donors. Simultaneously, the review examines how aid recipients can seek advantages beyond development or humanitarian assistance through aid-based bilateral relations. The following section then presents the analytical framework of the principal-agent problem that has been employed for this study. This is used to examine the complex motivations behind why the actors in the Korean Peninsula engage with aid. In the end, this chapter argues that the nature of aid on the Korean Peninsula and the question of whether altruism and camaraderie are the only shaping factors involved in inter-Korean support.

Why Aid to Conflict and Fragile States: Good Intentions or (Invisible) Influence Tug of Wars?

In development aid, donor motivations for aid are given under the guise of altruistic conceptions of support and camaraderie in pursuit of international development (Desai and Potter, 2014). Various aid motivations tend to be fronted as being based on the recipient state's needs and thus serve the aid requirements of the recipient (Nelson, 2012). This is however contested by the view that donors usually tend to provide aid with conditionalities, undermining the premise of pure altruism (Maizels and Nissanke, 1984). The intentions behind development aid, especially in conflict zones, have been examined as swinging between alleviating and supporting the recipients to increase their own donor's spheres of influence (Paragi, 2013; Wood, Hoy and Pryke, 2021). The relational approach understands spheres of influence as structured ties between actors: 'peripheral actors conform to the control and exclusion prerogatives of core actors when they are structurally dependent on them' (Jackson, 2020: 269). Aid is an activity that effectively restructures ties by putting the recipient under the donor's conditionalities, effectively increasing the sphere of influence (Fentanhun, 2023). Alrababa'h, Myrick and Webb (2020: 1) deem the two motivational categories as the 'humanitarian frame' and the 'political influence frame'. Similarly, Riddell (2007: 91) proposes that six main conditions influence the motivations behind international aid: '(1) to help address emergency needs; (2) to assist recipients to achieve their development (growth and poverty reduction) goals; (3) to show their solidarity; (4) to further their own national political and strategic interests; (5) to help promote donor-country commercial interests; and (6) because of historical ties'. These conditions are split into those that focus on the needs of the recipient state and those on the donor's egotistic state-centric ideals. Hence, motivations to provide aid are multifaceted and involve the interests of the donors and the recipients.

The chance of influencing the donor state's national security agenda, environmental concerns, and economic stability can also shape the premise and justification of development aid (Degnbol-Martinussen and Engberg-Pedersen, 2003; Streeten, 1987). Donors cannot instantly and intrinsically transform the recipient's country, neither its domestic politics and its overall development nor the overall influence. Rather, in order to influence the recipient's state, interventions must be consistent and planned accordingly for any intended fundamental change (Ashdown, Dixe and Talmage, 2020). In light of this, this literature review presents the case of aid, especially from the European Union (EU) to Central and East Europe (CEE), starting with the post-1989 aid programmes. This aid effectively ushered socio-political transformation in the recipient states through the expansion of the donor's sphere of influence, which ultimately led to the Europeanisation of CEE. The European experience exemplifies how a donor can superimpose the recipient's domestic politics and interests to trigger the change it desires through conditional aid.

Europeanisation under the Microscope: Conflict and Fragile States as Aid Recipients

The demise of the communist regimes that trickled down CEE from the late 1980s heralded the two simultaneous and irreconcilable processes of post-socialist transformation and Europeanisation. Although the transition was asynchronous and asymmetric as each country presented disparate levels of government resistance to change, civil society participation, violence, and foreign involvement, it was to a degree successful across the region (Bieber, 2003; Ekiert and Kubik, 1998; Opp, 1994; Visegrady, 1992). The achievement was not smooth in any case as each state encountered strong domestic opposition to the political incompatibilities of Europeanisation (Lindstrom, 2015). This accomplishment was owed in good part to the EU's passive leverage, understood as the traction instilled by the actor over the decision-makers in candidate states (Vachudová, 2005). This dominant influence from the EU to CEE began with a series of aid programmes and trade opportunities after 1989 that were directed to candidate states and carried economic and political conditionalities for the recipients (Grabbe, 2006). The phenomenon inspired rent-seeking behaviours from local elites in transitioning countries, which subsequently ushered them to brand the path forward as the way to 'Europe' (Lindstrom, 2015: 34).

'Europe' was as much a goal as it was an inspiration for the masses, as it carried hints of elements such as a free market economy, better ownership rights and civil rights, democracy, and economic prosperity (Sagan, 2010). Joining it would open up the way for these 'poor and weak countries to gain acceptance into a club of prosperous states, governed by rules that apply to all members' (Vachudová, 2005: 66), signifying better trading opportunities. Existing literature on European influence over credible candidates presents it through the 'external incentive model' (EIM) (Schimmelfennig and Sedelmeier, 2004, 2020). This prominent theoretical framework observes how countries calculate the benefits of joining the EU and abiding by its rules and norms in contrast to the expected political costs. The model observes that the benefits and membership are to an extent dependent on *acquis* conditionality, referring to the number of norms each country has adopted (Schimmelfennig and Sedelmeier, 2004: 671). Significant research has ratified this conditionality as states attempt to show compliance by assuming political costs, which has proven to be effective in the long run (Pataccini, 2022; Petrovic, 2020; Pridham, 2005).

The influence of Europe over these countries was not relegated only to passive leverage, but conditionality over membership actively intercepted political strategy and decision-making amongst CEE states. Those nations that desired to access the 'club of prosperous states' to incentivise cooperation, trade, and satisfy the rent-seeking behaviours of the respective elites (Vachudová, 2005: 66). To add to the bargain, the states were beneficiaries of Europe's development and humanitarian aid. Aid and cooperation are never *just* a means to support the recipient's development; rather, they are a means of influencing them politically as well (Yanguas, 2018). In light of this, aid effectiveness should not solely measure developmental progress but look at its influence on domestic politics on the receiving end, peacebuilding, and norm compliance (Browne, 2006). Moreover, development aid inflows promote peace in conflict areas and, its withdrawal, can potentially lead to a resurgence of violence or tensions (Campbell and Spilker, 2022; Matanock, 2020), and hence its contribution towards conflict prevention should not be overlooked (Fukuda-Parr, 2007).

Aid Conditionality in Conflict and Fragile States

Aid conditionality is a common yet criticised practice. Some, such as Yanguas (2018) and Fentanhun (2023), argue that depending on the historical and developmental background of the donor state itself, aid can be directed to serve and benefit the goals and interests of the donor state rather than those of the recipients. Issues such as colonial legacies, or as in the case of post-Soviet states, lingering spheres of influence are being contested, with new ideas being introduced from Western European states vis-à-vis the EU (Dasylva, 2021; Fagan, 2006). The so-called conditional aid has been used by donors to move beyond the developmental effects of aid in the recipient country to other purposes such as cultural, economic, or political (Lancaster, 2006). As such, this section explores how aid conditionality is used by donor countries to reshuffle dependency structures with the recipient country to understand fragile states accept aid terms that may not be of domestic interest.

Countries operationalise development aid under a variety of narratives and due to diverse, often interconnected, motivations that are pressed upon the recipients through framing, passive leverage, and conditionalities. Waving wealth over developing countries allows donors to overlap their voices with the recipients (Yanguas, 2018). The practice of impelling specific developments as conditionality for aid is, to an extent, a customary practice within the donor community, as it suggests donors have a substantial hold over the recipients' elites and policymaking (Kono and Montinola, 2009; Montinola, 2010). Whereas conditional aid can be more effective in democracies (Montinola, 2010), research suggests that it can also influence democratic transition (for example, Alesina and Dollar, 2000). This is one of the reasons the United States (US) geopolitical interests in the Middle East and Egypt led them to concentrate their conditional aid on the region. Similarly, France's aid outflows are influenced by strategic geopolitical strategies in past colonies to maintain a certain presence (Alesina and Dollar, 2000). As has been extensively presented earlier in this section, Europe has instilled longstanding influence and conditionality over CEE. These states, which had been considered to be Europe's underdogs (Visegrady, 1992: 246), such as post-conflict Bosnia and Herzegovina, became donor-reliant and thus more vulnerable to adapting to European conditions (Fagan, 2006; Sagan, 2010; Schimmelfennig and Sedelmeier, 2004).

Research shows development aid is more effective in democratic countries (Montinola, 2010) than in non-democracies due to interrelated elements such as weak institutions and higher corruption levels (Asongu, 2015). With this in mind, development aid under the premise of conflict prevention and peacebuilding remains useful for the donor states as they serve the strategic interest of asserting influence and promoting interests in the recipient state or region (Newman, 2010). In post-conflict developmental aid, power imbalances and inequality serve to prioritise the motivations of donor states while causing strains on the effectiveness of developmental aid (Goodhand and Sedra, 2009; Roesdahl and Varughese, 2017: 464).

Methodology and Theoretical Framework

Scholarship on aid motivation outlines how aid is directed to recipient states with the main consideration of what the benefits could be to the donor state, such as economic, political, and/or otherwise (Alesina and Dollar, 2000: 33; Milner, 2006). When analysing aid motivation with the case of South Korean aid to North Korea, this becomes an interesting question to examine. Based on the presumption that inter-Korean aid is given to solidify the longstanding relationship of inter-Korean brotherhood and camaraderie and restore the 'Korean National Community', it could be assumed that this is aid given without any other underlying motivations (Ministry of Unification, 2024).

In this chapter, the theory of incentives, otherwise known as the principal-agent problem or agency theory, has been employed to analyse and interpret South Korean aid towards North Korea. The principal-agent problem, founded in both economics and game theory, posits that the principal (the donor) is set to benefit from the agreement with the agent (the recipient). In turn, the agent is subject to a series of conditions to receive what they require from the principal (Rasmusen, 2006). Pundits propose that ideally, both the principal and the agent engage in a contract in which both parties are poised to benefit from (Miller and Whitford, 2002). However, in this contract, for the agent to benefit, they must 'take the appropriate actions to achieve these outcomes' (Gibson, 2005: 43). In analysing the tenets of this theory, game theorists infer that the principal-agent problem outlines the selfish nature of actors, which allows for the motivations of aid to be diverted and considerations of opportunistic, individual gains to be placed over the other norms that could inhibit this (Gibson, 2005; Perrow, 1986).

The argument that the imbalance of power found in a principal-agent relationship is unequally skewed in favour of the principal (South Korea) posits that the core focus of the aid under this relationship is primarily based on how the principal can gain or benefit from its aid giving (Saam, 2007). In this problem, the egotistic motivations of the donor could ultimately create obstacles for the recipient state to exercise sovereignty in their developmental processes paired with 'uncoordinated and suboptimal effort levels given by both parties' (Murshed, 2009: 420). Thus, this paradox in turn could create a plethora of challenges and can trap the recipient state in a paradigm of dependence on continual conditional aid from the donor state while the donor state places focus on its intrinsic motivations. This poses the argument that the principal sets to provide the agent with low-value incentives in return for high-value benefits on their end (Sappington, 1991).

However, while the argument posed in this theory tends to place its focus on the actions and motivations of the principal, it is also important to evaluate the role of the agent in this scenario. In this framework, agents should be willing to engage in the agreements and match the efforts of the principal to achieve positive outcomes for both parties (Killick, 1997: 487). Examinations that the power imbalance of this relationship lies entirely in the purview of the principal are a common oversight in the existing studies and are something that needs to be considered in this chapter, as an agent's behaviour and role in this relationship are often overlooked (Hawkins and Jacoby, 2006: 200). Especially when examining how North Korea as a recipient state engages in this relationship (Jung et al., 2021), understanding the exogenous and endogenous factors that motivate agent behaviour is important. Agents, like North Korea, may well be using this relationship with the principal to manipulate the outcome in their favour (Isopi and Mattesini, 2009).

This research is conducted based on a qualitative methodological approach to examine the incentives and motivations of South Korea's aid to North Korea, focusing on the motivations that reflect the element of altruism purported in inter-Korean relations. This chapter investigates how both South Korea as a donor and North Korea as a recipient use aid through the principal-agent relationship for their potential gains and benefits in the context of inter-Korean relations and peacebuilding. Factors such as South Korea's development trajectory and its role as a donor state will be analysed to determine whether they could shape or influence aid practices that go to North Korea. The existing data and statistics sourced from organisations such as the World Bank, the OECD, and the South Korean Ministry of Unification have been analysed. This has been further supported by extensive use of existing literature and data sourced from secondary sources to supplement the analysis and discussion of the motivating factors of South Korean aid to North Korea.

The North Korean Swing: Pressure and 'Aid Now, Rights Later' Tactics

South Korea's approach to North Korea has been susceptible to the predispositions of the incumbent administrations. Traditionally, progressive parties have been inclined to engage with North Korea as opposed to the most conservative ones, which have been more prone to adopting pressure tactics. Yoon Seok-youl's election in March 2022 has replaced the engagement policies pursued by Moon Jae-in's progressive administration with his 'audacious plan' (MoU, 2022c). The framework proposed by his administration seeks to develop reciprocal and mutually beneficial inter-Korean relations and establish the grounds for unification whilst maintaining a zero-tolerance policy towards military provocations from the North. This approach succeeded in the premature end of the détente that had come with the Pyeongchang Winter Olympics and the various inter-Korean summits in 2018. To follow through, one of the pillars of Yoon's North Korea policy rests in re-attempting normalising inter-Korean relations with an emphasis on humanitarian aid, exchange, and sustainable cooperation (MoU, 2022c).

The human rights-based approach of Yoon's North Korea policy breaks with Moon's 'aid now, rights later' strategies (Foster-Carter, 2022: 105). Moon's approach followed the tradition of other progressive parties combining 'low posture diplomacy' with constructive (Mosler, 2022: 16) or unconditional engagement (Drennan, 2005: 117). An example of this is Moon's approach, popularly named Moonshine Policy, and Kim Dae-jung's Sunshine Policy (Flake, 2005: 81). Yoon's pressure tactics have been partaken by previous conservative administrations with Lee Myung-bak's Principle of Coexistence and Co-prosperity and Park Geun-hye's Trust-Building Process (*trustpolitik*) on the Korean Peninsula (Park, 2022). The latter put forward the Vision Korea Project in 2013, which emphasised how South Korea's development assistance to North Korea was to be the key to trust-building, along with denuclearisation (MoU, 2013a: 17). In a sense, the North Korea policies pursued by South Korean conservative administrations have followed the carrot-and-stick approach in which development is used as the carrot, and pressure is the stick. Using carrots to bring peace has not only been a tactic used by South Korea's conservatives but also by other countries like Japan (Söderberg, 2006).

South Korean Aid to North Korea: A History

The OECD (2003) defines the collection of loans and grants that comprise development aid as 'flows of official financing administered with the promotion of the economic development and welfare of developing countries as the main objective, and which are concessional in character'. It falls into a diverse number of sectors, including food aid, economic and social infrastructure services, and environmental protection, amongst others (Cheng and Minhas, 2021). The core difference between development aid and humanitarian aid is that the latter has short-term goals as it deals with emergency responses, reconstruction, and prevention of disasters (Jakubik and Feuerriegel, 2022), whereas aid catered towards development has longer-term goals. Considering this, humanitarian operations attempting to fix crises in the long term, rather than aiding the immediate aftermath, are considered part of development aid (Jakubik and Feuerriegel, 2022).

South Korea is not unfamiliar with providing grants or loans to North Korea. Between the years 1995 and 2014, Seoul contributed approximately USD 3.41 billion in aid to Pyongyang (Hur, Park and Kim, 2017: 646). Whilst most of the outflows had to do with sectors traditionally identified as belonging to development aid, South Korea does not deem any of them as ODA. The reasoning for this is that as North Korea is considered part of South Korea as per the Constitution, Seoul is merely transferring to its own country and its own people (Howe, 2013; Hur et al., 2017). This section presents how different South Korean administrations have approached aid to North Korea as well as how Pyongyang has accepted it and reflects on the motivations each actor (principal/agent) observed according to their engagement with it.

In light of this, the MoU (2022a) keeps track of the capital disbursed to North Korea, whilst the Ministry of Foreign Affairs does the equivalent task with ODA. Figure 6.1 contrasts South Korea's ODA expenditure against capital spent towards North Korea in inter-Korean exchange and cooperation (economic aid and non-commercial trade such as the Light-Water Reactor (LWR) project and governmental assistance to NGOs), humanitarian aid, and food loans from 1995 to 1998. The ways in which governments allocate spending are a clear indication of their priorities (Dewan and Ettlinger, 2009). ODA is particularly prioritised for administrations that intend to remain relevant and influential by championing sustainable development in the receiving regions (Calleja, Hughes and Cichocka, 2021: 23–24).

General aid policies took a different approach, with conservative governments providing aid to states that had existing exchanges with South Korea and, thus, pursuing economic and social results. Progressive parties favoured states with low human development index (HDI) and with humanitarian and security concerns (Sohn and Yoo, 2015). However, aid to North Korea is not just foreign aid due to evident historical, geopolitical, and cultural matters that concern South Korea's security, economy, and the manner in which the Blue House interacts with other states and international bodies. Thus, support towards North Korea has not only been regulated by and provided by a different government body, yet it has still been influenced by the overall motivations and general policy directions of each administration.

Moon (2016: 279) defines the approaches partaken by the different leaders in the groups of restraint and confrontation between 1995 and 1997 with the first civil administration with Kim Young-sam; cooperative coexistence between 1998 and 2008 during Kim Dae-jung's and Roh Moo-hyun's administrations; and stagnation, starting with Lee Myung-bak's administration up until 2012. In contrast to North Korea policies, general aid policies show how progressive governments have been more inclined to respond to international pressure following international security issues outside of North Korea by switching more of their aid to be tied (Patterson and Choi, 2019). While, when dealing with North Korea, Kim Dae-jung and Roh Moo-hyun were more inclined to offer unconditional engagement and were criticised for ineffectively dealing with North Korea's threat due to their North Korea policies (Drennan, 2005; Kim, 2006). Unconditional is not, however, altruistic, as progressive governments held political, cultural, and diplomatic motivations just as equally as the conservative administrations did. Yet North Korea's choice in accepting aid was altered depending on the terms of this aid and, as it will be shortly presented, whether Pyongyang could mislead Seoul by accepting aid while expanding its military programmes.

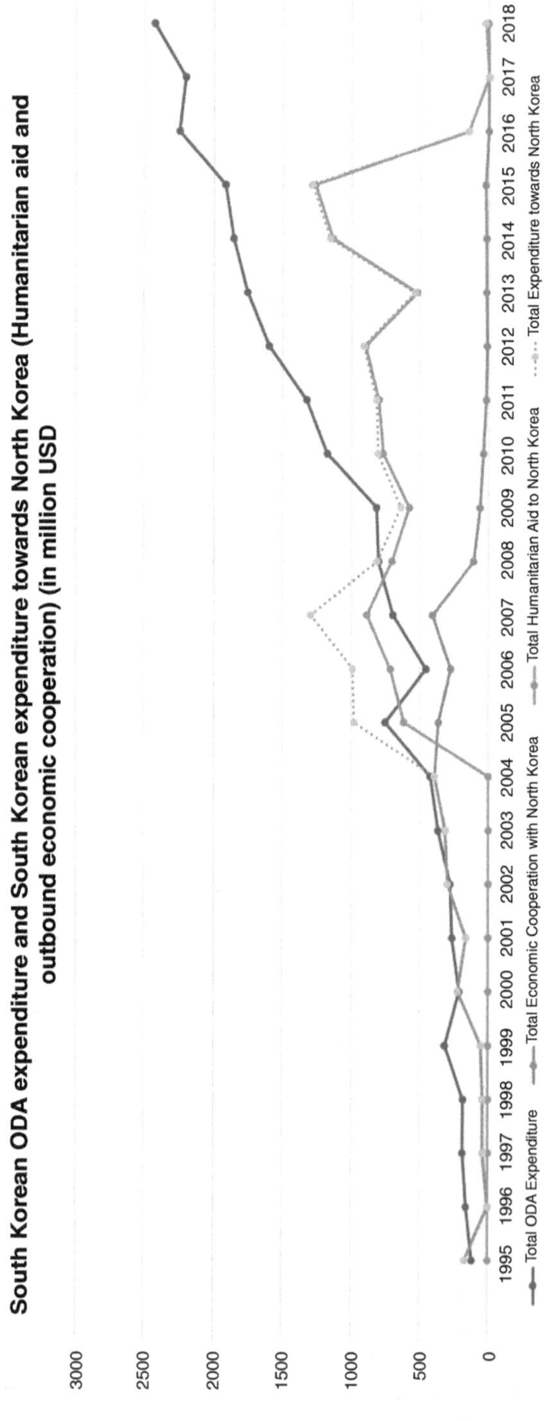

Figure 6.1 South Korean Aid to North Korea.

Source: Author's own compilation, based on World Bank (2022) and Ministry of Unification (2022a).

President Kim Young-sam took over the Blue House in 1993 and proposed the National Community Unification Formula (NCUF) to approach North Korea. The strategy followed the conservative tradition of his predecessors in a three-step plan that observed cooperation and reconciliation, a Korean commonwealth system, and finalised a united Korea (Park, 2014). Kim Young-sam's original inclination towards a more engaging approach was trumped by the 1994 North Korean nuclear crisis when Pyongyang withdrew from the Non-Proliferation Treaty (NPT) (Mosler, 2022). The switch towards a harsher line was declared with the lines that Seoul 'cannot shake hands with a partner with nuclear weapons' (Yoon, 1996: 513). President Kim Young-sam's office was taken over by his progressive rival Kim Dae-jung in 1998, and along with the administration change, North Korea's policies had a clear turn in consequence.

Kim Dae-jung's government initiated the Reconciliation and Cooperation Policy Towards the North, or Sunshine Policy, for which Seoul bowed to pursue reconciliation through cooperation and exchanges (Yoo, 2006). In doing so, expenditure on behalf of North Korea began resembling that which was provided for ODA for the first time in South Korea's history as an aid sender. The administration chose to provide development assistance towards areas that would improve living conditions in the long term, such as agriculture and medicine, and humanitarian aid remained negligible. Rather than providing humanitarian support directly to Pyongyang, Kim Dae-jung's office provided support to non-governmental organisations (NGOs) to conduct their own humanitarian aid campaigns in the North (Hur, 2017).

Kim Dae-jung's administration shifted South Korea's approach to North Korea as the economic and development gap between the two Koreas continued expanding, solidifying Seoul as the principal in inter-Korean relations that would increase in imbalance as time went on. The situation that had burgeoned from the 1990s famine had not only devastated North Korea but had complicated the path towards a smooth reunification (Hur, 2017; Kwon and Lim, 2006). Whereas Kim's approach in aid to North Korea aimed at its economic growth and the well-being of its people, the purpose was not only altruism but also diplomacy and policy. This worked, at the time, as North Korea accepted the diplomatic efforts and aid, as Pyongyang's interests aligned with the political premises of reunification and rapprochement. Whilst the Sunshine Policy had focused on exchange and cooperation, Kim Dae-jung's progressive successor, Roh Moo-hyun, inaugurated a period that focused on humanitarian aid. For the very first time, aid to North Korea surpassed ODA expenditure between the years 2005 and 2007. However, the continued support and 'strategic silence' that followed North Korea's missile tests flipped public opinion. North Korea had welcomed aid through the Sunshine Policy, perhaps due to its friendlier terms. Whereas the principal had approached it with the motivation of rapprochement, the agent had kept its ulterior interests. The efficiency of the Sunshine Policy was questioned (Kim, 2006: 50), and North Korea was pictured as an enemy following the reasoning that 'we provided rice, and it became nuclear bombs coming back at us' (Kim, 2015: 2).

The two conservative administrations that followed through, Lee Myung-bak's and Park Geun-hye's in 2008 and 2013, respectively, switched to pressure tactics.

Lee put forward Vision 3000, which proposed to raise North Korea's income to USD 3,000 per capita within ten years through the provision of 20 different projects (Kim, 2009: 2; Lankov, 2013: 174). In turn, Park Geun-hye emerged with the Vision Korea Project, pursuing economic development through cooperation and trust-building (MoU, 2013a). Both initiatives held an aid-for-development premise but were heavily political in response to the growing North Korean nuclear threat, which had turned into a more urgent matter after the Cheonan incident in 2010 (Kim, 2014).

The sinking of the military vessel culminated in the adoption of the 24 May Measures, which halted all inter-Korean cooperation apart from humanitarian aid targeting vulnerable groups such as flood victims and children and the Kaesong Industrial Complex (KIC) (Song and Hastings, 2020). Simultaneous to this initiative, local governments in South Korea stopped providing aid to the North, and all assistance has been relegated to NGOs since then (Song and Hastings, 2020). The common characteristics of both initiatives were that, firstly, they took a turn from previous administrations by providing solely conditional aid in the hope of denuclearising Pyongyang (Kim, 2016). The principal had provided aid with purposes beyond aid-for-development and of the political kind, driving them to prioritise aid with terms. Secondly, Kim Jong-un's utter rejection of the approaches dropped inter-Korean cooperation and exchanges to the bare minimum (Howe and Lee, 2016; KINU, 2009), while humanitarian aid remained relevant, as shown in Figure 6.1. As the principal-agent framework suggests, the agent participates in aid as long as it provides the benefits they seek. Pyongyang's decision to not engage in inter-Korean activities signals that its domestic interests were not met, and the terms of this conditional aid obstructed them.

Clashing Aid Motivations: A Cause of Inter-Korean Project Failures

Existing literature has shown scepticism over the potential of conditionality to increase aid effectiveness (Herbertsson and Paldam, 2007; Svensson, 2003) and analysed how underlying motivations behind development aid can trump aid effectiveness (for example, see Yanguas, 2018). Studies have readdressed the concept of effectiveness, reflecting on how aid contributes to donors expanding their dominion across regions (Alesina and Dollar, 2010; Newman, 2010). Accordingly, aid can be an effective tool in expanding spheres of influence as it rearranges structural dependencies. Aid recipients tend to become structurally reliant on the donors due to conditional terms. This has been noted in the literature review of this chapter when exploring how aid and trade conditionalities posed by the EU donor states to the CEE recipients created hierarchies in which the EU provided legitimacy and aid at the expense of the sovereignty of CEE states (Noutcheva, 2006). Aid provided by the EU after the 1980s was effective in 'Western-Europenising' CEE. The principal-agent theory introduces aid as an activity in which each party chooses to engage because it aligns with their interests. As opposed to current examples in which recipient states 'hammer compromises which they later try to sell to their domestic constituencies' (Petričušić and Erkan, 2010: 149), EU conditionalities helped legitimise the actions by CEE governments to their citizens (Grabbe, 2006).

Utilising aid as a tool to influence countries can lead to 'donor deafness', in which the concept defines the situation in which donors provide programmes of their interest but not the recipient's (Babaci-Wilhite et al., 2013: 741; Chan and Chung, 2015). Looking into the CEE case, the agent had to accept the trade-off of sovereignty in exchange for aid and legitimacy after the communist collapse (Grabbe, 2006). In this chapter, the concession Pyongyang accepts when engaging in inter-Korean cooperation and exchange is examined. The previous section has presented how the principal, Seoul, has approached aid to North Korea. Here, the cooperative projects are lined up to highlight the aims and potential benefits of these programs for both sides.

The MoU's White Paper on Korean Unification routinely includes sections covering exchange and cooperation with North Korea, humanitarian aid, and overviews of ongoing projects such as the KIC and the LWR Project. Prior to Lee Myung-bak's presidency in 2008, South Korea mostly focused on food aid and the LWR project when it came to aid to North Korea, which had followed the 1994 Agreed Framework between Pyongyang and Washington (MoU, 1993, 2001, 2005). The Korean Peninsula Energy Development (KEDO) initiative aimed to support North Korea's chronic energy shortages was eventually put on a 'temporary' suspension that never ceased (MoU, 2005: 120). Subsequent projects that followed the Green Détente approach included the Floor Prevention Projects in the Imjin River in 2009 and forest restoration activities (MoU, 2010; Song and Hastings, 2020).

The June 15 Joint Declaration in 2000 was adopted by both North and South, which looked to promote development in both countries and in which, amongst other concessions, the countries agreed to resolve commercial disputes among themselves (MoU, 2001). The scheme contributed to diplomacy and aimed to form commercial engagement, reinforcing development (Calleja et al., 2021). The projects that followed the joint declaration involved economic development through cooperation, such as the development of the KIC supported by Hyundai and Korea Land Corporation (KOLAND), the Mountain Geumgang Spring Water Project by Taechang, and joint software development with Samsung Electronics (MoU, 2001, 2005, 2010). Other initiatives looked to benefit Seoul's trade as a whole. They featured the three-way cooperation between South Korea, Russia, and North Korea, the Rajin-Hansan Logistics Partnership, and the restoration of the South Korean side of the Gyeongwon line (MoU, 2013b, 2014, 2016).

South-North cooperation is mutually beneficial, and thus both countries seek their own strategies. Yet it is noteworthy that Pyongyang has remained stoic throughout the years and particularly selective in terms of which aid was accepted into the country. Research has examined accepted projects that may play a part in the stakeholders' 'detailed strategies' (Kim, 2015: 20–21). Aid sent to North Korea is subject to terms posed not by the principal as it happened in the CEE case, but also by Pyongyang. Aid providers have limited access to ongoing projects outside

Pyongyang (Savage and the Nautilus Team, 2002). Research has examined this as a way in which North Korea restricts foreign influence inside the country (Carnegie and Dolan, 2021: 514). Yet aid does not reach the intended beneficiaries all the time. Studies have found that food aid rarely ends up in the hands of those who need it but, rather, those from the authorities and the military, which leads to believing Pyongyang's motivations behind accepting aid go beyond alleviating poverty (Manyin and Nikitin, 2009).

Both principal and agent states had foreseen an interest in engaging with aid programmes that had been achieved before completion or had ceased motivating them to continue in this relationship. Whereas economic projects were mutually beneficial and others, such as capacity building and environmental initiatives, were more advantageous for North Korea, practical and political complications tampered with success (for example, see MoU, 2010). This showcases the lack of harmonisation in cooperation that has misfired. The suspension of the Mountain Geumgang Tourist Resort in 2008 and the blow-up of the liaison office at the KIC in 2020 display both standards not being met.

Similar events to the aforementioned ones, such as the KIC closure in 2016, have been examined as Pyongyang shooting itself in the foot (Frank, 2016). Limited access and data validity challenge how to assess whether the projects had a socio-economic impact or potential for long-term environmental sustainability that North Korea could have originally sought. It is also possible that mutual accountability issues triggered the suspension of the projects due to the challenges created by North Korea and the initial lack of understanding or 'donor deafness' from South Korea (Babaci-Wilhite et al., 2013: 741). Yet, one of South Korea's goals and motivations behind providing aid is denuclearising the Peninsula, a target that has not been achieved and an element of contention between the two states. If Seoul's assessment of progress is linked to the advancement towards denuclearisation as aid progresses through the influence of donors in the country (Browne, 2006; Campbell and Spilker, 2022; Matanock, 2020), the initiatives have not been that successful (Park, 2014). And this diminishes the motivations a principal can have in continuing to engage in aid.

On the agent's side, if anything, the Kim regime has consistently rejected aid conditionality and international influence entering the country (Carnegie and Dolan, 2021: 514). In doing so, North Korea resists power imbalance and its adverse effects on Pyongyang's development goals (Roesdahl and Varughese, 2017). Disbursement of aid and cooperation activities has potentially prompted the emergence of rent-seeking behaviours from local elites and the military who have gotten hold of resources (Manyin and Nikitin, 2009: 14). Corruption on the recipient's side, inequality in distribution, lack of access, mutual accountability, and harmonisation could have triggered the early ends of mutual projects that both parties had originally accepted to engage with. Aid misuse hints that North Korea's priorities are not in aid reaching the intended targets. Challenges in aid provision through Pyongyang's terms point to how crucial it is for North Korea to restrict foreign influence in the country. As Lancaster (2006: 61) points out, when aid becomes politicised and challenged with conflicting purposes, it does not hit the target.

These limitations, in conjunction with the lack of progress in denuclearisation and harmony between the parties, would be the first signs for the principal donor, Seoul, that their interests would not be met through these activities.

Discussion: Green Paths to Green Goals, Motivating Factors in Sustainable Development Assistance

The concept of a green détente has been broached by several South Korean administrations as a tool to engage with North Korea without stepping into the realm of issues of high politics (Cho, 2013; Na, 2022). As observed in the policies of Lee and Park's administrations, they utilised the South-North Green Détente strategy focusing on climate change and the environment as a gateway to sustainable peace (MoU, 2014). Using a green détente to foster and encourage cooperation in pursuit of peaceful, sustainable development across the peninsula allows administrations an avenue to carefully navigate obstacles that arise as a result of the legal and geopolitical parameters of inter-Korean relations. Green issues, which preside predominantly in the realm of low politics, can be used to encroach on the issue of developmental support on the peninsula through aid and capacity-building mechanisms (Kim and Ali, 2016). These green matters, such as climate change adaptation and mitigation, can be argued to benefit both sides of the inter-Korean relationship for varying reasons, both cooperatively and individually.

Addressing environmental concerns through aid could be a motivating factor in engaging in inter-Korean cooperation activities, as while this is an avenue for South Korea to address peacebuilding and other issues, it is also a way to address the immediate concerns posed by environmental issues in North Korea. As a state, North Korea has a long history of suffering the consequences of climate change, experiencing natural disasters, land degradation, and extreme weather conditions, which in turn have impacted food security, agricultural stability, and infrastructure (Database Center for North Korean Human Rights (NKDB), 2021). As a fragile state in terms of its dysfunctional state mechanism, not the regime itself (Lim, 2021, 2023), North Korea's climate resilience is considered to be low, with a lack of structures in place to help the state adapt to increasing challenges posed by frequent natural disasters and the legacy of poor environmental management (Habib, 2009; Vivekananda, Schilling and Smith, 2014). Aid with a focus on these issues could help mitigate several environmental but also humanitarian concerns, based on the understanding that climate change poses itself as a driver of further problems (Habib, 2013). This is something that could benefit both the principal and the agent in this setting, as while the principal is set to benefit from this support as their commitment to green issues and global norms, the agent can address legitimate concerns posed by climate change while accepting aid not subject to the same barriers posed by sanctions and limitations (Zadeh-Cummings and Harris, 2020).

Both Koreas have identified how climatic challenges to sustainable development are posed to impact the peninsula; thus, this is reflected in legal frameworks, policies, and approaches to peaceful cooperation on both ends of the peninsula. Following the implementation of the UN Sustainable Development Goals (SDGs) in 2015 (United Nations General Assembly, 2015), assistance with a focus on green issues has been widely promoted as the de rigueur in supporting environmentally sustainable development. This is reflected in the shift of OECD DAC donors' bilateral ODA disbursements to addressing climate objectives, which was recorded as being 33.4 per cent of total allocations in 2020 (OECD, 2022a: 3). This demonstrates a dramatic shift in aid giving, with this figure increasing from 21.7 per cent and 23.3 per cent in 2013 and 2014, respectively (OECD, 2022b: 3). Seoul's ODA disbursements tend to reflect these trends, with both international and domestic commitments reflecting a policy direction and focus on sustainable development and climatic protections (as seen in Lee, 2010; Ministry of Economy and Finance, 2020). In 2020, a large focus of South Korea's total bilateral ODA was spent on environmental issues and addressing concerns posed by climate change, committing 12.7 per cent of total bilateral allocable aid towards these causes (OECD, 2022b).

The shift towards more environmentally sustainable ODA allocations and disbursements echoes both South Korea's domestic policy and its alignment with international norms. In 2008, the Lee Myung-bak administration introduced a shift in focus in South Korea towards green growth, with the idea of South Korea being a leader in environmentally considerate growth and development practices (Lee, 2010; Seong, 2011). This shift reflects a distancing of South Korea's own experience of development, which relied on 'brown growth' models of rapid industrialisation, which put economic growth above the interests of environmental protections or considerations (Kim, 2015). It can be pointed out that an element of irony surrounds South Korea's choosing to focus on promoting and pursuing environmentally friendly growth strategies as a recipient turned donor. While South Korea is praised for its shift from aid recipient to donor, the 'do as I say, not as I do' approaches to the environment and growth cannot be overlooked (Tonami and Müller, 2014: 209).

Although the trajectory in the commitment to green growth was lost in subsequent administrations and these policies have not been visible in environmental indices (Ayhan, 2019: 7), these policies can be perceived as a tool to position South Korea squarely into the frame of a responsible middle power focusing on green issues (Lee, 2016: 51; Blaxekjær, 2016). These domestic policies and focus on green matters influence the aid behaviours of Korea to be 'autobiographic' in that their aid giving mirrors not only its own developmental experiences but also domestic policies and motivations (Tonami and Müller, 2014: 194). The self-reflective nature of aid to Pyongyang foregrounds Seoul's commitment to international norms as it simultaneously attempts to align its support to North Korea with that of other developing states.

The IKCF infers that both parties are of equal standing and thus will work collaboratively to ensure the ultimate goal of peaceful cooperation is achieved. However, this financial support is usually subject to conditions, both intrinsic and extrinsic, which can mean that aid flows fluctuate based on geopolitical concerns and are usually given based on preconditions posed by the donor (Jung et al., 2021). This has been reaffirmed in policy reports such as the North Korean policy of the incumbent Yoon Suk-Yeol, which highlights how, based on the precondition of cooperation vis-à-vis denuclearisation, environmental cooperation projects can be pursued (MoU, 2022b). This unbalanced dynamic of inter-Korean cooperation allows South Korea to use the carrot of environmental cooperation under the premise of peacebuilding. This can thus be used to assert dominance in the relationship and balance their external motivations and needs above those of the recipient.

Although green issues reflect the paradigm shift towards addressing the pressing concern of climate change, the inter-Korean relationship exemplifies how both actors use the concept of aid, as a donor and a recipient, to benefit from this relationship. Using the lens of the principal-agent problem, it can be posited that both actors use the inter-Korean relationship to achieve relative gains on each side. On the South Korean side of this equation, one of the benefits of this relationship is that it opens the door to engage with Pyongyang through a 'depoliticised' lens like environmental issues. Simultaneously, it solidifies its commitment to green matters and adherence to international norms (Song and Hastings, 2020: 1817).

Conclusion

Camaraderie, brotherhood, peace, and building towards reunification have been at the core of South Korea's inter-Korean cooperation rhetoric. Simultaneously, aid is often linked to the premise of altruism, yet, as this chapter has examined, chronically unbalanced power dynamics and 'ulterior motives' play a considerable role in what motivates inter-Korean cooperation, aid, and support. Seoul's aid to Pyongyang is, for all intents and purposes, not considered ODA as, per the Constitution, South Korea's territory includes North Korea. This means that these contributions are not monitored nor recorded in the same way as ODA and have little breakdown. This stipulation also transforms any aid provided northward into cooperation, a notion that presupposes a mutually beneficial partnership that holds some sort of equality between the parties. Inter-Korean cooperation is characterised by pronounced politico-economic disparities that handicap equal power dynamics between North and South Korea.

Inter-Korean cooperation throughout the years has shown different trends that are telling about the dynamics of the relationship and the motivating factors that influence both parties in their roles as donor and recipient. South Korea's aid takes an autobiographical approach as it mirrors its own developmental experience while foregrounding commitment to international norms. At the same time, relations between Seoul and Pyongyang swing towards 'rights now, aid later' or active engagement whenever South Korea's Blue House is presided over by a conservative or a liberal president, respectively. This chapter poses green matters as an example of how issues like climate change that are traditionally considered to be low politics remain, in fact, singularly political when North Korea is at the aid-receiving end.

The premise of peacebuilding through sustainable development means that South Korea can, in principle, 'kill two birds with one stone' by addressing the environment while leveraging this support as a condition of peacebuilding and engagement (Ide, 2018: 328). Seoul's engagement reflects its commitment to pursuing green policies and its compliance with international norms. Likewise, Pyongyang has much to gain from engaging in this dynamic. Although environmental protection and assistance under the premise of environmental protections could be used to address legitimate concerns facing the state due to its vulnerability to climate change (Habib, 2009; Sarkodie and Strezov, 2019), it could also be used as a funding mechanism to support the financial qualms faced by North Korea (Habib, 2015). While camaraderie under the premise of a unified, homogenous population may be the main justification for inter-Korean support (MoU, 2022b). At the same time, extrinsic and intrinsic motivations may influence how each party manipulates the dynamic to their benefit in this relationship. Looking at the incentives of each side in engaging in this long-standing, highly complicated relationship, both parties seem to attempt to exploit and utilise it for their relative, intrinsic gains. These individual gains of both parties outline how, although peaceful cooperation may be the premise for engaging in the principal-agent contract, this is not the core motivation for either party.

Another element that shapes cooperation dynamics on both sides of the Peninsula is each party's 'ulterior motives' in pursuing engagement with the other actor. South Korea attempts to exert dominance over inter-Korean relations through cooperation, often through conditional aid targeting North Korea's denuclearisation or human rights. At the same time, Seoul's commitment to international norms as they provide aid benefits South Korea as it solidifies its international position. Although South Korea's motivations for engaging with North Korea can be observed, conditional aid and South Korea's goals are not always embraced by North Korea. The Kim regime is no stranger to manoeuvring the dynamics of the inter-Korean relationship to serve their interests and benefits. Pyongyang utilises Seoul's international position, its financial stability, and its commitment to green issues to its advantage in the prospects of attaining investments and fund projects that are beneficial for the North Korean economy and sustainable development.

The results of the tug-of-war in the power dynamics on the Korean Peninsula speak for themselves while bigger economic and environmental projects such as the KIC and the LWR have not stuck the landing, North Korea's nuclear program continues to endure. The road to development is paved with good intentions that frequently mix with the donor's own goals of extending areas of influence or having a certain domestic effect within the recipient's borders. South Korea's extrinsic and intrinsic motivations, including international norms and domestic politics, put these altruistic good intentions into question as they trump concerns about aid effectiveness and the long-term sustainability of cooperation projects. While South Korea's motivations are driven beyond altruism, North Korea as a recipient also makes its goalposts based on its motivations for picking and choosing to cooperate and receive aid. Ultimately, both parties exploit and manipulate this relationship for their gains, using the guise of peaceful cooperation being maintained to obscure questions of their own ulterior motives.

References

Alesina, Alberto, and Dollar, David. (2000). Who Gives Aid to Whom and Why? *Journal of Economic Growth,* 5(March): 33–63.

Alrababa'h, Ala', Myrick, Rachel, and Webb, Isaac. (2020). Do Donor Motives Matter? Investigating Perceptions of Foreign Aid in the Conflict in Donbas. *International Studies Quarterly*, 64(3): 748–757.

Ashdown, Brien K., Dixe, Alessa, and Talmage, Craig A. (2020). The Potentially Damaging Effects of Developmental Aid and Voluntourism on Cultural Capital and Well-Being. *International Journal of Community Well-Being*, 4(1): 113–131.

Asongu, Simplice A. (2015). Institutional Benchmarking of Foreign Aid Effectiveness in Africa. *International Journal of Social Economics*, 42(6): 543–565.

Ayhan, Kadir J. (2019). Rethinking Korea's Middle Power Diplomacy as a Nation Branding Project. *Korea Observer*, 50(1): 1–24.

Babaci-Wilhite, Zehlia, Geo-JaJa, Macleans A., and Shizhou, Lou. (2013). China's Aid to Africa: Competitor or Alternative to the OECD Aid Architecture? *International Journal of Social Economics*, 40(8): 729–743.

Blaxekjær, Lau. (2016). Korea as Green Middle Power: Green Growth Strategic Action in the Field of Global Environmental Governance. *International Relations of the Asia-Pacific*, 16(3): 443–476.

Bieber, Florian. (2003). The Serbian Opposition and Civil Society: Roots of the Delayed Transition in Serbia. *International Journal of Politics, Culture and Society*, 17(1): 73–90.

Browne, Stephen. (2006). *Aid and Influence. Do Donors Help or Hinder?* London: Routledge.

Calleja, Rachel, Hughes, Sam, and Cichocka, Beata. (2021). *Two Birds, One Budget: Using ODA for Influence and Development in the Indo-Pacific?* Washington, DC: Center for Global Development.

Campbell, Susanna P., and Spilker, Gabriele. (2022). Aiding War or Peace? The Insiders' View on Aid to Postconflict Transitions. *The Journal of Politics*, 84(3): 1370–1383.

Carnegie, Allison, and Dolan, Lindsay R. (2021). The Effects of Rejecting Aid on Recipients' Reputations: Evidence from Natural Disaster Responses. *The Review of International Organizations*, 16(3): 495–519.

Chan, Sheng-Ju, and Chung, Yi-Hsing. (2015). Trends and Challenges of Aid Effectiveness: The Rise of Asia. In: Cheng, I-Hsuan, and Chan, Sheng-Ju. (Eds.) *International Education Aid in Developing Asia: Policies and Practices.* New York: Springer, 11–24.

Cheng, Cindy, and Minhas, Shahryar. (2021). Keeping Friends Close, But Enemies Closer: Foreign Aid Responses to Natural Disasters. *British Journal of Political Science*, 51(3): 940–962.

Cho, Han-bum. (2013). *The 'Trust-building Process' Strategy for the Creative Restoration of the 'Korean-Ecosystem.'* Seoul: Korea Institute for National Unification.

Choi, Jin-Wook. (2010). From a Recipient to a Donor State: Achievements and Challenges of Korea's ODA. *International Review of Public Administration*, 15(3): 37–51.

Chun, Hong-Min, Munyi, Elijah N., and Lee, Heejin. (2010). South Korea as an Emerging Donor: Challenges and Changes on Its Entering OECD/DAC. *Journal of International Development*, 22(6): 788–802.

Dasylva, Oluwabemiga. (2021). The Politics of Development Economics and Peacebuilding: A Postcolonial Global North Hegemonic Agenda? *Journal of Management Policy & Practice*, 22(4): 60–69.

Database Center for North Korean Human Rights (NKDB). (2021). *A Human Rights-Based Approach to the SDGs in the DPRK.* Seoul: Database Center for North Korean Human Rights.

Degnbol-Martinussen, John, and Engberg-Pedersen, Poul. (2003). *Aid: Understanding International Development Cooperation.* London: Zed Books.

Desai, Vandana, and Potter, Rob. (2014). *The Companion to Development Studies.* London: Routledge.

Dewan, Sabina, and Ettlinger, Michael. (2009). *Comparing Public Spending and Priorities Across OECD Countries.* Washington, DC: Center for American Progress.

Drennan, William M. (2005). Altered States: The Future of U.S.-ROK Cooperation. In: Niksch, Larry A., Park, Jong-Chul, Paik, Hak-Soon, Flake, L. Gordon, Park, Young-Ho, Drennan, William M., and Park, Young-Kyu. (Eds.) *Implementing the Six-Party Joint Statement and the Korean Peninsula* (pp. 109–128). Seoul: Korea Institute for National Unification.

Ekiert, Grzegorz, and Kubik, Jan. (1998). Contentious Politics in New Democracies: East Germany, Hungary, Poland, and Slovakia, 1989–93. *World Politics*, 50(4): 547–581.

Fagan, Adam. (2006). Transnational Aid for Civil Society Development in Post-socialist Europe: Democratic Consolidation or a New Imperialism? *The Journal of Communist Studies and Transition Politics*, 22(1): 115–134.

Fentanhun, Getachew. (2023). Foreign Aid in the Post-colonial Africa: Means for Building Democracy or Ensuring Western Domination? *Cogent Social Sciences*, 9(1): 1–15.

Flake, L. Gordon. (2005). Sunshine or Moonshine? Inter-Korean Relations and their Impact upon the U.S.-DPRK Conundrum. In: Niksch, Larry A., Park, Jong-Chul, Paik, Hak-Soon, Flake, L. Gordon, Park, Young-Ho, Drennan, William M., and Park, Young-Kyu. (Eds.) *Implementing the Six-Party Joint Statement and the Korean Peninsula* (pp. 81–96). Seoul: Korea Institute for National Unification.

Foster-Carter, Aiden. (2022). North Korea: Options and Prospects. In: The International Institute for Strategic Studies (IISS) (Ed.) *Asia-Pacific Regional Security Assessment 2022* (pp. 80–109). London: Routledge.

Frank, Rüdiger. (2016). The Kaesong Closure: Punishment or Shot in the Foot? *38 North.* [Online]. February 12. [Accessed on 5 November 2022]. Available at: https://www.38north.org/2016/02/rfrank021216/

Fukuda-Parr, Sakiko. (2007). *Rethinking the Policy Objectives of Development Aid: From Economic Growth to Conflict Prevention.* UNU-WIDER (World Institute for Development Economic Research), Research Paper 32.

Gibson, Clark C., Andersson, Krister, and Shivakumar, Sujai. (2005). *The Samaritan's Dilemma: The Political Economy of Development Aid.* Oxford: OUP Oxford.

Goodhand, Jonathan, and Sedra, Marj. (2009). Who Owns the Peace? Aid, Reconstruction, and Peacebuilding in Afghanistan. *Disasters*, 34: 78–102.

Grabbe, Heather. (2006). *The EU's Transformative Power Europeanization through Conditionality in Central and Eastern Europe.* London: Palgrave Macmillan.

Habib, Benjamin Luke. (2009). The Implications of Climate Vulnerability for North Korean Regime Stability. *The International Journal of Climate Change: Impacts and Responses*, 1(1): 83–104.

Habib, Benjamin Luke. (2013). DPRK Meets UNFCCC: An Introduction to North Korea's Interactions with the International Climate Change Regime. *International Review of Korean Studies*, 10(1): 65–90.

Habib, Benjamin Luke. (2015). Balance of Incentives: Why North Korea Interacts with the UN Framework Convention on Climate Change. *Pacific affairs*, 88(1): 75–97.

Hawkins, Darren G., and Jacoby, Wade. (2006). How Agents Matter. Delegation and Agency in International Organizations. In: Hawkins, Darren G., Lake, David A., Nielson, Daniel L., and Tierney, Michael J. (Eds.) *Delegation and Agency in International Organizations*. Cambridge: Cambridge University Press, 199–228

Herbertsson, Tryggvi Thor, and Paldam, Martin. (2007). Does Development Aid Help Poor Countries Converge to Our Standard of Living? *Danish Journal of Economics*, 145: 188–214.

Howe, Brendan. (2013). South Korea's Contribution to the Promotion of Human Security. *The Protection and Promotion of Human Security in East Asia* (pp. 213–236). London: Palgrave Macmillan.

Howe, Brendan, and Lee, Kyoungmin. (2016). Trustpolitik: The Failure to Build Trust in Inter-Korean Relations. *Journal of Peace and Unification*, 6(2): 95–124.

Hur, Jaeyong, Park, Jiyoung, and Kim, Youngwan. (2017). Same Money, Different Names: Analysis of South Korean Aid to North Korea. *Asian Perspective*, 41(4): 645–671.

Hur, Mi-yeon. (2017). Reassessing the Sunshine Policy in the Light of Conflict Transformation Theory. *Journal of Conflict Transformation & Security*, 6(1): 79–99.

Ide, Tobias. (2018). The Impact of Environmental Cooperation on Peacemaking: Definitions, Mechanisms, and Empirical Evidence. *International Studies Review*, 21(3): 327–346.

Isopi, Alessia, and Mattesini, Fabrizio. (2009). *Good Donors or Good Recipients? A Repeated Moral Hazard Model of Aid Allocation*. Research Paper, No. 09/10. Nottingham: CREDIT.

Jackson, Van. (2020). Understanding Spheres of Influence in International Politics. *European Journal of International Security*, 5(3): 255–273.

Jakubik, Johannes, and Feuerriegel, Stefan. (2022). Data-driven Allocation of Development Aid toward Sustainable Development Goals: Evidence from HIV/AIDS. *Production and Operations Management*, 31(6): 2739–2756.

Jeon, Kyeong-woong. (2019). *"제재 곧 해제"... 대북 무상원조 준비하는 KOICA* ["Sanctions Will Be Lifted Soon." KOICA Is Preparing to Send Free Aid to North Korea]. *News Daily*. [Online]. March 20. [Accessed on 17 January 2023]. Available at: https://www.newdaily.co.kr/site/data/html/2019/03/20/2019032000182.html

Ji, Dagyum. (2019). South Korea Seeking Ways to Streamline Delivery of Development Aid to the North. *NK News*. [Online]. March 20. [Accessed on 17 January 2023]. Available at: https://www.nknews.org/2019/03/south-korea-seeking-ways-to-streamline-delivery-of-development-aid-to-the-north/

Jung, Heon Joo, Park, Geonwoo, Ji, Myeonggeun, and Rich, Timothy S. (2021). Why Help North Korea? Foreign Aid to North Korea and Its Determinants, 2002–2018. *Pacific Focus*, 36(2): 202–228.

Jung, Jione, and Yoo, Aila. (2021). Korea as an OECD DAC Member: 10-Year Achievements and Way Forward. *KIEP Research Paper, World Economy Brief*: 21–11.

Killick, Tony. (1997). Principals, Agents and the Failings of Conditionality. *Journal of International Development: The Journal of the Development Studies Association*, 9(4): 483–495.

Kim, Don Jin. (2015). Aid to the Enemy: Linking Development and Peacebuilding on the Korean Peninsula. *The Pacific Review*, 29(4): 1–26.Kim, Hong Nack. (2006). South-North Korean Relations under the Roh Moo-hyun Government. *International Journal of Korean Studies*, 10(1): 37–59.

Kim, Hyosook. (2018). The Political Drivers of South Korea's Official Development Assistance to Myanmar. *Contemporary Southeast Asia*, *40*(3): 475–502.

Kim, Jinhee, and Garland, Joshua. (2019). Development Cooperation and Post-Colonial Critique: An Investigation into the South Korean Model. *Third World Quarterly*, 40(7): 1246–1264.

Kim, Jiyoung. (2014). The Politics of Foreign Aid in North Korea. *The Korean Journal of International Studies*, 12(2): 425–450.

Kim, Kisang, Choi, Esther S., and Chung, Suh-Yong. (2023). Mainstreaming Climate Change into Emerging Donor's Official Development Assistance: The Case of South Korea. *Progress in Development Studies*, 23(1): 44–64.

Kim, Kyuryoon. (2009). Implementation of the Vision 3000: Development Aid Projects to North Korea. In: Kim, Kyuryoon. (Ed.) *Modernization and Opening-Up of North Korean Economy: Roles and Efforts of Neighboring Countries*. Seoul: Korea Institute for National Unification, 1–12.

Kim, Rakhyun, and Ali, Saleem H. (2016). Green Diplomacy-An Opportunity for Peace-Building? *Enviromental Policy and Law*, 46(1): 86–96.

Kim, Soyeun, and Gray, Kevin. (2016). Overseas Development Aid as Spatial Fix? Examining South Korea's Africa Policy. *Third World Quarterly*, 37(4): 649–664.KINU. (2009). *The Lee Myung-bak Government's North Korea Policy: A Study on Its Historical and Theoretical Foundation*. Seoul: Korea Institute for National Unification.

Kono, Daniel Yuichi, and Montinola, Gabriella R. (2009). Does Foreign Aid Support Autocrats, Democrats, or Both?. *The Journal of Politics*, 71(2): 704–718.

Korea Law Translation Centre. (2019). *Inter-Korean Exchange and Cooperation Act, Statutes of the Republic of Korea*. [Online]. [Accessed on 16 January 2023]. Available at: https://elaw.klri.re.kr/eng_mobile/viewer.do?hseq=22377&type=part&key=1

Kwon, Eundak, and Lim, Jae-Cheon. (2006). Crossing the River that Divides the Korean Peninsula: An Evaluation of the Sunshine Policy. *International Relations of the Asia-Pacific*, 6(2): 129–156.

Lancaster, Carol. (2006). *Foreign Aid: Diplomacy, Development, Domestic Policies*. Chicago: The University of Chicago Press.

Lankov, Andrei. (2013). *The Real North Korea*. Oxford: Oxford University Press.

Lee, Kyung Suk. (2016). New Approach of South Korea's Middle Power Diplomacy: Focusing on Global Agenda Setting. *Global Politics Review*, 2(2): 40–57.

Lee, Myung-bak. (2010). Shifting Paradigms: The Road to Global Green Growth. *Global Asia*, 4(4): 8–12.

Lee, Suk. (2012). ROK Policy on North Korea and Inter-Korean Economic Cooperation: Prospects and Analyses. *International Journal of Korean Unification Studies*, 21(1): 1–31.

Lim, Sojin. (2014). Compliance with International Norms: Implementing OECD DAC Principles in South Korea. *Globalizations*, 11(6): 1–17.

Lim, Sojin. (2019). Determinants of Aid Modalities: A Case of South Korea on Triangular Cooperation and Its Implication towards North Korea. *North Korean Review*, 15(Spring): 73–93.

Lim, Sojin. (2021). The Paradox of Unsustainability in UN Sustainable Development Goals (SDGs): The North Korean Case in the Context of Accountability and the Fragile States under Sanctions. *Journal of Peace and Unification*, 11(1): 55–78.

Lim, Sojin. (2023). *International Aid and Sustainable Development in North Korea: A Country Left Behind with Cloaked Society*. London: Routledge.

Lindstrom, Nicole. (2015). *The Politics of Europeanization and Post-Socialist Transformations*. London: Palgrave Macmillan.

Maizels, Alfred, and Nissanke, Machiko K. (1984). Motivations for Aid to Developing Countries. *World Development*, 12(9): 879–900.

Manyin, Mark E., and Nikitin, Mary Beth. (2009). *Assistance to North Korea*. Washington, DC: US Congressional Research Service.

Matanock, Aila M. (2020). How International Actors Help Enforce Domestic Deals. *Annual Review of Political Science*, 23(1): 357–383.

Miller, Gary J., and Whitford, Andrew B. (2002). Trust and Incentives in Principal-Agent Negotiations: The 'Insurance/Incentive Trade-off.' *Journal of Theoretical Politics*, 14(2): 231–267.

Milner, Helen V. (2006). Why Multilateralism? Foreign Aid and Domestic Principal-Agent Problems. In: Hawkins, Darren G., Lake, David A., Nielson, Daniel L., and Tierney, Michael J. (Eds.) *Delegation and Agency in International Organizations*. Cambridge: Cambridge University Press, 107–139.

Ministry of Economy and Finance. (2020). *The Korean New Deal: National Strategy for a Great Transformation*. Seoul: Ministry of Economy and Finance.

Ministry of Unification. (1993). *White Paper on Korean Unification 1996*. Seoul: Ministry of Unification.

Ministry of Unification. (2001). *White Paper on Korean Unification 2001*. Seoul: Ministry of Unification.

Ministry of Unification. (2005). *White Paper on Korean Unification 2005*. Seoul: Ministry of Unification.

Ministry of Unification. (2010). *White Paper on Korean Unification 2010*. Seoul: Ministry of Unification.

Ministry of Unification. (2013a). *Trust-building Process on the Korean Peninsula*. Seoul: Ministry of Unification.

Ministry of Unification. (2013b). *White Paper on Korean Unification 2013*. Seoul: Ministry of Unification.

Ministry of Unification. (2014). *White Paper on Korean Unification 2014*. Seoul: Ministry of Unification.

Ministry of Unification. (2016). *White Paper on Korean Unification 2016*. Seoul: Ministry of Unification.

Ministry of Unification. (2019). *White Paper on Korean Unification 2019*. Seoul: Ministry of Unification.

Ministry of Unification. (2022a). *Data & Statistics. Inter-Korean Exchanges & Cooperation*. [Online]. [Accessed on 17 January 2022]. Available at: https://www.unikorea.go.kr/eng_unikorea/relations/statistics/exchanges/

Ministry of Unification. (2022b). *Unification and North Korea Policy of Yoon Suk Yeol Government*. Seoul: Ministry of Unification.

Ministry of Unification. (2022c). *2022 Ministry of Unification Work Plan* [Press Release]. [Accessed on 24 July 2022]. Available at: https://www.unikorea.go.kr/eng_unikorea/news/releases/?boardId=bbs_0000000000000034&mode=view&cntId=54275

Ministry of Unification. (2023). *Inter-Korean Exchanges & Cooperation, Ministry of Unification* [Online]. [Accessed on 17 January 2023]. Available at: https://www.unikorea.go.kr/eng_unikorea/relations/statistics/exchanges/

Ministry of Unification. (2024). *Humanitarian Assistance* [Online]. [Accessed on 24 April 2024].

Montinola, Gabriella R. (2010). When Does Aid Conditionality Work?. *Studies in Comparative International Development*, 45: 358–382.

Moon, Kyungyon. (2016). The Influence of South Korean NGOs on State Aid Policy. *Asian Perspective*, 40(2): 271–297.

Mosler, Hannes B. (2022). *Lessons Learned? South Korea's Foreign Policy toward North Korea under the Moon Jae-in Administration. Working Papers on East Asian Studies*, 132. Duisburg: University of Duisburg-Essen, Institute of East Asian Studies (IN-EAST).

Murshed, S. Mansoob. (2009). On the Non-Contractual Nature of Donor-Recipient Interaction in Development Assistance. *Review of Development Economics*, 13(3): 416–428.

Na, Youngwoo. (2022). Sustainable Peace through South-North Green Détente. *Korean Institute for National Unification.* [Online]. [Accessed on 5 November 2022]. Available at: https://www.kinu.or.kr/pyxis-api/1/digital-files/b7fbb577-e838-40c0-8970-4b8d89a2779b

Nelson, Travis. (2012). Determinants of Disaster Aid: Donor Interest or Recipient Need? *Global Change, Peace & Security*, 24(1): 109–126.

Newman, Edward. (2010). Peacebuilding as Security in 'Failing' and Conflict-Prone States. *Journal of Intervention and Statebuilding*, 4(3): 305–322.

OECD. (2003). *Official Development Aid Assistance (ODA).* [Online]. [Accessed on 20 October 2022]. Available at: https://stats.oecd.org/glossary/detail.asp?ID=6043.

OECD. (2005). *Paris Declaration on Aid Effectiveness*. Paris: OECD Publishing.

OECD. (2008). *The Paris Declaration on Aid and Effectiveness and the Accra Agenda for Action*. Paris: OECD Publishing.

OECD. (2011). *Busan Partnership for Effective Development Co-operation: Fourth High Level Forum on Aid Effectiveness, Busan, Republic of Korea,* 29 November to 1 December 2011. Paris: OECD Publishing.

OECD. (2022a). *"Korea", in Development Co-operation Profiles.* Paris: OECD Publishing.

OECD. (2022b). *Climate-related Official Development Assistance: A Snapsho*t. Paris: OECD Publishing.

Opp, Karl-Dieter. (1994). Repression and Revolutionary Action: East Germany in 1989. *Rationality and Society*, 6(1): 101–138.

Paragi, Beata. (2013). First Impressions and Perceived Roles: Palestinian Perceptions on Foreign Aid. *Society and Economy*, 35(3): 389–410.

Park, Geun-Hye. (2011). A New Kind of Korea: Building Trust between Seoul and Pyongyang. *Foreign Affairs,* 90: 13–20.

Park, Jin, and Lee, Jiwon. (2011). The Direction of Inter-Korean Cooperation Fund Based on ODA Standard. *KDI School of Pub Policy & Management Paper*, 11(5): 1–22.

Park, Jong-Chul. (2022). Tasks of North Korea Policy of the Yoon Suk-yeol Government: Déja Vu or a New Paradigm. *International Journal of Korean Unification Studies*, 31(1): 1–35.

Park, Young Ho. (2014). South and North Korea's Views on the Unification of the Korean Peninsula and Inter-Korean Relations. *KRIS Brookings*, 21: 1–21.

Pataccini, Leonardo. (2022). Europeanisation as a Driver of Dependent Financialisation in East-Central Europe: Insights from the Baltic States. *New Political Economy*, 27(4): 646–664.

Patterson, Dennis, and Choi, Jangsup. (2019). Policy and Practice in ODA Disbursements: An Analysis of Changes in South Korea's Official Development Assistance. *Journal of East Asian Studies*, 19(2): 239–264.

Perrow, Charles. (1986). Economic Theories of Organization. *Theory and Society*, 15(1): 11–45.

Petričušić, Antonija, and Erkan, Ersin. (2010). Constitutional Challenges Ahead the EU Accession: Analysis of the Croatian and Turkish Constitutional Provisions that Require Harmonization with the Acquis Communautaire. *Review of Interational Law and Politics*, 6(22): 133–151.

Petrovic, Milenko. (2020). The Post-Communist Transition of the Western Balkans: EUropeanisation with a Small Enlargement Carrot. In: Akimov, Alexandr, and Kazakevitch, Gennadi. (Eds.) *30 Years since the Fall of the Berlin Wall.* Singapore: Palgrave Macmillan, 57–82.

Pridham, Geoffrey. (2005). *Designing Democracy: EU Enlargement and Regime Change in Post-Communist Europe*. Basingstoke: Palgrave Macmillan.

Rasmusen, Eric. (2006). *Games and Information: An Introduction to Game Theory*. Malden, MA: Blackwell Publishing.

Republic of Korea. (1948). *Constitution of the Republic of Korea*. [Online]. [Accessed on 17 January 2023]. Available at: https://www.refworld.org/docid/3ae6b4dd14.html

Riddell, Roger. (2007). *Does Foreign Aid Really Work?* Oxford: Oxford University Press.

Roesdahl, Mie, and Varughese, George. (2017). Development Aid Architecture and the Conditions for Peacebuilding and Human Rights: Does the Framework Fit the Purpose? *Journal of Human Rights Practice*, 9(3): 457–468.

Saam, Nicole J. (2007). Asymmetry in Information versus Asymmetry in Power: Implicit Assumptions of Agency Theory? *The Journal of Socio-Economics*, 36(6): 825–840.

Sagan, Iwona. (2010). Post-Socialist Transformation, European Neighbourhood and Civil Society Networks between Poland, Russia and Ukraine: A Case of Multi-level Contingency. *European Integration*, 32(5): 439–456.

Sappington, David E. (1991). Incentives in Principal-Agent Relationships. *Journal of Economic Perspectives*, 5(2): 45–66.

Sarkodie, Samuel Asumadu, and Strezov, Vladimir. (2019). Economic, Social and Governance Adaptation Readiness for Mitigation of Climate Change Vulnerability: Evidence from 192 Countries. *Science of the total Environment*, 656: 150–164.

Savage, Timothy, and Nautilus Team. (2002). NGO Engagement with North Korea: Dilemmas and Lessons Learned. *Asian Perspective*, 26(1): 151–167.

Schimmelfennig, Frank, and Sedelmeier, Ulrich. (2004), Governance by Conditionality: EU Rule Transfer to the Candidate Countries of Central and Eastern Europe. *Journal of European Public Policy*, 11(4): 661–679.

Schimmelfennig, Frank, and Sedelmeier, Ulrich. (2020). The Europeanization of Eastern Europe: The External Incentives Model Revisited. *Journal of European Public Policy*, 27(6): 814–833.

Seong, Jieun. (2011). The Green Growth Policy of the Lee Myung-bak Government: Policy Integration Perspectives for System Transition. *STI Policy Review*, 2(2): 11–24.

Song, Annie Young, and Hastings, Justin V. (2020). Engaging North Korea: Environmental Cooperation in Peacebuilding. *Third World Quarterly*, 41(11): 1809–1827.

Söderberg, Marie. (2006). Can Japanese Foreign Aid to North Korea Create Peace and Stability? *Pacific Affairs*, 79(3): 433–454.

Sohn, Hyuk-Sang, and Yoo, Nari. (2015). Motivation for Aid Allocation and Political Ideology: A Case Study of South Korea. *Pacific Focus*, 30(3): 344–371.

Streeten, Paul. (1987). National Food Security and Food Aid. In: Paul Streeten. (Ed.) *What Price Food? Agricultural Price-Policies in Developing Countries*. London: Palgrave Macmillan, 39–44.

Svensson, Jakob. (2003). Why Conditional Aid Does Not Work and What Can be Done about It? *Journal of Development Economics*, 70(2): 381–402.

Temple, Jonathan. (2014). Aid Conditionality. In: Desai, Vandana, and Potter, Rob. (Eds.) *The Companion to Development Studies*. Third Edition. Abingdon: Routledge, 569–572.

Tonami, Aki, and Müller, Anders Riel. (2014). Trajectories of Japanese and South Korean Environmental Aid: A Comparative Historical Analysis. *The Journal of Environment & Development*, 23(20): 191–219.

UNESCAP. (2018). *Achieving the Sustainable Development Goals through Enhanced Development Cooperation in East and North-East Asia*. [Online]. Incheon: UN ESCAP. [Accessed on 17 January 2023]. Available at: https://repository.unescap.org/bitstream/handle/20.500.12870/363/ESCAP-2018-RP-Achieving-SDGs-enhanced-development-cooperation-East-North-East-Asia.pdf?sequence=4&isAllowed=y

United Nations General Assembly. (2015). *Resolution 70/1: Transforming Our World: The 2030 Agenda for Sustainable Development (21 October 2015).* [Online]. A/RES/70/1. [Accessed on 2 September 2023]. Available at: https://www.un.org/en/development/desa/population/migration/generalassembly/docs/globalcompact/A_RES_70_1_E.pdf.

Vachudová, Milada Anna. (2005). *Europe Undivided: Democracy, Leverage, and Integration after Communism*. Oxford: Oxford University Press.

Visegrady, Antal. (1992). Transition to Democracy in Central and Eastern Europe: Experiences of a Model Country – Hungary. *Illiam and Mary Bill of Rights Journal*, 1(2): 245–266.

Vivekananda, Janani, Schilling, Janpeter, and Smith, Dan. (2014). Climate Resilience in Fragile and Conflict-affected Societies: Concepts and Approaches. *Development in Practice*, 24(4): 487–501.

Wood, Terence, Hoy, Chris, and Pryke, Jonathan. (2021). The Effect of Geostrategic Competition on Public Attitudes to Aid. *Journal of Experimental Political Science*, 8(3): 285–295.

World Bank. (2022). *Net ODA Provided, Total (Current US$) – Korea, Republic.* [Online]. [Accessed on 20 October 2022]. Available at: https://data.worldbank.org/indicator/DC.ODA.TOTL.CD?locations=KR

Wright, Peter, Mukherji, Ananda, and Kroll, Mark J. (2001). A Reexamination of Agency Theory Assumptions: Extensions and Extrapolations. *The Journal of Socio-Economics*, 30(5): 413–429.

Yanguas, Pablo. (2018). *Why We Lie About Aid. Development and the Messy Politics of Change*. London: Zed Books.

Yoo, Ho-Yeol. (2006). The Sunshine Policy and the Inter-Korean Relations in the 21st Century. In: *Cooperation and Conflict in Northeast Asia: The Korean Role, 10–11 October,* Santiago, Chile. [Online]. Santiago: Institute of International Studies, University of Chile. [Accessed on 2 November 2022]. Available at: https://web.uchile.cl/facultades/estinter/centros/cap/doctos/yoo-Ho-Yeol.pdf

Yoon, Sanghyun. (1996). Korea's Kim Young Sam Government: Political Agendas. *Asian Survey*, 36(5): 511–522.

Zadeh-Cummings, Nazanin, and Harris, Lauren. (2020). The Impact of Sanctions Against North Korea on Humanitarian Aid. *Journal of Humanitarian Affairs*, 2(1): 44–52.

Index

Note: **Bold** page numbers refer to tables; *italic* page numbers refer to figures and page numbers followed by "n" denote endnotes.

Kolibri 360 GmbH
Ferdinand-Jühlke-Straße 7
99095 Erfurt, Deutschland
produktsicherheit@kolibri360.de